To Mum – the silver lining ...

GRUMPY OLD WIT

ROSEMARIE JARSKI

An exclusive edition for

ALLSORTED.
for all your gift books and gift stationery

Watford, Herts, U.K. WD19 4BG

1 3 5 7 9 10 8 6 4 2

This edition first published in Great Britain in 2014
An exclusive edition for Allsorted, Watford, Herts, UK, WD19 4BG

First published in 2007 by Ebury Press, an imprint of Ebury Publishing
A Random House Group company

Introduction and compilation copyright © Rosemarie Jarski 20007

Rosemarie Jarski has asserted her right to be identified as the author of this Work in
accordance with the Copyright, Designs and Patents Act 1988

The Random House Group Limited Reg. No. 954009

Addresses for companies within the Random House Group can be found at
www.randomhouse.co.uk

A CIP catalogue record for this book is available from the British Library

The Random House Group Limited supports the Forest Stewardship Council® (FSC®),
the leading international forest-certification organisation. Our books carrying the
FSC label are printed on FSC®-certified paper. FSC is the only forest-certification
scheme supported by the leading environmental organisations, including Greenpeace.
Our paper procurement policy can be found at www.randomhouse.co.uk/environment

Printed and bound in Great Britain by Clays Ltd, St Ives PLC

ISBN 9780091917838

To buy books by your favourite authors and register for offers visit
www.randomhouse.co.uk

If there is anyone here whom I have not insulted, I beg his pardon.

Johannes Brahms

CONTENTS

GRUMPY HOME & FAMILY

GRUMPY WORK & MONEY

GRUMPY TRANSPORT & TRAVEL

GRUMPY SPORT & LEISURE

GRUMPY NATURE

GRUMPY ARTS & ENTERTAINMENT

INTRODUCTION

They're gobby, arsey, cussed and downright rude. Thank goodness for grumpy old wits. They don't get the credit they deserve. The popular view of '*homo grumpius*' is of a miserable old codger waving their fist in the air and ranting about 'bloody this' and 'bloody that' in a gravy-stained cardie. But in a society polluted by political correctness and stultified by 'health and safety', grumpies are a breath of fresh air. They stand up and say what the rest of us are thinking. Far from being figures of fun, they should be recognised and celebrated for what they are: defenders of free speech, fighters against officiousness, railers against received opinion, enemies of pretension, upholders of justice. In short, heroes.

Evelyn Waugh, one of our greatest grumpy old wits, identified the most deadly sin of the twentieth century as 'too much tolerance', and contended that there were 'still things worth fighting *against*'. Were he around to witness current events, doubtless he'd be saying the same. John Mortimer believes 'causing offence is important and beneficial to humanity. People should be offended three times a week and twice on Sunday.' Bertrand Russell summed it up succinctly: 'Dissent is life, conformity, death.'

But it's not about sounding off for the sake of it. Grumpy old wits always have a good reason for their anger. They're rebels *with* a cause. Terry Wogan talks about a certain type of person who sits with their ear glued to their radio waiting to be offended. It's the same type V.S. Pritchett describes, who, after tea and toast each morning, 'looks eagerly to see what was annoying in the papers – some new annoyance to add to a lifetime's accumulation of annoyances'. They're the type who sign their letters, 'Disgusted of Tunbridge Wells'.

Grumpy old wits are not like this. They don't go looking for trouble. Ordinarily, they're decent, upstanding, mild-mannered citizens, going about their day, minding their own business. Only when something happens to upset or offend their keen sense of right and reason do they react. As that splendidly splenetic grump of yesteryear, Gilbert Harding, explains: 'I am full of the milk of human kindness, damn it. My trouble is that it gets clotted so easily.'

So, what turns peace-loving pussycats into wolves baying for blood? Lawyers, naturally; other drivers, of course; politicians, certainly. Then there are traffic wardens, cold-callers, mothers-in-law, joggers, journalists – how long do you have? In two words: Other People. 'Hell is other people,' said Jean-Paul Sartre, but try saying that in our 'caring society'. It's easier to come out as a gay than it is a misanthrope.

Popular culture continues to peddle the fanciful idea that we're all one big happy family. But as Henry Miller said, 'It is silly to go on pretending that under the skin we are all brothers, the truth is more likely that under the skin we are all cannibals, assassins, traitors, liars, hypocrites, poltroons.' Not the most flattering take on mankind, perhaps, but grumpy old wits are not in the business of airbrushing. They have not only removed their rose-tinted specs, they have smashed the lenses, bent the frames, snapped off the arms and stamped the shattered remains into the ground, thereby improving their vision one hundred per cent. I can see clearly now the bullshit's gone.

So, what else brings grumpies out in an allergic rash? Christmas, holidays, parties, theme parks – anything promising to be 'a fun time' is, by definition, not going to be. 'The prospect of a long day at the beach makes me panic,' says Philip Lopate. 'There is no harder work I can think of than taking myself off to somewhere pleasant, where I am forced to stay for hours and "have fun".' It's a well-documented fact that suicide hotlines are busiest during holiday times, and ring off the hook over the Christmas period. If you're going to be murdered, the date it's most likely to happen is 1 January. Worth bearing in mind when you're planning which auld acquaintance you're going to see in the New Year with.

Life's Little Annoyances also rank high on the grumpy hit list. 'How little it takes to make life unbearable,' said H.L. Mencken. 'A pebble in the shoe, a cockroach in the spaghetti, a woman's laugh' (and don't you just know he had a particular woman's laugh in mind when he mentioned that). Anthony Trollope talked about 'the little daily lacerations upon the spirit' (and no doubt his 'day job' working for the Post Office provided an unlimited supply of these). H.P. Lovecraft describes the cumulative effect: 'The ugly trifles of existence began to drive me to madness, like the small drops of water torturers let fall ceaselessly upon one spot of their victim's body.'

Which of us doesn't know the relentless drip, drip, drip of life's little vexations. The question is, why do we rail most against the small things? Simply because we have no control over the big things. Death, War, Famine, Pestilence and Peter Andre are beyond the control of most of us, so, instead, we bang on about the selfish sod who had 11 items in the 'Ten Items or Less' queue at the supermarket, or the bastard who cut us up on the dual carriageway on the way home from work. There's a telling moment in *One Foot in the Grave* when the godfather of grumps, Victor Meldrew, thinks he's died and gone to heaven. Meeting his maker for the first time, it's Victor's big chance to confront Him with all the big questions that have plagued him during his life on earth. What, you wonder, will he ask: 'Why is there war? Why is there disease? Why is there starvation?' What Victor actually says is: 'God! Why did you let them kick me out of my job? Why do you let people throw crisp packets in other people's gardens? Why can't you make Rich Tea biscuits easier to open?' We may laugh, but which of us, in the same position, wouldn't likely say the same.

Whether it's litter on the lawn or impenetrable packaging, we all have our list of pet hates. 'I don't have pet peeves,' says Whoopi Goldberg, 'I have whole kennels of irritation.' Woof woof to that. The real pleasure is in comparing our list with others' and discovering that we're not alone in our hatred of people who say, 'At the end of the day', people who nick our parking space, noisy eaters, warm beer, waiting rooms, anchovies, Sarah Beeny, practical jokes, people who walk round town bare-chested (of either sex), surprises, Sudoku, sniffers, snorers, skinny girls who complain about being fat, noisy neighbours, nosy neighbours, neighbours, American chocolate, public displays of affection, dream sequences in movies, hearing the sound of a toilet being flushed on the other end of the phone, magic tricks, Mr Bean, the smell of horseradish, catchphrases, muzak, mosquitoes – oh, excuse me... got a bit carried away there. At the end of the day, the point is this: a pet hate shared is a stress halved. Give your pet hates an airing and it's as good as a dose of prunes. Prunes! Ugh! Put them on the list too.

Of course, what's on your list isn't necessarily going to coincide with what's on somebody else's. In fact, one man's pet hate could well be another man's beloved 4x4. But that doesn't preclude you from appreciating a witty barb even if it's directed at something you hold in high regard. For example, you can idolise Barbra Streisand yet still appreciate John Simon's critique of her in *A Star is Born* as a dazzling display of virtuoso wit *per se*: 'O for the gift of Rostand's Cyrano to invoke the vastness of that nose alone as it cleaves the giant screen from east to west, bisects it from north to south. It zigzags across our horizon like a bolt of fleshy lightning; it towers like a ziggurat made of meat.'

Nothing personal, Mr Simon would say. Still, it's doubtful Ms Streisand was straight on the phone congratulating him on being right on the nose. Celebrities, whose egos can be even bigger than their pre-nose job schnozzes, respond to censure with varying degrees of graciousness. When a couple criticised his performance in a Noël Coward play, Rupert Everett sent them a clump of his pubic hair. Not lice – I mean, nice. To journalists who pooh-pooh her in print, Sharon Osbourne sends a pile of her own faeces 'gift-wrapped' in a Tiffany box tied with a white bow. Now that's just plain wrong. Surely it should be a *red* bow.

While suppressing a snigger, grumpy old wits would condemn such crude acts of vengeance as, at best, juvenile, at worst, cowardly. Seek revenge by all means, but there's no need to sink to gutter-level tactics. Not when you can be smart and sharp and thereby secure the last laugh for yourself. Just like Al Gore. You remember, the 'former next President of the United States'. Poor old Al had long been the butt of endless quips about his wooden demeanour. But he turned it all around in a speech he made to thousands of delegates in California. (By the way, for the purposes of this story, you might need to be reminded that Al has a wife named Tipper.) He stood up and began reeling off all the jokes that had been made about him: '"Al Gore is an inspiration to millions of Americans who suffer from Dutch Elm Disease." "If you use a strobe light, it looks like Al Gore is actually moving." "He's so stiff, racks buy their suits off Al Gore." I've heard 'em all,' he told the cheering crowd, 'and each time I say, "Very funny, Tipper."' Russell Lynes sums up the advice: 'If you can't ignore an insult, top it; if you can't top it, laugh it off; and if you can't laugh it off, it's probably deserved.'

But fielding an insult is the easy part. Coming up with the killer line in the first place is what's tough. There's a difference between profanity and invective. Profanity can be heard everywhere, from the football terraces to the kitchens of Michelin-starred restaurants. Grumpy old wits know all the naughty words and aren't afraid to use them for dramatic effect, but they prefer to set the bar higher. They know that a single, literate, well-wrought insult is more effective than any amount of cheap, vulgar abuse, if you get my meaning, you stupid fucking moron.

Grumpy Old Wit is packed to the gills with the very best invective from the wittiest grumps ever. It's invidious to single out anyone in particular but who doesn't have a soft spot for Les Dawson, who was that contradiction in terms – a cuddly curmudgeon. Then there's Dave Allen, as 'bracing as a shot of Irish whisky'. Also up there are George Carlin, Joan Rivers, Jeremy Clarkson, A.A. Gill, Victor Lewis-Smith, Jack Dee, Jeremy Hardy and Mark Lamarr. And let's not forget Rodney Dangerfield, that 'heroic mess of a man' whose catchphrase, 'I don't get no respect,' could be the motto for grumpies everywhere. This self-styled loser carried his self-deprecating style right to the grave, where his headstone reads: 'Rodney Dangerfield: There goes the neighbourhood.'

In political circles, none can rival 'the great panjandrum', Benjamin Disraeli, whose rumbles in the political jungle with William Gladstone, in particular, are the stuff of legend. (How fitting, then, that these two political sparring partners should grace the cover of a book celebrating grumpy old wits.) Their mutual loathing makes Blair and Brown seem like Romeo and Juliet, and inspired such gems as this from Dizzy: 'The difference between a misfortune and a calamity is this: if Gladstone fell into the Thames, it would be a misfortune, and if someone hauled him out again, that would be a calamity.'

Great fictional grumpies, so vividly realised that it's impossible to believe they don't actually exist, include Victor Meldrew (David Renwick), Rab C. Nesbitt (Ian Pattison) and Basil Fawlty (John Cleese and Connie Booth). Ranking among the top grumpy double acts are Steptoe and Son (Galton and Simpson), Sophia and Dorothy in *The Golden Girls*, and Karen and Rosario in *Will and Grace*. In each of these relationships, the vitriol flung back and forth between the characters is so vicious, so vile, so venomous, that their deep love for each other shines through. Insults not compliments make the best glue. They also make the best aphrodisiac as evidenced by any film noir of the 1940s and any romantic comedy ever made. *Grumpy Old Wit* includes some cracking examples.

What's so refreshing about grumpy old wits is that they're not image-conscious. They don't suffer with that distinctly modern disease, which afflicts so many people today, from reality TV contestants to presidents: a desperate need to be loved. Because they're not obssessing about what others think of them, they are free to say whatever they damn well please and hang the consequences. None are likely to be appointed H.M. Ambassador any time soon. Most are graduates of the Jeremy Clarkson School of Diplomacy, adept at pouring oil on troubled water then setting a lighted match to it. Born curmudgeons, they don't suffer fools gladly, take no prisoners, and have their phasers set to vaporise not stun. 'I'm not passive-aggressive,' says Mark Lamarr, 'I'm aggressive-aggressive.' Drama critic Kenneth Tynan kept this injunction above his desk: 'Raise tempers, goad and lacerate, raise a whirlwind.' You can never accuse them of being boring.

Perhaps you're wondering if you yourself are a grump. Let's see. Do you believe the toast will always land butter-side down? Do you think the light at the end of the tunnel is an oncoming train? Do you prefer a whisky sour to a sweet sherry, an elegy to an ode, the dark side of the moon to the sunny side of the street, 'Woe, woe, and thrice woe' to 'Yabba dabba do', the Addams Family to the Brady Bunch, Edvard Munch to Norman Rockwell, Orla Guerin to Natasha Kaplinsky, gadflys to butterflies, E minor to C major, anti to pro? Is your spiritual home on Henman Hill, Wimbledon SW19? If so, you're well on your way. Ask yourself this clincher: 'Am I a grump?' If you answer 'no', then yes, you most likely are. For the very definition of a grump is that they don't think of themselves as such – at least, not consciously. The tagline of *Curb Your Enthusiasm*, starring the maestro of mope, Larry David, is: 'Deep inside you know you're him.'

Grumpiness is the only rational response to the world we live in. 'My thoughts, I guess, are bitter,' said Mignon McLaughlin. 'Who but the bitter have thoughts?' Who, indeed. Consider those who never get pissed off: born-again Christians and Mouseketeers. Would you really want to swap places with any of these? Happy people are scary; they're mentally unbalanced. Grumpiness is a more interesting, more creative mindset and, crucially, it leaves something to hope for: happiness. Not that we grumpies would probably want it even if we got it. Ah well, we'll just have to learn to be happy without it.

GRUMPY
LIFE

PROBLEMS

I'm a Jew...I'm small...I'm homosexual...and I live in Sheffield. I'm
fucked.
                                        Posner, *The History Boys*

We're all fucked. I'm fucked. You're fucked. The whole department's
fucked. It's been the biggest cock-up ever and we're all completely fucked.
            Sir Richard Mottram, Her Majesty's Permanent Secretary at the
            Department for Transport, after the 'good day to bury bad news' debacle

—You're just making a mountain out of a molehill.
—Five years of molehills – they add up.
                    Dorothy Zbornak and Sophia Petrillo, *The Golden Girls*

—It's a Catch 29 situation.
—You mean Catch-22.
—No, it's worse than that.   **Patient and psychiatrist, *Help***

I feel like Korky the Cat, who has been run over by a steamroller, got up
and had someone punch him in the stomach.   **Howard Wilkinson**

If my life gets any worse, I'm phoning hell to ask about their exchange
programme.   **Frasier Crane, *Frasier***

It's like I'm roasting on a spit in hell, and you two are there with chefs'
hats and barbecue tongs.   **Zoey Woodbine, *Cybill***

—Are you in town?
—I'm in deep shit – Deep Shit, Arkansas.
                    Darryl and Thelma Dickinson, *Thelma and Louise*

This is a crisis, a large crisis. In fact, it is a twelve-storey crisis with a
magnificent entrance hall, carpeted throughout, 24-hour porterage and an
enormous sign on the roof saying, 'This is a Large Crisis.'
                            Edmund Blackadder, *Blackadder Goes Forth*

I have here an accident policy that will absolutely protect you – no matter what happens. If you lose a leg, we'll help you look for it.

Groucho Marx

—But eventually you'll solve my problem, right?
—Sure, if your problem is too much optimism.

Scott Adams

At the drabber moments of my life (swilling some excrement from the steps, for instance, or rooting with a bent coat-hanger down a blocked sink) thoughts occur like 'I bet Tom Stoppard doesn't have to do this' or 'There is no doubt David Hare would have deputed this to an underling.'

Alan Bennett

My neck…continues to click and hurt… Worse at the moment is having inadvertently stopped the sink up with boiled rice, having had to send my amplifier to the repair shop, and having a sticking accelerator on my car.

Philip Larkin

Remember that every life is a special problem, which is not yours but another's; and content yourself with the terrible algebra of your own.

Henry James

Ladies in love with buggers, and buggers in love with womanisers, and the price of coal going up too. Where will it all end?   Lytton Strachey

There can't be any crisis next week. My schedule is already full.

Henry Kissinger

One miracle always leads to problems, like Lazarus had to die again.   Dennis Potter

The human race never solves any of its problems. It merely outlives them.

David Gerrold

SADNESS & DEPRESSION

—How ya doin', Norm?
—I'm on top of the world! It's a dismal spot in Greenland somewhere.
Norm Peterson and 'Coach' Pantusso, Cheers

God knows life sucks. It's right there in the Bible. The book of Job is all about Job asking God to take away pain and misery. And God says, 'I can't take away pain and misery because then no one would talk to me.'
Bill Maher

Life is divided into the terrible and the miserable.
Woody Allen

He's going round looking like a depressed hedgehog in search of a lorry.
Philip Norman

He looks as if his idea of fun would be to find a cold damp grave and sit in it.
Richard Winnington, on Paul Henreid

Eeyore without the *joie de vivre*.
Mike Selvey

I think if we all acted the way we felt, four out of eight people at a dinner table would be sitting there sobbing.
Jim Carrey

I felt pretty good – like an amputated leg.
Philip Marlowe, Murder, My Sweet

In a real dark night of the soul it is always three o'clock in the morning, day after day.
F. Scott Fitzgerald

'Heaven Knows I'm Miserable Now'.
The Smiths, song title

We would have shone at a wake, but not at anything more festive.
Mark Twain

Freddie experienced the sort of abysmal soul sadness which afflicts one of Tolstoy's peasants when, after putting in a heavy day's work strangling his father, beating his wife, and dropping the baby into the city reservoir, he turns to the cupboard, only to find the vodka bottle empty.

P.G. Wodehouse

So this is what it feels like when doves cry.

Milhouse Van Houten, The Simpsons

You can't spend the rest of your life crying. It annoys people in the movies.

Oscar Madison, The Odd Couple

I have wept only three times in my life: the first time when my earliest opera failed; the second time when, with a boating party, a truffled turkey fell into the water; and the third time when I heard Paganini play.

Gioacchino Rossini

I think that people *ought* to be upset, and if I ran a paper I would upset them all the time; I think that life is so important and, in its workings, so upsetting, that nobody should be spared.

J.R. Ackerley

The average man is a conformist, accepting miseries and disasters with the stoicism of a cow standing in the rain.

Colin Wilson

If ever tempted by depression I repeat three things to myself: I am an Englishwoman. I was born in wedlock. I am on dry land.

Blanche Warre-Cornish

A new study shows that licking the sweat off a frog can cure depression. The downside is, the minute you stop licking, the frog gets depressed again.

Jay Leno

We either make ourselves happy or miserable. The amount of work is the same.

Carlos Castenada

FUTILITY & APATHY

Why get up? What for? There's nothing to do... And if I got up, what then? More of the same, if not worse. At least here in bed I am minimising my debts.   **Simon Munnery**

I don't fuckin' drink, I don't fuckin' smoke (except a pipe – aaooh!), I don't fuckin' fuck women – I might as well be fuckin' dead.   **Philip Larkin**

What's the point of going out? We're just going to wind up back here anyway.

Homer Simpson

In the small hours when the acrid stench of existence rises like sewer gas from everything created, the emptiness of life seems more terrible than its misery.   **Cyril Connolly**

Everything is worth precisely as much as a belch, the difference being that a belch is more satisfying.   **Ingmar Bergman**

Howard Hughes said one time: 'My God, Mitch, you're just like a pay toilet. You don't give a shit for nothing.'   **Robert Mitchum**

Way I see it, we're all on the *Hindenburg*; no use fighting over the window seat.   **Richard Jeni**

I wore a neck-brace for about a year. I wasn't in an accident or anything. I just got tired of holding my head up.   **Margaret Smith**

—You despise me, don't you?
—If I gave you any thought, I probably would.
                    Ugarte and Rick Blaine, *Casablanca*

We know life is futile. A man who considers that his life is of very wonderful importance is awfully close to a padded cell.   Clarence Darrow

There are two possibilities, one can either do this or do that. My honest opinion and friendly advice is this: do it or do not do it, you will regret both.   Søren Kierkegaard

The day will happen whether or not you get up.   John Ciardi

DAYS

Good moaning!   Officer Crabtree, 'Allo, 'Allo

What a beautiful day – the kind of day that starts with a hearty breakfast and ends with a newsreader saying, '…before turning the gun on himself.'
                                        Dan Conner, Roseanne

Another day, another dolour.   Matthew Engel

…moanday, tearsday, wailsday, thumpsday, frightday, shatterday…

James Joyce

Sunday is always a bad day. A sort of grey purgatory that resembles a bus station with broken vending machines. God is dead, and denied the last word on things, is acting like a real baby. Sunday is some sort of revenge.
                                        Lorrie Moore, Anagrams

Oh dear, oh dear. Ohhh dear me. I dunno. I'm fed up! You sure it's only two o'clock? Doesn't the time drag? Ooh, I do hate Sundays. I'll be glad when it's over. Drives me up the wall just sitting here looking at you lot. Every Sunday it's the same. Nowhere to go, nothing to do, just sit here waiting for the next lot of grub to come up.
                                        Tony Hancock, Hancock's Half Hour

It was the Sunday afternoons he couldn't cope with, and that terrible listlessness that sets in at about 2.55, when you know you've taken all the baths you can usefully take that day, that however hard you stare at any given paragraph in the newspaper you will never actually read it, or use the revolutionary new pruning technique it describes, and that as you stare at the clock the hands will move relentlessly on to 4 o'clock, and you will enter the long dark teatime of the soul.

Douglas Adams, *Life, the Universe, and Everything*

How was my day? Like the rubber-glove part of a physical examination.

Drew Carey

On Monday morning I am dedicated to the proposition that all men are created jerks.

H. Allen Smith

It's been a rough day. I got up this morning, put a shirt on and a button fell off. I picked up my briefcase, and the handle came off. I'm afraid to go to the bathroom.

Rodney Dangerfield

I try to take one day at a time, but sometimes several days attack me at once.

Jennifer Unlimited

Life has to be a little nuts sometimes. Otherwise it's just a bunch of Thursdays strung together.

Beau Burroughs, *Rumor Has It...*

Well, today was a total waste of make-up.

Clare Mason

The trouble with, 'Have a nice day,' is that it puts all the pressure on you. Now you've gotta go out and somehow manage to have a good time – all because of some loose-lipped cashier.

George Carlin

If anyone tells me to 'Have a nice day,' I usually say, 'Thanks, but I have other plans.'

Paul Fussell

If someone says, 'Have a nice weekend,' I never say, 'You too.' Because I never know if, perhaps, by the time the weekend rolls around, I will have other plans for that person. Come Friday, I may wish to have them slain.

George Carlin

I was once reduced to mild hysteria by an American who said to me, 'Have a nice tomorrow!'

Norman St John-Stevas

Have a nice day, dear. Don't drive over any mines or anything.

Basil Fawlty, *Fawlty Towers*

Have a nice goddamn day.

Ian Shoales

DISAPPOINTMENT

I knew an old lady who'd never seen the sea. So, I took her there and she watched it for a while, then said: 'Is that all it does?'

Michael Howard

Disappointing.

Oscar Wilde, on the Atlantic Ocean

Like most things connected in their first association with school books and school time, the Leaning Tower of Pisa was too small. I felt it keenly.

Charles Dickens

When I was a boy, my parents told me to reach for the stars. Sadly, I later learned that stars are just massive fiery balls of gas, which, were I to reach one, would vaporizse me instantly.

Frasier Crane, *Frasier*

Age does not diminish the extreme disappointment of having a scoop of ice cream fall from the cone.

Jim Freiberg

Diogenes, asked why he had been begging for money from a statue, replied, 'I am practising disappointment.'

Bernard Levin

When I complained that the firework display was over after an underwhelming two minutes, my wife said, 'Tell me about it.'

David Letterman

I'm English and, as such, I crave disappointment. I actively seek it out. That's why I buy Kinder Eggs – crap chocolate, crap toy.

Bill Bailey

The name Hanger Lane Gyratory System is perhaps as bitter a disappointment as anyone could hope for. The name seems dark and intriguing, bristling with a thousand possibilities – it just oozes Heath Robinson with a hint of Hieronymous Bosch. So what could be more of a let-down than to discover that it's just a big roundabout with a pretentious name?

IanG, BBC website

George Moorman, an artist whose latest work is made entirely of chocolate, says he is 'disappointed' after it was eaten by visitors to an exhibition. Exhibition director Gerrit Bosch confirmed: 'On the first day, I noticed small teeth marks in the chocolate. But the speed by which it disappeared surprised me.'

Sunday Times, 2002

He looked like one who has drained the four-ale of life and found a dead mouse at the bottom of the pewter.

P.G. Wodehouse

He wanted friendship and got friendliness; he wanted steak and they offered Spam.

Bernard Malamud

He had the look of a frustrated tiger whose personal physician had recommended a strict vegetarian diet.

P.G. Wodehouse

Opera-lover Fred Harrop was surprised when friends sent him a book of pornographic photographs for his 80th birthday. The Internet book service Amazon.com had mistakenly sent him *Literate Smut*, containing 35 pictures of sex, instead of *Backstage At The Opera With Cecilia Bartoli*. Amazon has apologised for the error, and also for the remark of a company spokesman who told Harrop's friends: 'If you think Mr Harrop was disappointed, imagine how the guy who got the opera book feels.'

The Times

Blessed is he who expects nothing, for he shall never be disappointed.

Jonathan Swift

BOREDOM

Oh God, look who's coming in! He's the biggest bore in London – second only to Edward Knoblock.

John Gielgud, lunching with Edward Knoblock

A very decent chappie, but rather inclined to collar the conversation and turn it in the direction of his home-town's water supply system.

P.G. Wodehouse

Isn't your story over yet? I've passed kidney stones less painful than this.

Sophia Petrillo, *The Golden Girls*

It's a good job we're not having soup, or else I'd put me head in it and drown meself.

Shirley Valentine, *Shirley Valentine*

—Do you have any idea how difficult it is to feign interest in the same old stories over and over again?
—And you call yourself a psychiatrist?

Frasier and Niles Crane, *Frasier*

Oh, William, dear, if you weren't such a great man you would be a terrible bore.

Catherine Gladstone

Highly educated bores are by far the worst: they know so much, in such fiendish detail, to be boring about.

Louis Kronenberger

...and thirteenthly...

Oxford Don, overheard

—Stan is the second most boring man on earth when he's depressed.
—Who's the first?
—Stan when he's not depressed.

Dorothy Zbornak and Rose Nylund, *The Golden Girls*

He's always grabbing my arm when he talks to me. I guess it's because so many people have left in the middle of his conversation.

Jerry Seinfeld

Bore: a person who lights up a room simply by leaving it.
Laurence J. Peter

Under pressure, people admit to murder, setting fire to the village church or robbing a bank, but never to being bores.

Elsa Maxwell

A yawn is more disconcerting than a contradiction.

Mason Cooley

The word 'boredom' did not enter the language until the eighteenth century... Was it because people were not bored before the eighteenth century? Was it because people were bored but didn't have a word for it? Was it because people were too busy trying to stay alive to get bored?

Walker Percy

A bore is a man who, when you ask him how he is, tells you.

Bert Leston Taylor

I never ask anybody how he is. I follow Franklin P. Adams's practice: I saw him encounter one of the bores at the club one time and Frank said, 'Hello, Fred, howareyouthatsfine.'

Frank Sullivan

We are almost always bored by just those whom we must not find boring.
La Rochefoucauld

Idle people are often bored and bored people, unless they sleep a lot, are cruel. It is no accident that boredom and cruelty are great preoccupations in our time.

Renata Adler

I find that a most effective way of quelling bores is simply to say, suddenly and irrelevantly, 'Now, Singapore – does that mean anything to you?'
                                                                    Peter Ustinov

The surest way to get rid of a bore is to lend him money.
                                                            Paul Louis Courier

LONELINESS

Alone: in bad company.   Ambrose Bierce

I'm no VIP, I'm not even an IP. I'm just a lonely little P, sitting here in the gutter.   Robin Scherbastsky, *How I Met Your Mother*

If you're sat all alone in a room and feeling lonely, break wind. You can guarantee someone will immediately walk in.   Terry Wogan

If you think nobody cares if you're alive or dead, try missing a couple of car payments.   Flip Wilson

One of the advantages of living alone is that you don't have to wake up in the arms of a loved one.   Marion Smith

STRESS & ANXIETY

I was walking the streets of Glasgow and I saw this sign: 'This door is alarmed.' I said to myself, 'How do you think I feel?'   Arnold Brown

Margaret's not a lot better yet. The doctor says it's nervous exhaustion. It's been building up over the last 35 years.
                                            Victor Meldrew, *One Foot in the Grave*

I'm not saying my wife's a nervous type...but she has to knock back two large gins to calm her down so she can get the top off her tranquilliser bottle.
Les Dawson

She's as nervous as a very small nun at a penguin shoot.
DCI Gene Hunt, *Life on Mars*

He lives on a diet of fingernails and coffee.
May Livingstone

You can't so much as suck a Polo without crunching it. You go right through the entire packet like a beaver in one of those old cartoons.
Margaret Meldrew, *One Foot in the Grave*

You're the only man in the world with clenched hair.
Oscar Madison, *The Odd Couple*

In the library where my son Malcolm works he became convinced that people were taking out large-print books who didn't really need them. He became withdrawn and worried, sick about the injustice of it all. Sometimes I wish he didn't work in such a volatile environment.
Mrs Merton

He looked haggard and careworn, like a Borgia who has suddenly remembered that he has forgotten to shove cyanide in the consommé, and the dinner-gong due any moment.
P.G. Wodehouse

I get very tense around apples – well, I get very tense generally. I think I've fallen into the trap of blaming fruit.
Jeff Murdoch, *Coupling*

If I knew what I was so anxious about, I wouldn't be so anxious.

Mignon McLaughlin

I was once thrown out of a mental hospital for depressing the other patients.
Oscar Levant

—I feel like a lost sock in the laundromat of oblivion.

—Jim, my pet, is it angst, or too much lager?

Chris Garratt and Mick Kidd, *BIFF*

WORRY

We experience moments absolutely free from worry. These brief respites are called panic.

Cullen Hightower

The reason why worry kills more people than work is that more people worry than work.

Robert Frost

Beneath the strain of expectation even the little iced sugar cakes upon the tea-table looked green with worry.

Ronald Firbank

Whenever he thought about it, he felt terrible. And so, at last, he came to a fateful decision. He decided not to think about it.

Will Cuppy

We poison our lives with fear of burglary and shipwreck and, ask anyone, the house is never burgled and the ship never goes down.

Jean Anouilh

Everybody is afraid for himself, and everybody thinks his neighbours' fears are ridiculous, as they generally are.

J.A. Spender

This is the secret to life...replace one worry with another.

Charles Schulz

Don't worry about tomorrow; who knows what will befall you today?

Yiddish saying

LUCK

Remember, no matter how bad things get, there's always someone worse off than yourself: me.
Les Dawson

The only reason I get up in the morning is to see if my luck's changed. And it never bloody has.
Andy, *Brassed Off*

You may already be a loser.   **Rodney Dangerfield, opening a sweepstakes letter**

I am so unlucky. The other night, I was mugged by a Quaker.
Woody Allen

I'm like King Midas in reverse. Everything I touch turns to shit.
Tony Soprano, *The Sopranos*

If Jordan were to have triplets, he'd be the one in the middle – sucking his thumb.
Roy Brindley

He felt like a man who, chasing rainbows, has had one of them suddenly turn and bite him in the leg.
P.G. Wodehouse

All my life I've arrived at the station just after the *Orient Express* has left.
Dawn Powell

I'm always getting screwed by the system. That's my lot in life. I'm the system's bitch.
Drew Carey

Fate waits around every corner with a sock full of wet sand.
P.G. Wodehouse

What people call fate is mostly their own stupidity.   **Arthur Schopenhauer**

You know when you get a piece of toilet paper and blow your nose with it, that piece of toilet paper probably considers itself lucky. What about recycled toilet paper, how does that feel? 'We have to go through that shit again…'
Jimeoin

The mayfly lives only one day. And sometimes it rains. George Carlin

A man walks into a pub and walks up to the bar, and he sees a tramp at the condom machine repeatedly feeding money in it, with condoms pouring out. He says, 'Would you mind moving? I want to use it.' The tramp says, 'No, I'm on a winning streak here!' Lenny Henry

If everything is coming your way, then you're in the wrong lane.

Bumper sticker

OPTIMISM & PESSIMISM

There are moments when everything goes well; don't be frightened, it won't last. Jules Renard

I'm so discouraged, sometimes I wish Noah had built the *Titanic*.

Jimeoin

Things are going to get a lot worse before they get worse. Lily Tomlin

I always like a little accident early; it makes us safe for the rest of the day. William Dean Howells

I wanted wine, women and song. I got a drunk woman singing.

Simon Munnery

I can endure my own despair, but not another's hope. William Walsh

What is hope? Nothing but the paint on the face of Existence; the least touch of truth rubs it off, and then we see what a hollow-cheeked harlot we have got hold of. Lord Byron

I hate the saying, 'Always a bridesmaid, never a bride.' I like to put things into perspective by thinking, 'Always a pallbearer, never a corpse.'
Laura Kightlinger

Always borrow money from a pessimist. They don't expect to be paid back.
Anon

An optimist is someone who hasn't got round to reading the morning papers.
Earl Wilson

I find nothing more depressing than optimism.
Paul Fussell

An optimist is one who goes after Moby Dick in a rowboat and takes the tartar sauce with him.
Zig Ziglar

The place where optimism most flourishes is the lunatic asylum.
Havelock Ellis

I'm an incurable optimist, that's the misery of it.
Patrick, *Treats*

People seem to enjoy saying, 'Is this glass half full or half empty?' They stop smiling when I say, 'It'll be empty when I pour it over your head.'
Jimmy Fallon

When I see a glass, it's not half empty. It's not half full. It just needs topping up.
Bill, *Weak at the Top*

He had the look of one who had drunk the cup of life, and found a dead beetle at the bottom.
P.G. Wodehouse

My pessimism goes to the point of suspecting the sincerity of pessimists.
Jean Rostand

—Cheer up. Remember what the *Monty Python* boys say.
—Always look on the bright side of life?
—Nobody expects the Spanish Inquisition.
James Hammerton and Helen Quilley, *Sliding Doors*

I wish I could think of a positive point to leave you with. Will you take
two negative points? Woody Allen

FEAR

My biggest fear is that there's no such thing as PMS and that this is who
I really am. Carol Weston, *Empty Nest*

Don't be alarmed, it's only my wife laughing. Basil Fawlty, *Fawlty Towers*

One of my big fears in life is that I'm gonna die and my parents are going
to come to clean out my apartment and find that porno wing I've been
adding onto for years. Bill Hicks

Flying my first mission over Baghdad, frankly, I don't think you could
have driven a needle up my sphincter using a sledgehammer.
Colonel Barry Horne, F-117 pilot

I'm afraid of the dark and suspicious of the light. I have an intense desire
to return to the womb – anybody's. Woody Allen

As Mr Blackadder says, when the going gets tough, the tough hide under
the table. Baldrick, *Blackadder the Third*

Women are afraid of mice and murder, and of very little in between.
Mignon McLaughlin

Man is the only animal of which I am thoroughly and cravenly afraid...
There is no harm in a well-fed lion. It has no ideals, no sect, no party.
George Bernard Shaw

Panicky with fear of burglars from childhood, I have ripened into someone afraid of everything – debtors, enemies, a knock at the door, a telephone call (these all represent demands on time and courtesy), teachers, doctors, admirers (these may be disappointed in me), my clothes, my work, editors, strange houses, familiar houses (I might get trapped in them), invitations, no invitations, businessmen, friends of friends, other races, dumb people, head waiters, elevator boys, mirrors, political thinkers, musicians, women and children. Nothing in my life has ever reassured me. My mind is as filled with terrors as my closet is with moths. I am not afraid of criticism or death or pain.

Dawn Powell, *Diaries*

Be Afraid. Be Kind of Afraid.

Tagline, *Scooby-Doo*

A new survey has found that one of the top fears of British people is going to the dentist. Which proves the theory that what frightens us most is the unknown.

Conan O'Brien

I wrote the scenes by using the same apprehensive imagination that occurs in the morning before an afternoon's appointment with my dentist.

John Marquand

I'm afraid to close my eyes, I'm afraid to open them.

Heather Donahue, *The Blair Witch Project*

Fear is the foundation of most governments.

John Adams

Once you stop fearing government, the government fears you.

Robert D. Graham

PARANOIA

I told my psychiatrist that everyone hates me. He said I was being ridiculous; everyone hasn't met me yet.

Rodney Dangerfield

I'm not suggesting my old lady's neurotic but she was watching a Leeds versus Hull Kingston Rovers match and every time they went into a scrum she thought they were talking about her. **Les Dawson**

You may think you're paranoid, but are you paranoid *enough*?
William Gibson

There's one thing I've noticed in life, and that's how paranoid a person up a ladder gets if a complete stranger starts climbing up after him. **Michael Redmond**

You know what's embarrassing? When you look through a keyhole and you see another eye. **Henny Youngman**

Sometimes paranoia's just having all the facts. **William S. Burroughs**

The biggest conspiracy has always been the fact that there is no conspiracy. Nobody's out to get you. Nobody gives a shit whether you live or die. There, you feel better now? **Dennis Miller**

SUICIDE

I feel like committing suicide, but I've got so many problems, that wouldn't solve them all. **Jerry Falk, *Anything Else***

There have been times when I've thought about suicide – but with my luck it would probably turn out to be only a temporary solution. **Woody Allen**

I'd kill myself tomorrow if I didn't think hell was worse. **Alan Beasley**

'I wish I was dead' is a terrible thing to say because it's 'I wish I *were* dead' – conditional tense. **Jeremy Hardy**

—Did you ever know anyone who committed suicide?
—Plenty. I used to live in Seattle, remember.

Tony and Janice Soprano, *The Sopranos*

Guns are always the best method for private suicide. Drugs are too chancy. You might miscalculate the dosage and just have a good time.

P.J. O'Rourke

I know him. He's too nervous to kill himself. He wears his seat-belt in a drive-in movie.   **Oscar Madison, *The Odd Couple***

Not another suicide attempt! If Dottie isn't careful she's going to hurt herself one of these days.   **Alexander Woollcott, on Dorothy Parker**

He won't kill himself. It'd please too many people.

Oliver Webb, *Twentieth Century*

Our governess – would you believe
It? – drowned herself on Christmas Eve!
This was a waste, as, anyway,
It would have been a holiday.   **Harry Graham, *Waste***

After a ripple or two, the water closes over your head as if you had never existed. You are not indispensable, after all… Your fellow townsmen will have something to talk about for a few days. Your neighbours will profess shock and enjoy it. One or two might miss you, perhaps your family, who will also resent the disgrace. Your creditors will resent the inconvenience. Your lawyers will be pleased. Your psychiatrist will be displeased. The priest or minister or rabbi will say a few words over you and down you will go on the green tapes and that's the end of you. In a surprisingly short time, everyone is back in the rut of his own self as if you had never existed.   **Walker Percy**

Anyone desperate enough for suicide…should be desperate enough to go to creative extremes to solve problems: elope at midnight, stow away on the boat to New Zealand and start over, do what they always wanted to do but were afraid to try.   **Richard Bach**

The question is whether suicide is the way OUT, or the way IN.
Ralph Waldo Emerson

Doesn't it seem a little like going where you haven't been invited?
Richard Eberhart

As a very tired rich man said to his chauffeur, 'Drive off that cliff, James, I want to commit suicide.'
Adlai Stevenson

Why kill yourself? Life will do it for you.
Anon

I've discounted suicide in favour of killing everyone else in the world instead.
Spider Jerusalem, *Transmetropolitan*

PSYCHOANALYSIS

'I'm not aware of your problem,' the psychiatrist said, 'so perhaps you should start at the beginning.' 'Very well,' replied the patient. 'In the beginning, I created the heavens and the earth...'
Anon

—Where were you, Mr Groomkirby, before you came here today?
—I was living in a world of my own, sir.
—Where, roughly, would this be in relation to, say, Chester-Le-Street?
—Quite some way away.
N.F. Simpson, *One Way Pendulum*

You're Norman Bates with a briefcase.
Gail Platt, on Richard Hillman, *Coronation Street*

You know those drugstore kits that tell you when you're pregnant? They should have one that tells you when you're sane.
Kay Chandler, *Random Hearts*

I didn't have a nervous breakdown. I was clinically fed up for two years.
Alan Partridge

There is nothing evil or degrading in believing oneself a teapot, but it argues a certain inaccuracy of the thought processes.   **P.G. Wodehouse**

Lunatics often reason with great acuteness, like the mad don who thought the don underneath was trying to shoot him through the floor, and consequently always sat on the table until at last he grew to believe that he was a teapot.   **R.A. Knox**

There are hardly any excesses of the most crazed psychopath that cannot easily be duplicated by a normal, kindly, family man who just comes in to work every day and has a job to do.   **Terry Pratchett**

Is he genuinely mad? Or has he just put his underpants on his head and stuffed two pencils up his nose?   **General Melchett, *Blackadder Goes Forth***

What sane person could live in this world and not be crazy? Ursula K. LeGuin

These days, you can't tell the difference between those who are mad and those who are on their hands-free.   **Rosie Bales, *Jam and Jerusalem***

When you think about it, attention deficit disorder makes a lot of sense. In this country there isn't a lot worth paying attention to.   **George Carlin**

And though washing one's hands twenty to thirty times a day would be considered obsessive-compulsive, please bear in mind that your husband *is* a coroner.   **Dr Frasier Crane, *Frasier***

I think love lyrics have contributed to the general aura of bad mental health in America.   **Frank Zappa**

Last week I told my psychiatrist, 'I keep thinking about suicide.' He told me from now on I have to pay in advance.   **Rodney Dangerfield**

My psychiatrist says I have a messiah complex. But I forgave him.   **Jim Carrey**

He's nuttier than a squirrel turd.

Lieutenant Gerke, *Me, Myself and Irene*

[*Looking through a telescope into a mirror*] What is this but
psychoanalysis?   Simon Munnery

—Your therapist rang yesterday.
—Well, tell him he's sacked. And then ask him how that makes him feel.
Donna and Eddie Doig, *Mobile*

I no longer see a psychoanalyst. He was meddling too much in my
private life.   Tennessee Williams

The neurotic would like to trust his analyst – if only because he's paying
him so much money. But he can't – because if the analyst really cared,
he'd be doing it for nothing.   Mignon McLaughlin

Psychiatrists are terrible ads for themselves, like dermatologists with acne.
Mignon McLaughlin

I got sent to a psychiatrist who put me on Xanax when I was 13. I went
back for my next visit, and he had killed himself. I swear to God, it's
true. I had to wait for the rest of the hour for my mom to pick me up.
Sarah Silverman

Freud was a man so dissatisfied with his own mother and father that he
devoted his own life to convincing everyone who would listen – or better
still, talk – that their parents were just as bad.   John Ralston Saul

Sigmund Freud was a half-baked Viennese quack. Our literature, culture,
and the films of Woody Allen would be better today if Freud had never
written a word.   Ian Scholes

The Freudian technique can be applied to anything at all with equally
ridiculous results.   Flannery O'Connor

I don't go in for this auto-cannibalism. Very damaging.   Peter O'Toole

I never stand aside and look at myself in case I find out how I tick.

Peter Ustinov

I suspect that our own faith in psychiatry will seem as touchingly quaint to the future as our grandparents' belief in phrenology seems now to us.

Gore Vidal

If you have an ounce of common sense and one good friend you don't need an analyst.

Joan Crawford

I never know whether to pity or congratulate a man on coming to his senses.

William Makepeace Thackeray

HAPPINESS

Start off every day with a smile and get it over with.

W.C. Fields

She's perky all right. Makes you want to sneak up behind her with a pillow and suffocate her.

Helen Sinclair, *Bullets Over Broadway*

Oh, happy. Ah yes, I remember that.

Basil Fawlty, *Fawlty Towers*

In Glasgow there is no such word as 'happy'. The nearest we have is 'giro' or 'blootered'.

Rab C. Nesbitt, *Rab C. Nesbitt*

He's never blissful. There's always a 'Yeah, but'.

Steve Adams, on Larry David

The happiest moments of your life are those that occur when someone who has an appointment to see you is prevented from coming.

Peter Medawar

And when the doctor said I didn't have worms any more, that was the happiest day of my life.

Ralph Wiggum, *The Simpsons*

Happiness is the sight of one's constituency slowly disappearing in the rear-view mirror.
Alistair, MP, *Whipping It Up*

The trouble with man was, even while he was having a good time, he didn't appreciate it. Why, thought Milligan, this very moment might be the happiest in my life. The very thought of it made him miserable.
Spike Milligan

If life on Planet Earth was really supposed to be a picnic, we would all have been born clutching gingham tablecloths.
Jonathan Cainer

I only had to look at my parents to see the misery that happiness could bring.
Rab C. Nesbitt, *A Stranger Here Myself*

A lifetime of happiness: no man alive could bear it; it would be hell on earth.
George Bernard Shaw

Happiness is a good martini, a good meal, a good cigar, and a good woman – or a bad woman, depending on how much happiness you can stand.
George Burns

Happiness is not a circus clown rolling around in a big tractor tyre so that his arms and legs form 'spokes'. Happiness is when he stops.
Jack Handey

Mine is a most peaceable disposition. My wishes are a humble cottage with a thatched roof, but a good bed, good food, the freshest milk and butter, flowers before my window, and a few fine trees before my door; and if God wants to make my happiness complete, He will grant me the joy of seeing some six or seven of my enemies hanging from those trees.
Heinrich Heine

If one only wished to be happy, this could be easily accomplished; but we wish to be happier than other people, and this is always difficult, for we believe others to be happier than they are.　　　　Montesquieu

LIFE & LIVING

If people knew the story of their lives, how many would then elect to live them?　　　　Cormac McCarthy

—My life just flashed before my eyes.
—What was it like? A Bergman film without the jokes?
　　　　Saffie and Edina Monsoon, *Absolutely Fabulous*

What an awful thing life is. It's like soup with lots of hairs floating on the surface. You have to eat it nevertheless.　　　　Gustave Flaubert

Life is a blister on top of a tumour, and a boil on top of that.
　　　　Sholem Aleichem

Life is like an enema; you get out of it what you put into it, plus a load of crap.　　　　Ira Levin

Not only is life a bitch, it has puppies.　　　　Adrienne E. Gusoff

Life – with a capital F.　　　　Lilian Baylis

I ask only two things of life, courage and dignity. Well, three things if you include the ability to shit Maltesers.　　　Rab C. Nesbitt, *A Stranger Here Myself*

In the chocolate box of life the top layer's already gone. And someone's pinched the orange cream from the bottom.　　　Bob Ferris, *The Likely Lads*

Life is like a box of chocolates – a cheap, thoughtless, perfunctory gift that nobody ever asks for.　　　　William B. Davies

Life is like a box of chocolates...you never know which one might be a laxative.
Louie, *Lucky Louie*

Life can be one big toilet, so for all our sakes, don't make waves.
Forrest Gump

I am proud of my cake-making image but life is not that perfect. There are socks in my fruit bowl.
Jane Asher

The total history of almost anyone would shock almost everyone.
Mignon McLaughlin

Every time I try to take out a new lease on life, the landlord raises the rent.
Ashleigh Brilliant

If life hands you lemons, make lemonade. However, if life hands you pickles, you might as well give up because pickleade is disgusting.
Clifton J. Gray

Reality continues to ruin my life.
Bill Watterson

Life isn't like coursework, baby. It's one damn essay crisis after another.
Boris Johnson

Half of life is fucking up, the other half is dealing with it.
Henry Rollins

He who has never envied the vegetable has missed the human drama.
E.M. Cioran

You live your life by the three Rs: rage, ringworm and roll-ups.
Mary Nesbitt, *Rab C. Nesbitt*

There are three Gs to avoid in life: golf, gardening and gonorrhoea.
Dom Joly

Most people think life sucks, and then you die. Not me. I beg to differ. I think life sucks, then you get cancer, then your dog dies, your wife leaves you, the cancer goes into remission, you get a new dog, you get remarried, you owe ten million dollars in medical bills but you work hard for thirty-five years and you pay it back and then – one day – you have a massive stroke, your whole right side is paralysed, you have to limp along the streets and speak out of the left side of your mouth and drool but you go into rehabilitation and regain the power to walk and the power to talk and then – one day – you step off a kerb at 67th Street, and BANG you get hit by a city bus and then you die. Maybe.
                                                                    Denis Leary

You live 80 years, and at best you get about 6 minutes of pure magic.
                                                                  George Carlin

Life is what happens when you're not watching television.   Jason Love

The life of man in this world is like the life of a fly in a room filled with a hundred boys, each armed with a fly-swatter.   H.L. Mencken

Why won't life leave me alone?   W.N.P. Barbellion

To live is to war with trolls.   Henrik Ibsen

When his life was ruined, his family killed, his farm destroyed, Job knelt down on the ground and yelled up to the heavens, 'Why, God? Why me?' and the thundering voice of God answered, 'There's just something about you that pisses me off.'   Stephen King

My one regret in life is that I am not someone else.
                                                                  Woody Allen

It's just life…wake up and smell the thorns.   Bill Parrish, *Meet Joe Black*

Life is like an Etch-a-Sketch. You know where you want to go, but you're darned if you can figure out how to get there.   Kate Clinton

Life is like jay-walking at Le Mans.   **William McIlvanney**

Life is a rainbow which also includes black.   **Yevgeny Yevtushenko**

Life is a cement trampoline.   Harold Nordberg

My life is like a porno movie, without the sex.   **Anon**

Life is unfair. With that face you should know that already.
                                    Germaine Greer, to John McCririck

Of course life is hard. After all, it kills you.   **Katharine Hepburn**

Life is a bountiful murderer. It comes to us bearing an armful of gifts, of
which the last is a knife to the heart. It is like a Christmas morning on
which one of the presents is a letter bomb. That is if one is lucky.
                                                        Kenneth Tynan

We all start off as sperm and end up as ash; our life amounts to jacking
off into an ashtray.   **Sean Hughes**

Life can little more supply than a few good fucks and then we die.
                                                        John Wilkes

Life is hard. Then you die. Then they throw dirt in your face. Then the
worms eat you. Be grateful it happens in that order.   **David Gerrold**

Life is like an ice-cream cone. You have to lick it one day at a time.
                                                        Charlie Brown

Everyone has a purpose in life. Perhaps yours is watching televison.
                                                        David Letterman

GRUMPY CHARACTER

HATE

I'm Worried That I'm Starting To Hate Almost Everyone In The World.
Mark Watson, title of Edinburgh show

How do I loathe thee? Let me count the ways.
Tagline, *Ten Things I Hate About You*

There are only two things I dislike about you – your face.
Marina Rudd, *The Mirror Crack'd*

'I hate you, I hate you!' cried Madeline, a thing I didn't know anyone ever said except in the second act of a musical comedy. **P.G. Wodehouse**

I do not want people to be very agreeable, as it saves me the trouble of liking them a great deal. **Jane Austen**

She hands me her hatred done up like a fruitcake soaked six months in sherry. **William H. Gass**

Rolf Harris is a difficult man to hate, but that doesn't mean we shouldn't try. **A.A. Gill**

I have always hated my personality – it's one of the most unfortunate I've ever encountered. **Percy Grainger**

Try not to despise yourself too much – it is only conceit. **P.J. Kavanagh**

Everybody hates me because I'm so universally liked. **Peter de Vries**

It does not matter much what a man hates, provided he hates something.
Samuel Butler

From the deepest desires often come the deadliest hate. **Socrates**

The worst, the least curable hatred, is that which has superseded deep love. **Euripedes**

We hate you so much because we loved you so much.

**Banner seen in the crowd at footballer Luis Figo's first game
in Barcelona after transferring from Barcelona to Real Madrid**

I never hated a man enough to give him his diamonds back.

Zsa Zsa Gabor

PET HATES

What do you despise? By this you are truly known.   **Frank Herbert**

My loathings are simple: stupidity, oppression, crime, cruelty, soft music.

Vladimir Nabokov

Yapping dogs. Cigarette slobs. Richard Seifert.   **Spike Milligan**

Walking through a narrow, dirty street, behind a fat person.

James Beresford

People who carry golfing umbrellas the size of Croydon. It's only a bit of
rain, not a monsoon. They nearly 'ave me eye out.   **Paul O'Grady**

People who do not turn down the ringing tone on their mobile phones.

Jaci Stephen

People that have porn films on their iPods... They always position
themselves so I can never see over their shoulder.   **Roger Feldman**

I don't like liars, I don't like cheats, I don't like bullshitters, I don't like
arse-lickers.   **Sir Alan Sugar**

People who step off escalators and stop dead in front of you, just gazing
around. They need to be fitted with brake lights. The same applies to
people who walk through shop doors and stop.   **Wendy Leddin**

Houses with paranoid security lights that switch themselves on accusingly as you pass their front gates. People at checkout tills who hand you back your change with a £5 or £10 note spread out flat and the coins balanced on top of it. Cars that thud with the mindless music being played by their ditto drivers.

Philip Norman

...ginger hair and butter beans and Scotsmen sitting in Westminster and caravans and any talk of global warming by people who don't know what they're on about and the Toyota Prius and books with no plot and costume dramas on ITV and anything with Jade Goody in it...

Jeremy Clarkson

Reading a favourite book from the library, which has, *very obviously*, passed through the unwashed hands of all the subscribers.

James Beresford

Trying in vain to effect a union between unsoftened butter and the crumb of a very stale loaf, or a quite new one.

James Beresford

People who say *ciao* (other than Italians); socks with sandals; radio phone-ins; people who put clothes on dogs; people who wear sunglasses indoors; the mint Magic Tree air fresheners (they're always in mini cabs and make you feel queasy when you've had one too many).

Dan Fielder

Attempting to erase a mistake, but, in fact, only scratching holes in the paper.

James Beresford

I loathe A.A. Gill. And okra.

Gordon Ramsay

Cold coffee, lukewarm champagne and overexcited women.

Orson Welles

Everyone hates mimes. Mother Teresa would punch a mime.

John Waters

Squatting plump on an unsuspected cat in your chair.

James Beresford

People being rude to waiting staff. It's weird that people think they're buying status with a meal.   **Edith Bowman**

Toddlers in restaurants. What they do for a living is make noises, smell, bang their spoons, dribble and cough up purée. They're all called Zac and Molly. I blame the 'new age' parents.   **Ricky Gervais**

I very much dislike people who pick their teeth with a covering hand.

Peter Ustinov

Biting a piece of cheek almost out, and then perpetually catching it between your teeth for a fortnight afterwards.   **James Beresford**

I hate seeing trees chopped down.   **Cliff Richard**

Wire coat-hangers.   **Laurence Olivier**

Loudspeaker announcements about late train arrivals that apologise for any inconvenience they 'may' have caused. Tourists who enter crowded trains or lifts wearing backpacks almost as big as themselves. Prices in odd pence ('Large cappuccino – £2.87, please') that indicate they're always edging higher and higher.   **Philip Norman**

Letting fall (of course on the buttered side) the piece of roll, or muffin, on which you had set your heart.   **James Beresford**

Marmalade pudding. Cockroaches. 'Long Vehicle' on the back of lorries on the road (rousing immediate fury on the part of the driver behind them).   **Agatha Christie**

Other drivers.   **Michael Aspel**

Posh women in 4x4s who *never* say thank you when I pull over to let their tanks by.   **Fiona Phillips**

Traffic wardens and wardenesses. Taxi drivers who don't stop. Taxi drivers who tell you how they would like to help people with their luggage, but can't because they aren't insured once they leave their cab, and therefore if they fell down and hurt themselves, they wouldn't have a leg to stand on.   Mel Calman

Waiting for the operation of an emetic.
James Beresford

Those lavatory doors which open inwards in such a way you have to back up on to the seat to get out. Golfing stories. Marzipan.
Denis Norden

Dropping something, when you are either too lame or too lazy to get up for it; and almost breaking your ribs, and quite throwing yourself down, by stretching down to it over the arm of your chair, without, at last, reaching it.   James Beresford

I have a horror of sunsets. They are so romantic, so operatic.
Marcel Proust

I hate walking uphill.   Richard Briers

I can't stand it when people put used matches back in the box. I'm not wild about toads either.   Jilly Cooper

Cutting bread and butter with a knife, the handle of which has been touched by someone whose fingers have come in contact with honey. Then, being hurried away, without a moment allowed for washing your hands.   James Beresford

People who leave doors open, who boast about their *faux pas*, who presume you know who is talking when they telephone. People who play radios which can be heard out of doors, wealthy communists, smokers with coughs but no matches or ashtrays, upper-class youths who adopt Cockney accents.   Cecil Beaton

Obliged, out of politeness, to caress your hostess's favourite lap-dog, which has sore eyes and bad breath.   James Beresford

This week, penny collector Gene Sukie went to the bank and cashed in 10,000 pounds of pennies he had collected over 34 years, which were worth over 14,000 dollars. And, of course, I was in line behind him.
                                        Tina Fey

Queue-jumpers. I've stood in queues and a fella's nipped in and I go, 'Eh? Eh! Oi! Hey, you! There's a queue.' And the fella goes, 'Oh, I'm sorry, I didn't notice it.' And I'll go, 'You didn't notice it? Eight people standing behind each other? What did you think it was – a gang bang?'
                                        Dave Allen

People who have no sense of humour, i.e. don't laugh at my jokes.
                                        Mel Calman

Feeling a great insect dash into your eye – then, after carrying it home in agony, and sitting for an hour while the socket is rummaged with the corner of a handkerchief, your eye left sorer than ever, the animal seeming considerably grown, since he first took shelter under your penthouse lid.   James Beresford

Living with, or even visiting, one whose feelings differ widely from your own with regard to the admission of fresh air.   James Anderson

People who take for ever rearranging the luggage in the racks on planes, holding up 200 passengers behind them. Loud music in shops. People who chew loudly. People who sniff loudly. Noisy children. Parents who let their noisy children play in the street right outside my house.
                                        Jaci Stephen

Slugs, poets and caddies with hiccups.   P.G. Wodehouse

People who say 'Take care' instead of 'Goodbye'; the packaging around sticking plasters making it impossible to unwrap them in your moment of need; people who insist on telling you what's going to happen next in a film.   Teresa Holt

People who ask, 'What is (TV personality) *really* like?' I always answer, 'Worse.'
Denis Norden

I hate TV presenters who, just before an ad break, say, 'Don't go away!' As a matter of principle, I immediately reach for the remote and flick over just to show the bastards that *I'll* decide what I do, thank you very much.
Paul Fletcher

I abominate muted but intrusive melodies on tape that presume to be soothing in a supermarket, restful in a restaurant, elevating in a lift or tranquillising in a trans-continental aeroplane. They set my teeth on edge... I look forward to the time when we're grown-up enough not to need music, like chips, with everything.
Humphrey Lyttelton

Wives who are too lazy to cook their husbands a proper meal when they come home from work, and men who are so meek they put on a plastic apron and wash up.
Barbara Cartland

Being seized with a violent bowel complaint whilst you are riding on horseback with two young ladies, to one of whom you are paying your addresses, being obliged to alight in great confusion, telling your fair companions that there is an exquisite bit of scenery round a hedge, which they have just passed, and which you should very much like to sketch, assuring them that you will return in five minutes, and remembering afterwards that it is well known that you never drew in your life.
James Beresford

Invited to a party and given a warm gin and tonic.
Ernie Wise

Knocking at a door, and, by a horrible and unaccountable lapse of memory, forgetting the name of the master or mistress of the house.
James Beresford

Sitting down alone in a large party upon a sofa that makes an *equivocal* noise.
James Beresford

Endeavouring to make violent love under the table, and pressing the wrong foot.
James Beresford

Pomposity   Barabara Castle

Anyone who advises you of his virtues by declaring them as vices: 'My trouble is, I care about people too passionately.'

Denis Norden

People who 'know'. The 'knowers' who get me are those with the *answer* for all the world's problems – Northern Ireland, the England football team, immigration – they've got the solution, black and white, straight from the shoulder, no messing about. And all they can't understand is why nobody else can see how *simple* it all is...

Terry Wogan

John Osborne's hate-objects included the Arts Council, people called Debbie and Kevin, charities with names like Aids Concern, the smoke police, Australians, vegetarians, Euro-MPs, and a Bishop of Bromley who now wears jeans and says, 'What is Christianity but a one-parent family?'

Benedict Nightingale

Two of my pet aversions are dried coconut and seed cake. The others I will not mention for fear of the law of libel.

Lady Stocks

—What annoys you? What would you like to change?
—Everything.

Michael Parkinson and Ian Hislop

OVERRATED THINGS

The four most overrated things in life are champagne, lobster, anal sex and picnics.

Christopher Hitchens

Anything written in French, painted by Germans or composed by Englishmen; footballers; anyone who uses the word 'deconstruct' or 'discourse'.

Soldier Palmer

Front-row seats at sporting events; doctor's advice; Robin Williams.

Jubal, The Dead Parrot Society

Mozart was the Victor Sylvester of his day, churning out dance music for the court.

Jeremy James

I have never visited IKEA, drunk Coca-Cola, worn denim, seen *The Mousetrap*, liked the Beatles, owned a mobile phone or iPod, eaten in a cinema, been to a disco in Ibiza, eaten Pot Noodles, had a body piercing, finished a D.H. Lawrence novel, found *Little Britain* funny.

John Hopkinson

ANGER

There are three groups that no British Prime Minister should provoke: the Vatican, the Treasury and the Miners.

Stanley Baldwin, *attrib.*

If not actually disgruntled, he was far from being gruntled.

P.G. Wodehouse

You looked so intense, the way you pointed your little alarm thingy at the car, like, 'Fuck you, car. *Now* you're locked!'

Dave Attell, *Arrested Development*

Road rage, air rage. Why should I be forced to divide my rage into separate categories? To me, it's just one big, all-around, everyday rage. I don't have time for fine distinctions. I'm busy screaming at people.

George Carlin

I screamed a lot, but it was that or firearms.

Roseanne

It's true, I'm a rageaholic! I just can't get enough rageohol!

Homer Simpson, *The Simpsons*

Bloody woman. Bloody birthdays. Bloody everything. Bloody hell. Bloody footmark on the carpet. Bloody people coming in with wet shoes...

Victor Meldrew, *One Foot in the Grave*

He looked like a Welsh rarebit about to come to the height of its fever.

P.G. Wodehouse

If someone had annoyed him, if a barman hadn't brought him his drink quick enough, say, it would be simmering away inside him. He would walk into the kitchen and hurl the cutlery drawer at the ceiling. All the knives and forks and spoons would come crashing down. The noise was terrifying. I would be rooted to the spot, knowing that he was going to make me pick them up, one by one.

Celia Carman, ex-wife, on George Carman, QC

There are two kinds of angry people: explosive and implosive. Explosive is the type of individual you see screaming at the cashier for not taking his coupon. Implosive is the cashier who remains quiet day after day and then finally shoots everyone in the store. **Buddy Rydell, *Anger Management***

Heav'n has no rage, like love to hatred turn'd, nor Hell a fury, like a woman scorn'd. **William Congreve**

I could see that she was looking for something to break as a relief for surging emotions...and courteously drew her attention to a terracotta figure of the Infant Samuel at Prayer. She thanked me briefly and hurled it against the opposite wall. **P.G. Wodehouse**

Great fury, like great whisky, requires long fermentation. **Truman Capote**

Ice formed on the butler's upper slopes. **P.G. Wodehouse**

Beware the fury of a patient man.   John Dryden

If only Edward Heath had lost his temper in public the way he does in private he would have become a more commanding and successful national leader.   William Davis

The full potentialities of human fury cannot be reached until a friend of both parties tactfully interferes.   G.K. Chesterton

When you see a married couple coming down the street, the one who is two or three steps ahead is the one that's mad.   Helen Rowland

I'd rather fight with you than make love with anyone else.
                                                    Nick Mercer, *The Wedding Date*

ARGUMENT

I had an interesting morning; I got into an argument with my Rice Krispies. I distinctly heard, 'Snap, crackle, fuck you!'   George Carlin

—I'm told you left *Saturday Night Live* because of creative differences. Is that true?
—Yes, I was creative and they were different.
                                                    Interviewer and Harry Shearer

Between friends differences in taste or opinion are irritating in direct proportion to their triviality.   W.H. Auden

Everything you do irritates me. And when you're not here, the things I know you're gonna do when you come in irritate me.
                                                    Oscar Madison, *The Odd Couple*

There are two theories to arguing with a woman. Neither one works.
                                                    Will Rogers

We had rowed in Malibu, Montpellier, a stretch of beach between Los Angeles and San Francisco, the desert in the Nevada Valley, Dodge City, the doorway of a shop in France and almost every lay-by in England.
Carla Lane, *Instead of Diamonds*

Bathrooms are always popular for rows – we discovered early on that tiles provide a wonderful ring of tight resonance that adds something to even the most trivial of shouting matches.
Mil Millington

—What does Stevie Wonder's wife do when they've had a fight?
—She rearranges the furniture.
Anon

There's no arguing with Johnson; for when his pistol misses fire, he knocks you down with the butt end of it.
Oliver Goldsmith, on Dr Samuel Johnson

A sure way of getting the last word in an argument is to say, 'You're right.'
Anon

Will you stop agreeing with me! It makes me feel I must be wrong.
Bill Hoest

Men are convinced of your arguments, your sincerity, and the seriousness of your efforts only by your death.
Albert Camus

We're not fighting! We're in complete agreement! We hate each other!
Lily Marton, *The Band Wagon*

And upsetting my tea, I fell over the dog (of course there was a dog); and away I went in rage.
Frederick Rolfe

INSULTS

—I'm Yosemite Sam. The meanest toughest rip-roaringest Edward Everett-Hortensist hombre what ever packed a six-shooter.
—Ya don't say? Well, come here, Shorty.
Yosemite Sam and Bugs Bunny

You great…soft…sissy…girlie…nancy…French…bender…Man-United-supporting poof!   **DCI Gene Hunt,** *Life on Mars*

You are a hateful and despicable person and I hate and despic you.
                                                        Tom Ballard, *Waiting for God*

—You bastard!
—Yes, sir. In my case an accident of birth. But you, sir, you're a self-made man.   **J.W. Grant and 'Rico' Fardan,** *The Professionals*

—I think you've forgotten who you're talking to.
—An overweight, over-the-hill, nicotine-stained, borderline-alcoholic homophobe with a superiority complex and an unhealthy obsession with male bonding.
—You make that sound like a bad thing.
                              DCI Gene Hunt and DCI Sam Tyler, *Life on Mars*

I'd call him a sadistic, hippophilic necrophile, but that would be beating a dead horse.   **Woody Allen**

—You are a dyed-in-the-wool Fascist reactionary squalid little know-your-place don't-rise-above-yourself don't-get-out-of-your-hole, complacent little turd… You're mentally, physically, spiritually a festering fly-blown heap of accumulated filth.
—What do you want for your tea?
                              Harold and Albert Steptoe, *Steptoe and Son*

I want his balls on a platter.   **Malika Zidane**

You'll have to sew 'em back on first!   **Basil Fawlty,** *Fawlty Towers*

Best taken, like strychnine, in small doses.
                                              Cecil Day Lewis, on Maurice Bowra

I never liked him and I always will.   **Dave Clark**

He rang my secretary last month, and asked her sharply, 'Where's your boss?' When she replied, 'On safari,' he snapped, 'Well, I hope he meets a hungry lion.'
                                                        Alan J. Lerner, on Rex Harrison

He is one of those people who would be enormously improved by death. Saki

'Very good,' I said coldly. 'In that case, tinkerty-tonk.' And I meant it to sting.
                                                        P.G. Wodehouse

Ashley, if you're here, who's running hell?
                                                        Pete Dunville, *Two Guys, a Girl and a Pizza Place*

Tracy Barlow! I mean, even her initials are a killer disease!
                                                        Eileen Grimshaw, *Coronation Street*

That's strange. I usually get some sign when she's in town – dogs forming into packs, blood weeping down the walls...   Niles Crane, *Frasier*

Let's face it, she's not Mother Teresa. Gandhi would have strangled her.
                                                        Ken Kessler, *Ruthless People*

Come on in, and try not to ruin everything by being you.
                                                        Carol Connelly, *As Good as It Gets*

Ooh, she's so cold. I'll bet she has her period in cubes.
                                                        Edina Monsoon, *Absolutely Fabulous*

People light up when they see me. No, I don't mean cigarettes.
                                                        Dame Edna Everage

You wouldn't exude warmth even if you were on fire.
                                                        Jason Gardiner, to Kay Burley

Is it true you make your own yoghurt? You get a pint of milk and stare at it.   Ted Robbins, to Anne Robinson

If I see that woman again I'm going to pull out every hair on her chin.
Tallulah Bankhead

Today I'm handing out lollipops and ass-whoopin's, and right now, I'm all out of lollipops!
Grace Adler, *Will and Grace*

—You probably just think I'm some ghastly American bitch, don't you?
—God, no. I thought you were Canadian.
Sylvia Plath and Professor Thomas, *Sylvia*

He is at his wits' end – it is true that he had not far to go.
Lord Byron

—My brother is not too smart.
—Genetics is a powerful force.
Henry and Dr House, *House*

—You know, Spock, at times you seem quite human.
—Captain, I hardly believe that insults are in your line as my commanding officer.
Captain James T. Kirk and Mr Spock, *Star Trek*

—I like him. He's honest and he's got a good heart.
—Then it's true what they say: opposites attract.
Verna and Tom Reagan, *Miller's Crossing*

You know, Sheridan, you have one great advantage over everyone else in the world. You've never had to meet Sheridan Whiteside.
Maggie Cutler, *The Man Who Came to Dinner*

You're so full of piping hot crap the mention of your name draws flies.
Belize, *Angels in America*

—Can I get you a drink?
—How about a hot cup of shut-the-fuck-up?
George and Roxy, *Dead Like Me*

—Wanna bite of my chocolate bar?
—Not if you skipped it to me over a pool of disinfectant.

Bob 'Bulldog' Bristoe and Frasier Crane, *Frasier*

—Hi all. Feed me.
—To what?

Charley Dietz and Carol Weston, *Empty Nest*

Jealousy is a very ugly thing, Dorothy, and so are you in anything backless.

Sophia Petrillo, *The Golden Girls*

—I'm not a whore.
—I wouldn't pay.

Alice and Larry, *Closer*

Your smile is like a crack in the gates of hell. One can smell the sulphur and hear the screams of the damned through your smiles.

Tom Ballard, *Waiting for God*

Don't look now, but there's one too many in this room and I think it's you.

Groucho Marx

I'd like to ask you to stay and have a drink, but I'm afraid you might accept.

Lynn Markham, *The Female on the Beach*

—How do you like your coffee?
—Alone.

Drummond Hall and Lynn Markham, *The Female on the Beach*

Karen, you can't just devastate me and kick me out. You're not my lover.

Jack McFarland, *Will and Grace*

Get out before I cut your head off, scoop out the insides and give it to your mother as a vase.

Edmund Blackadder, *Blackadder II*

I wouldn't live with you if the world were flooded in piss and you lived in a tree.

Julie Higgins, *Parenthood*

Your lips say goodbye, but your ass says still here!

Mimi Bobeck, *The Drew Carey Show*

THREATS & CURSES

If you bother me again I shall visit you in the small hours of the night
and put a bat up your nightdress.   **Basil Fawlty, *Fawlty Towers***

I hope someone slams a door in your face, you sneeze and your head
explodes.   **Louie De Palma, *Taxi***

I'm gonna reach right down his throat and take out his lungs with an ice-
cream scoop.   **Senate Majority Leader, *The West Wing***

—I hope you get jury duty!
—I hope you're on trial!
          Mailman and Pete Dunville, *Two Guys, a Girl and a Pizza Place*

May you put your dentures in backwards and chew your head off!
          Sophia Petrillo, *The Golden Girls*

May your marinara sauce never stick to your pasta!
          Angela, *The Golden Girls*

May you marry a ghost, may it bear you a kitten, and may the Good
Lord give it the mange.   **Irish curse**

May the French ulcer love you and the Lord hate you.
          Arab curse [the 'ulcer' is syphilis]

May the fleas of a thousand camels infest your armpits.   **Arab curse**

May you tan and freckle!   **Jack McFarland, *Will and Grace***

May all your teeth drop out, except one – so you may have a permanent
toothache.   **Yiddish curse**

May your tapeworm develop constipation!   **Yiddish curse**

May the doctors name a disease after you! **Yiddish curse**

May your opera box be full of cellophane-crinklers and the stage
swarming with stand-bys! **Niles Crane, *Frasier***

May you always live in interesting times. **Chinese curse**

May the curse of Mary Malone and her nine blind illegitimate children
chase you so far over the hills of Damnation that the Lord himself cannot
find you with a telescope. **Irish curse**

May your every wish be granted. **Ancient Chinese curse**

We need new curses that really mean something, like, 'Oh, yeah? Audit
you, buddy!' **Elayne Boosler**

SWEARING

—How do you get an old lady to shout 'Cunt!'
—Get another to shout 'Bingo!' **Anon**

Yes, I swear a lot. But the advantage is that having played football
abroad, I can choose a different language to the referee's. **Jürgen Klinsmann**

Arabs love to cuss in English. They won't do it in Arabic because then
God could hear them. But God doesn't speak English. **Aron Kader**

Once a policeman approached Sidney Morgenbesser, Professor of
Philosophy, and told him there was no smoking on the subway.
Morgenbesser responded that he was leaving the subway and hadn't lit
up yet. The cop said, 'If I let you do it, I'd have to let everyone do it.'
Morgenbesser replied, 'Who do you think you are – Kant?' The cop
mistook this German philosopher for a vulgar epithet, and Morgenbesser
had to explain it all down at that police station. **Gary Shapiro**

Ineffable: describes someone you absolutely cannot swear in front of, such as the Queen Mum.

Jessica Henig

On TV today, you can say I pricked my finger, but you can't say it the other way around.

George Carlin

If I had a large amount of money I should found a hospital for those whose grip upon the world is so tenuous that they can be severely offended by words and phrases yet remain all unoffended by the injustice, violence and oppression that howls daily.

Stephen Fry

Take not God's name in vain: select a time when it will have an effect.

Ambrose Bierce

Under certain circumstances, profanity provides a relief denied even to prayer.

Mark Twain

The dirtiest four-letter word: nice.

New York Times

Let us swear while we may, for in Heaven it will not be allowed.

Mark Twain

CRUELTY

Laugh and the world laughs with you. Stub your toe and the world laughs whether you do or not.

Linda Perret

People say you've got to be cruel to be kind. I say why can't you just be cruel? Leave it at that.

Rory Bremner, as Michael Howard MP, *Bremner, Bird and Fortune*

All cruel people describe themselves as paragons of frankness.

Tennessee Williams

Not only does he shit on our heads, we're supposed to say thanks for the hat.

Brendan Filone, *The Sopranos*

SCHADENFREUDE

Aw, honey. I know what would make you feel better. But I'll never leave you, not in a million years.   **Peggy Bundy, *Married With Children***

Happiness: an agreeable sensation arising from contemplating the misery of another.   **Ambrose Bierce**

There is no spectacle more agreeable than to observe an old friend fall from a roof-top.   **Confucius**

Rejoice! Rejoice! Rejoice!
          Edward Heath, on hearing of Margaret Thatcher's fall from power, *attrib*.

Whenever a friend succeeds, a little something dies in me.   **Gore Vidal**

I couldn't give a fuck what that jumped-up little French twat, Raymond Blanc, thinks. The only reason he's in Britain is because he failed in France. When I heard Maison Blanc had gone tits up, it added two inches to my cock.   **Gordon Ramsay**

We're not happy until you're not happy.   **Kinky Friedman**

I love to be in Britain when it's hot weather. I love it when you get four or five days of hot weather, because then people in Kent run out of water, don't they? Know what I like to do? I like to ring them up, and play the sound of running water down the phone... 'Hello, I just washed my car. Probably water the lawn in a minute. Might have a bath, might not, see how I feel. I'll probably fill the bath, not even use it.'   **Jack Dee**

The best reason to read about the rich, of course, is to be reassured that money cannot buy happiness – and, indeed, often seems to buy trouble.   **Maureen Dowd**

I hate flying. When I had to go to Australia, a friend bought me a fear-of-flying course at Heathrow. The scene on the plane was like Armageddon. One woman was literally tearing great clumps of hair out of her head, and one man had gripped the seat arms so tight, it took six people to uncurl his fingers. It was all positively biblical. The friend who had bought me the course came along and spent the day killing himself laughing.

Jo Brand

The best thing about visiting a hospital is that you see a lot of people who are much sicker than you, and it kind of makes you feel good.

George Carlin

We all like to see people sea-sick when we are not, ourselves.   Mark Twain

It's one of my favourite things to do: get shitty songs stuck in people's heads. You should try it. It's your own little form of terrorism. You're not blowing up buildings, but you can ruin someone's afternoon if you want. Just sneak up behind somebody you don't like and go, 'If you like piña coladas...'

Christian Finnegan

If you want to cheer yourself up this is what I recommend: first, catch an aeroplane to the most miserable country in the world; second, search out the most miserable street in the most miserable country; third, find the most miserable person in the most miserable street in the most miserable country; and then enjoy a bloody good laugh.

Peter Cook

GRUDGE & FORGIVENESS

Of course I am prepared to bury the hatchet – right in the back of his head.

Brian Clough

Every time I offer her an olive branch, she snaps it in two, sets it on fire, and writes 'No' with the ashes.

Frasier Crane, *Frasier*

When a female colleague enraged him with her primness, John Osborne inserted a used condom into her sandwich. The prank was more than three decades in the past when he wrote his autobiography, but he remained emphatic that the woman deserved it.   **Rhoda Koenig**

To have a grievance is to have a purpose in life.   **Eric Hoffer**

A bloody good grudge was like a fine old wine. You looked after it carefully and left it to your children.   **Terry Pratchett**

If you see him running awkwardly you'll know where I've stuck his olive branch.   **Dave Bassett**

I never trouble to be avenged. When a man injures me, I put his name on a piece of paper and lock it up in a drawer. It is marvellous to see how the men I have thus labelled have the knack of disappearing.   **Benjamin Disraeli**

It is far pleasanter to injure and afterwards beg forgiveness than to be injured and grant forgiveness. He who does the former gives evidence of power and afterwards of kindness of character.   **Friedrich Nietzsche**

Saying 'I'm sorry' is the same as saying 'I apologise'. Except at a funeral.   **Demetri Martin**

If I die, I'm sorry for all the bad things I did to you. If I live, I'm sorry for all the bad things I'm gonna do to you.   **Joe Gideon, *All That Jazz***

MANNERS & ETIQUETTE

[*Knock on the door*] Come the fuck in or fuck the fuck off.   **Malcolm Tucker, *The Thick of It***

Who are you, and why should I care?   Bender, *Futurama*

—I'm Bart Simpson. Who the hell are you?
—I'm Dave Shutton, and I must say that in my day, we didn't talk that
way to our elders.
—Well, this is my day, and we do...
                              Bart Simpson and Dave Shutton, *The Simpsons*

I don't mind if you don't like my manners. I don't like them myself.
They're pretty bad. I grieve over them long winter evenings.
                                      Philip Marlowe, *The Big Sleep*

In England people do not speak to you unless they are firmly introduced
with no hope of escape.   **Learie Constantine**

The word 'lady' is most often used to describe someone you wouldn't
want to talk to for even five minutes.   **Fran Lebowitz**

Maybe, just once, someone will call me 'sir' without adding, 'you're
making a scene'.   **Homer Simpson**

It's not a slam at *you* when people are rude – it's a slam at the people
they've met before.   **F. Scott Fitzgerald**

There is a politeness so terrible that rage beside it is calm. Minna Thomas Antrim

There's a sort of person who rushes out of the house to shake hands with
you in order not to have to take you inside.   **Frederic Raphael**

One of the miseries of town life is stopping in the street to address a
person whom you know rather too well to pass without speaking, and yet
not quite well enough to have a word to say to – he feeling himself in the
same dilemma, so that, after each has asked, and answered, the question
'How do you do?', you stand silently face to face, apropos to nothing, for
a minute; and then part in a transport of awkwardness.   **James Beresford**

[Meeting an acquaintance in the street] *What you say*: Well, I mustn't keep you. *What you mean*: I have run out of things to say and want you to carry on walking.   Jeremy Hardy

I cannot tolerate civility unless one is actually paying for it.

Robert Morley

Monstrous behaviour is the order of the day. I'll tell you when to be shocked. When something human and decent happens.   Lucille Kallen

PUNCTUALITY

Okay, I'll meet you in front of Jordan's at 4.30 sharp. How late will you be?   Bill Hoest

Oh, sorry I'm late. I wanted to make sure I missed most of dinner.

Karen Walker, *Will and Grace*

Lateness really really winds me up. I'm never late. I was born a week premature. No excuse is good enough. Not even family bereavement 'cause I'll go, 'Well, you knew she was ill, she's been ill for ages, plan ahead!'   Ricky Gervais

—How many times have I told you not to come in here until I call you?
—Well, I don't like to be late, sir.
—How can you be late if you come in here before I even know I want you?   Henry Braymore and Radar, *M*A*S*H*

I have noticed that people who are late are often so much jollier than the people who have to wait for them. I am a believer in punctuality though it makes me very lonely.   E.V. Lucas

The early bird gets the worm. The early worm…gets eaten.

Norman R. Augustine

—Complete this famous saying, 'Better late than...'
—Pregnant!   Guy Corbin and Blanche Devereaux, *The Golden Girls*

If I'm not back in five minutes...wait longer.
                                   Ace Ventura, *Ace Ventura: Pet Detective*

It's okay to be late, so long as you bring big doughnuts.   Jason Love

EGO

'So,' said Lynn Barber, sitting down opposite me and switching on her tape recorder, 'is it true you Google yourself every day?'   Toby Young

I don't go scouring the web for mentions of my name. It's a depressing exercise. At best, it's like looking at yourself in a fractured mirror. At worst, it's a funhouse mirror.   David Gerrold

Whenever I am sent a book on the lively arts, the first thing I do is look for myself in the index.   Julie Burchill

So you're the Toby Young you write so much about...
                                               Private Eye magazine

He is just about the nastiest little man I've ever known. He struts sitting down.   Mrs Dykstra, on Thomas E. Dewey

...an ego like the liver of a Strasbourg goose.   Alice Thomas Ellis

He thinks his fart as sweet as musk.   Proverb

—You know who finds you absolutely fascinating?
—Who?
—You.   Mrs Merton and Edwina Currie, *The Mrs Merton Show*

She had the expression of someone who would not be surprised to find her portrait on a postage stamp.   Penny Patrick

She's totally wrapped up in herself. If she were a meringue, she'd eat herself.
                                                    John McCririck, on Brigitte Nielsen

—Cancer?! I mean, why? Why me? Why does everything happen to *me*?
—Look, love, it'll be okay. Let's keep this in perspective. It's *me* who's got the cancer.
                                                    Jill and Terry Tyrrel, *Nighty Night*

—There is no 'I' in team.
—There is no 'F' in way.
                                                    Tim and Lee, *Not Going Out*

Hello, Sam. You're almost as good-looking as Diane says you think you are.
                                                    Diane's mother, *Cheers*

My wife said to me in bed, 'God, your feet are cold!' I said, 'You can call me Brian in bed, dear.'
                                                    Brian Clough

—You're dreaming about a girl you've never met?
—Come on, Fonz, haven't you ever dreamed?
—Hey, I'm not the dreamer. I'm the dreamee.
                                                    The Fonz and Richie Cunningham, *Happy Days*

Humility is a good quality, but it can be overdone.
                                                    Conrad Black

I am not conceited. It's just that I have a fondness for the good things in life and I happen to be one of them.
                                                    Kenneth Williams

When I think of me, I smile.
                                                    'Reverend Jim' Ignatowski, *Taxi*

It's the greatest love story since *Tristan and Isolde*, and he plays both parts.
                                                    Daniel Wolf, on Ed Koch

A truly honest personal ad would say, 'I want to date myself, only with more money.'
                                                    Maureen Brownsey

Nottingham is a beautiful city with lovely people. The River Trent is lovely, too. I know, I've walked on it for 18 years.
                                                    Brian Clough

This plane isn't going to crash. *I'm* on it.   Muhammad Ali

One of the best temporary cures for pride and affectation is seasickness; a man who wants to vomit never puts on airs.   Josh Billings

CLASS & SNOBBERY

Good Lord, I can't believe I'm at a public pool. Why doesn't someone just pee on me directly?   **Karen Walker,** *Will and Grace*

It's always best to have two private planes because however well one plans ahead, one always finds one is on the wrong continent.   **Barbara Amiel**

We've got to have two toilets because I don't want the crew coming through our cabin to use the one at the back.   **Barbara Amiel, on one of her private planes**

I have flown economy and haven't had a problem with it. It's good discipline.   **Peter Hill-Wood**

You snobs! You stupid, stuck-up, toffee-nosed, half-witted, upper-class piles of pus!   **Basil Fawlty,** *Fawlty Towers*

England is the most class-ridden country under the sun. It is a land of snobbery and privilege, ruled largely by the old and silly.   **George Orwell**

The more I see of the moneyed classes, the more I understand the guillotine.   **George Bernard Shaw**

People think there's a rigid class system here, but dukes have even been known to marry chorus girls. Some have even married Americans.   **Prince Philip**

To marry an American is bad enough, but a *poor* American...   **Cynthia Asquith**

An aristocracy is like cheese; the older it is the higher it becomes.

David Lloyd George

The great and very obvious merit of the English aristocracy is that nobody could possibly take it seriously.

G.K. Chesterton

'There's been an accident!' they said,
'Your servant's cut in half; he's dead!'
'Indeed!' said Mr Jones, 'and please
Send me the half that's got my keys.'

Harry Graham, 'Mr Jones'

An ideal title for a book on how to be condescending would be: *Even You Can Learn How To Be Condescending*.

Richard Henry

I don't like country music, but I don't mean to denigrate those who do. And for the people who like country music, 'denigrate' means 'put down'.

Bob Newhart

Olive oil? Asparagus? If your mother wasn't so fancy, we could just shop at the gas station like normal people.

Homer Simpson

It's a damn shame we have this immediate ticking off in the mind about how people sound. On the other hand, how many people really want to be operated upon by a surgeon who talks broad Cockney?

Eileen Atkins

Working-class men exist only to the middle classes as occupations: the plumber, the gas man, the mugger or the joyrider.

Rab C. Nesbitt, *A Stranger Here Myself*

You might be a redneck if...
Your ironing board doubles as a buffet table.
You work without a shirt on...and so does your husband.
You go to the family reunion to meet women.

Jeff Foxworthy

I'm not working class. I come from the criminal classes.

Peter O'Toole

What a curse these social distinctions are. They ought to be abolished.
I remember saying that to Karl Marx once, and he thought there might
be an idea for a book in it. **P.G. Wodehouse**

There is no better antidote to snobbery and racism than genealogy.
Daily Telegraph

Will you excuse me, I must work the hall.
Barbara Amiel, to Prince Charles, at the Royal Opera House

RACE & PREJUDICE

'Ebony and ivory live together in perfect harmony, side by side on my
piano keyboard, oh Lord, why can't we?' You know, you can play that
song just on the white notes. *In One Ear*

—Hello, Mom.
—Hello, dear. I hear you're marrying a gay, black guy. Wouldn't it be
easier to just run me over? **Grace and Bobbie Adler, *Will and Grace***

If you're black, you gotta look at America a little bit different. You gotta
look at America like the uncle who paid for you to go to college but
molested you. **Chris Rock**

Remember the crayon box with the flesh-coloured crayon? Little white
kids: 'I'm going to draw my mother and father.' Black kids: 'I don't know
nobody who looks like this.' 'Don't throw it out, I can use it to draw the
police.' **D.L. Hughley**

I got pulled over when I was behind the wheel of a Porsche in Philly once
for what we call DWB – Driving While Black. **Charles Barkley**

This is the worst kind of discrimination. The kind against me.
Bender, *Futurama*

Superior? You're not superior to an amoeba with special needs.

DCI Sam Tyler, *Life on Mars*

I ain't bigoted. I'm always the first to say, 'It ain't your fault you're coloured.'

Archie Bunker, *All in the Family*

No bum that can't speak perfect English oughta stay in this country. They oughta be de-exported the hell outta here.

Archie Bunker, *All in the Family*

Now there sits a man with an open mind. You can feel the draught from here.

Groucho Marx

Enoch's dreaming of a White Christmas, just like the ones he used to know...

Albert Steptoe, *Steptoe and Son*

—Why does Stevie Wonder always smile?
—No one told him he's black.

Anon

It just occurred to me, Mickey Mouse is black.

Mike Stivic, *All in the Family*

At that moment I discovered one of life's greatest secrets – black guy, plus basketball, equals white girl.

Chris Rock, *Everybody Hates Chris*

We came up with a wonderful tactic: instead of confronting the Klu Klux Klan with angry epithets and rocks, we lined up on both sides of the street and mooned them as they marched by.

Molly Ivins

I don't care if you think I'm racist. I just want you to think I'm thin.

Sarah Silverman

I am free of all prejudice. I hate everyone equally.

W.C. Fields

SUCCESS

I didn't get where I am today without knowing there isn't any fun in getting where I am today.
C.J., *The Fall and Rise of Reginald Perrin*

Success is having to worry about every damn thing in the world, except money.
Johnny Cash

—Has the success of *Titanic* changed your husband?
—No, he's always been a jerk.
Reporter and Mrs James Cameron (now ex)

As every cockroach knows, thriving on poisons is the secret of success.
Mason Cooley

If at first you don't succeed, buy her another beer.
Slogan on T-shirt, withdrawn from Asda supermarkets after complaints

If at first you don't succeed, lower your standards.
Tagline, *Tommy Boy*

I might have been a fairly good violinist, maybe the second best. But who cares about the second best? This way it's fine. I'm the world's worst violinst.
Jack Benny

I've often thought people reach the top of the tree because they haven't got the qualifications to detain them at the bottom. A very good lawyer tends to stay in the law. The one who's not quite as gifted becomes Richard Nixon.
Peter Ustinov

He was a self-made man who owed his lack of success to nobody.
Joseph Heller

I hate to lose more than I like to win. I hate to see the happiness on their faces when they beat me.
Jimmy Connors, tennis player

The most dementing of all modern sins: the inability to distinguish excellence from success.
David Hare

Nothing is more humiliating than to see idiots succeed in enterprises we have failed in.   Gustave Flaubert

—What is the victory of a cat on a hot tin roof?
—I wish I knew. Just staying on it, I guess, as long as she can.
                                    Brick and Maggie Pollitt, *Cat on a Hot Tin Roof*

FAILURE

Come forth, Lazarus! And he came fifth, and lost the job.   James Joyce

I see my local science fiction club is holding a *Star Wars* Costume Competition. Remember, in that competition there are no winners or losers. Only losers.   Jo Caulfield

A club for UFO spotters in Salisbury, Wiltshire, has been wound up after five years because members have failed to spot any UFOs.
                                                          Birmingham Evening Mail

I used to play football and you'd be lined up waiting to be picked for the team and you didn't want to be the last one picked because everyone would think you were a wimp... And they'd say, 'You can't play today, Sean, because there's an odd number.' Fair enough, I'll go and write some poetry or something. I know, I'll take my dog for a walk. Come on, Patch – we don't need *them*. 'Sean...' Yes? 'Patch is picked.'   Sean Hughes

The world is made up of people who never quite get into the first team and who just miss the prizes at the flower show.   Jacob Bronowski

—You know, Charlie Brown, they say we learn more from losing than from winning.
—Then that must make me the smartest person in the world.
                    Linus Van Pelt and Charlie Brown, *A Boy Named Charlie Brown*

Some people are so far behind in the race that they actually believe they're leading.
                                    Corrado 'Junior' Soprano, *The Sopranos*

Mike nodded. A sombre nod. The nod Napoleon might have given if somebody had met him in 1812 and said, 'So, you're back from Moscow, eh?'
                                    P.G. Wodehouse

I shoulda quit while I was behind.
                                    Sidda Walker, *Divine Secrets of the Ya-Ya Sisterhood*

—You win some, you lose some.
—That would be nice.
                                    Lucy and Charlie Brown

You win some, you lose some, and then there is that little-known third category...
                                    Al Gore

ADVICE

The most basic rule for survival in any situation is: never look like food.
                                    Park ranger

Don't be too sweet lest you be eaten up; don't be too bitter lest you be spewed out.
                                    Jewish proverb

My wife said, 'Don't try to be charming or witty, or debonair. Just be yourself.'
                                    George W. Bush

Speak softly and carry a big stick.
                                    Teddy Roosevelt

Walk softly and carry an armoured tank division.
                                    Colonel Jessop, *A Few Good Men*

Never touch shit, even with gloves on. The gloves get shittier, the shit doesn't get any glovier.
                                    Ferenc Molnar

Don't cross this field unless you can do it in 9.9 seconds. The bull can do it in 10. **Sign on a bison range, Illinois**

Be kind to your knees. You'll miss them when they're gone. **Mary Schmich**

You should always unplug appliances before going to bed at night. There are two exceptions to this rule: fridges and life-support machines. Otherwise you could end up wasting a lot of vegetables. **Jimmy Carr**

Create a 'To Don't' list that contains tasks, rituals and meetings that you should never waste your time on again. Then stick to it. **Tom Peters**

I have adopted the last sentence of Philip Roth's *Everyman* as a response to politics, most other books I read, and almost all the films I see: 'Just as I feared from the start.' **John Irving**

Accept certain inalienable truths: prices will rise, politicians will philander, you too will get old, and when you do you'll fantasise that when you were young prices were reasonable, politicians were noble and children respected their elders. **Mary Schmich**

Every now and then say, 'What the fuck.' 'What the fuck' gives you freedom. Freedom brings opportunity. Opportunity makes your future. **Miles, *Risky Business***

Whenever you're called on to make up your mind, and you're hampered by not having any, the best way to solve the dilemma, you'll find, is simply by spinning a penny. No – not so that chance shall decide the affair while you're passively standing there moping; but the moment the penny is up in the air, you suddenly know what you're hoping. **Piet Hein**

When things get too unpleasant, I burn the day's newspapers, pull down the curtains, get out the jugs, and put in a civilised evening. **H.L. Mencken**

Good advice is never as helpful as an interest-free loan. **Mason Cooley**

Smile! It irritates people. **Anon**

GRUMPY
RELATIONSHIPS

PEOPLE

They say 'love thy neighbour as thyself'. What am I supposed to do?
Jerk him off too?   Rodney Dangerfield

I hate people. People make me pro-nuclear.   Margaret Smith

There are too many people, and too few human beings.   Robert Zend

People are okay taken two or three at a time. Beyond that number they
tend to choose up sides and wear armbands.   George Carlin

I hate mankind, for I think myself one of the best of them, and I know
how bad I am.   Joseph Baretti

We're a virus with shoes, okay? That's all we are.   Bill Hicks

—Why do you always assume the worst of people?
—Statistics.   Matt and Gwyn Marcus, *Miami Rhapsody*

Some people are alive simply because it is against the law to kill them.

Mark Meyer

I can't stand people who order a salad for themselves then keep nicking
the chips off your plate. People who stick up for the person you're
bitching to them about. People behind you in a queue at the supermarket
who then dash ahead of you when a new till opens up. People who are in
the north but say, 'I'm going UP to London,' and people who are in the
south but say, 'I'm going DOWN to London.'   Karen Wilson

I can think of many people who could and should be removed from the
scene in such a way that no one can really explain what happened.
George Monbiot. Ken Livingstone. Various hardline Muslim fanatics.
Most human rights lawyers. Anyone with a rally jacket. People in

Babyshambles. People with beards. Anyone with a sign on their desk that says 'You don't have to be mad to work here', anyone in a jungle in Australia, anyone who claps along to the oompah music at the Horse of the Year Show, and everyone at the Ideal Home Exhibition.

Jeremy Clarkson

People who should be phased out... Guys who wink when they're kidding. Guys who always harmonise the last few notes of 'Happy Birthday'. Guys who still smell like their soap in the late afternoon. People who give their house or car a name. Blind people who don't want any help. Old people who tell me what the weather used to be where they used to live.

George Carlin

People don't bother me until they get teeth.

Dr House, *House*

I know there are people in the world who do not love their fellow human beings and I hate people like that.

Tom Lehrer

The only thing that could spoil a day was people. People were always the limiters of happiness except for the very few that were as good as spring itself.

Ernest Hemingway

It's not catastrophes, murders, deaths, diseases, that age and kill us; it's the way people look and laugh, and run up the steps of omnibuses.

Virginia Woolf

We cough because we can't help it, but others do it on purpose.

Mignon McLaughlin

P.G. Wodehouse's fear of contact with the human race was so great that he could not overcome it... Sitting in a room in New York with Guy Bolton on an occasion when his wife Ethel was going out to look for a flat, he called to her: 'Get one on the ground floor.' 'Why?' she asked, and he replied: 'I never know what to say to the lift boy.'

Frances Donaldson

Mirrors and copulation are abominable since they both multiply the numbers of people.

Jorge Luis Borges

One of the worst things in life is not how nasty the nasty people are. You know that already. It is how nasty the nice people can be.

Anthony Powell

The more I see of man, the better I like my dog.   Frederick the Great

Inanimate objects were often so much nicer than people, she thought. What person, for example, could possibly be so comforting as one's bed?

Barbara Pym

This House looks forward to the day when the inevitable asteroid slams into the earth and wipes humans out thus giving nature the opportunity to start again.   **Tony Banks, MP, excerpt from a Commons motion**

MANKIND

Descended from the apes? My dear, we will hope it is not true. But if it is, let us pray that it may not become generally known.

Wife of a canon of Worcester Cathedral

I worked some gigs in the Deep South, Alabama. You talk about Darwin's waiting room. There are guys in Alabama who are their own father.   **Dennis Miller**

A man thinks he amounts to a great deal, but to a flea or a mosquito, a human being is merely something good to eat.   **Don Marquis**

What is man, when you come to think upon him, but a minutely set, ingenious machine for turning, with infinite artfulness, the red wine of Shiraz into urine?   **Isak Dinesen**

I sometimes think that God in creating man somewhat overestimated his ability.   **Oscar Wilde**

The evolution of the brain not only overshot the needs of prehistoric man, it is the only example of evolution providing a species with an organ which it does not know how to use.   Arthur Koestler

Pop culture has turned the brain into the body's new appendix; no real function and it could quite possibly blow up and kill you. As organs go, you just don't need your brain any more.   Dennis Miller

I believe I've found the missing link between animal and civilised man. It is us.   Konrad Lorenz

GENDER

—Men, or women?
—Oh…*definitely*.   Teddy Bass and Harry, *Sexy Beast*

When I was a kid, I asked my mother, 'Mum? What's a transvestite?' She said. 'That's your father, son. I'm over here.'   Stephen K. Amos

Lorenz Hart? His Broadway colleagues knew him as 'Bitched, Buggered and Bidildoed'.   Anon

I think that a lifetime of listening to disco music is a high price to pay for one's sexual preference.   Quentin Crisp

Didn't gays used to be a better class of person?   B.J. Cox

—What's a gay masochist?
—A sucker for punishment.   Anon

There is probably no sensitive heterosexual alive who is not preoccupied with his latent homosexuality.   Norman Mailer

I thought I was gay, for a bit. Then I found out about the prohibitive standards of hygiene.   Bernard Black, *Black Books*

I was definitely a gay kid. My tree house had a breakfast nook.

Bob Smith

I'm 33, single, with neat hair. Even I think I'm gay.

Patrick Maitland, *Coupling*

—He's a bum bandit. D'you understand? A poof. A fairy. A queer.
A queen. Fudge packer. Uphill gardener. Fruit-picking sodomite.
—He's gay?
—As a bloody Christmas tree!

DCI Gene Hunt and DCI Sam Tyler, *Life on Mars*

I'm just a man who's very good to his mother.

John 'I'm Free' Inman

When I came out as gay, my mom, she said, 'I'd love you even if you were a murderer.'

Marc Cherry

She was so far in the cupboard she was in danger of being a garment bag.

Rita Mae Brown, on Martina Navratilova

I wish that homosexuals were born with a little horn in the middle of their foreheads so we couldn't hide so easily. At least if you can't hide, you have to stand up and fight.

Harvey Fierstein

Seventy per cent of the gay population were born that way. The other thirty per cent were sucked into it.

Anon

Years ago, if you were gay, your only options were the clergy or suicide. Or presenting a game show.

Lilian, *The Smoking Room*

In the Royal Navy in the 1960s, any hint that you were gay would lead to an immediate discharge.

Gay rights activist

Sex is out of the question. I don't even like seeing your head poke out through your sweater.

Will Truman, to Jack McFarland, *Will and Grace*

Homosexuality is a sickness, just as are baby-rape or wanting to become the head of General Motors.   **Eldridge Cleaver**

Texas senator John Cornyn's argument against gay marriage is, 'If your neighbour marries a box turtle, it doesn't affect your everyday life. But that doesn't make it right.' I myself was not a psychology major, but I think it's safe to assume that at one point or another, Senator Cornyn has thought about making love to a box turtle.   **Aziz Ansari**

I support gay marriages. I believe they have the right to be as miserable as the rest of us.   **Kinky Friedman**

FRIENDS

I'm just a really nice guy. If I had friends, you could ask them.
                              Walter Kornbluth, *Splash*

On his 70th birthday, I suggested we hire a telephone box and invite all his friends to a party.   **Doug Haywood, on Rex Harrison**

This is Milhouse. He's my best friend because – well, geographical convenience.   **Bart Simpson, *The Simpsons***

You should never be in the company of anyone with whom you would not want to die.   **Frank Herbert**

There's nothing I wouldn't do for Bing, and there's nothing he wouldn't do for me. And that's the way we go through life – doing nothing for each other.   **Bob Hope, on Bing Crosby**

—I'm perfectly capable of being friends with women without some kind of agenda.
—For how long?
—As long as it takes.   **Patrick Maitland and Steve Taylor, *Coupling***

Friendship is more lasting than love and more legal than stalking.

Jane Christie, *Coupling*

When a stranger identifies you from a friend's description, it's just as well you didn't hear the description.

Mignon McLaughlin

If you want to know who your friends are, get yourself a jail sentence.

Charles Bukowski

One good reason for maintaining only a small circle of friends is that three out of four murders are committed by people who know the victim.

George Carlin

True friends stab you in the front.

Oscar Wilde

I don't like any of my friends... No, I like acquaintances: a wide circle of faintly familiar people who smile and wave but whose names escape me. An acquaintance has all the expectation, desire to please and vivacity of a first date. They flash wit and compliments and don't expect you to call or go to their children's weddings.

A.A. Gill

I sometimes felt I was the perfect customer for a much-needed but never-produced Hallmark card that would read, 'We've been friends for a very long time,' followed on the inside by, 'What do you say we stop?'

Joseph Epstein

ENEMIES

He was probably his own worst enemy, although there was plenty of competition.

Roy Boulting, on Peter Sellers

Most women have all other women as adversaries; most men have all other men as their allies.

Gellett Burgess

When the news of Napoleon's death came, before the King had been informed of it by his ministers, Sir Edward Nagle, anxious to communicate the welcome tidings, said to him, 'Sir, your bitterest enemy is dead.' 'Is she, by God!' said the tender husband.   Henry Edward Fox

Enemies, as well as lovers, come to resemble each other over a period of time.   Sydney J. Harris

A priest asks a dying Spaniard, 'Do you forgive your enemies?' The dying Spaniard replies, 'I have no enemies. I have shot them all.'   W.H. Auden

MEN

'You're a man among men, Sully,' she said. 'Thanks,' he said. 'It wasn't a compliment,' she assured him.   Richard Russo

Men are rats, they're lower than rats, they're fleas on rats, worse than that, they're amoebas on fleas on rats. I mean, they're too low for even the dogs to bite. The only girl a man can depend on is her daddy.   Frenchy, *Grease*

—These Addams men, where do you find them?
—It has to be damp.   Debbie Jellinsky and Gomez, *Addams Family Values*

—Why did God invent men?
—Because a vibrator can't mow the lawn.   Anon

Men are like public toilets – they're either vacant, engaged or full of shit.   Anon

He may have hair upon his chest but, sister, so has Lassie…   Katharine, *Kiss Me, Kate*

The American male doesn't mature until he has exhausted all other possibilities.   Wilfred Sheed

Men are just schoolboys in uniforms diddling with their little peckers.
Bob Shacochis, *Easy in the Islands*

Horny.
Terry Wallis, when asked how he was feeling
after waking from a coma after 19 years

My dears, apart from Anatole France and Albert Schweitzer, there is no man interested in anything but sex.
Barbara Amiel

We are all only human, men in particular.
Alexander McCall Smith

Men are delusional. Hugh Hefner lounges around in a bathrobe with three live-in girlfriends. You know guys are sitting at home watching the Playboy channel and thinking, 'That could be me. *I've* got a bathrobe.'
Denise Munro Robb

The four pillars of the male, heterosexual psyche: naked women, stockings, lesbians, and Sean Connery the best James Bond.
Steve Taylor, *Coupling*

I know what men want. Men want to be really, really close to someone who will leave them alone.
Elayne Boosler

There are three things all men should know: you're never going to be famous. You're fatter than you think. And most important of all, they don't keep wearing stockings.
Steve Taylor, *Coupling*

WOMEN

People say to me, 'You're not very feminine.' Well, they can just suck my dick.
Roseanne

Being a woman is a terribly difficult task, since it consists principally in dealing with men.
Joseph Conrad

Men should only believe half of what women say. But which half?
Jean Giraudoux

I'm a woman! We don't say what we want, but we reserve the right to get pissed off if we don't get it. That's what makes us so fascinating – and not a little bit scary.
Lydia, *Sliding Doors*

Women do not find it difficult nowadays to behave like men, but they often find it extremely difficult to behave like gentlemen.
Compton Mackenzie

[Wife to husband] If you ask me what's wrong one more time, I'm going to tell you.
David Sipress

—The trouble with you women is you have no sense of humour.
—Nonsense! After all, one of us married *you*.
Mark Stone and Ellen Parker

Never make a joke about a woman's hair, clothes or menstrual cycle.
James Hammerton, *Sliding Doors*

I hate women because they always know where things are.
James Thurber

Bints, they're only saft on the ooside. On the inside, they've got hearts on them as hard as Hygena worktops.
Rab C. Nesbitt, *Rab C. Nesbitt*

Do they have to have all these lipsticks and bottles everywhere? And the smells! Why can't women smell of something that isn't a smell?
Bob Geldof

That's what a woman should smell like – Lemon Pledge and meat sauce.
Ray Barone, *Everybody Loves Raymond*

Women should wear white like domestic appliances and they should not be allowed out. You don't take washing machines out of the house, do you?
Bernie Ecclestone

You should treat women the same way as a Yorkshire batsman used to treat a cricket ball. Don't stroke 'em, don't tickle 'em, just give 'em a ruddy good belt.
Fred Trueman

If a woman voices her opinion in the woods, and nobody hears her, is she still a bitch?
Anon

'An Alpine Idyll' by Ernest Hemingway is a simple anecdote about a Swiss peasant: waiting until spring to carry his wife's corpse to burial in the village, he puts her in the woodshed, where she freezes stiff, and he finds her open jaw a handy place to hang his lantern at night.
Justin Kaplan

Never try to impress a woman, because if you do she'll expect you to keep up to the standard for the rest of your life.
W.C. Fields

—Why does it take a woman with PMS four hours to cook a chicken?
—BECAUSE IT JUST FUCKING DOES, OKAY?
Anon

When it concerns a woman, does anybody ever really want the facts?
Philip Marlowe, *The Lady in the Lake*

BATTLE OF THE SEXES

—I'm sorry.
—What for?
—I don't know yet.
Ted Hughes and Sylvia Plath, *Sylvia*

Maybe women are completely different when we're not with them. Maybe they're not cross all the time.
Jeff Murdock, *Coupling*

Why do women insist on asking men what they're thinking? We're thinking: 'Fuck, better think of something to say.' Either that or we're imagining that we're spies.
Ed Byrne

If you want to know the most fundamental difference between men and women, look in a lavatory... Women can talk and micturate at the same time. Men can't. Women actually go into the loo to talk to one another. If anyone talks to you in a gents, it's heresy.   A.A. Gill

I think men talk to women so they can sleep with them and women sleep with men so they can talk to them.   Jay McInerney

The average man speaks 25,000 words a day. The average woman says 30,000 words a day. Unfortunately, when I get home at night, I've spoken my 25,000 but my wife doesn't start hers until we get into bed.
                              Michael Collins

We are men. We are different. We have only one word for soap. We do not own candles. We have never seen anything of any value in a craft shop. We do not own magazines full of photographs of celebrities with their clothes on.   Steve Taylor, *Coupling*

My wife comes home, and I've spread crap all over the house. I come home, and she's organised the refrigerator magnets in a grid pattern. Tell me again which one of us is crazy.   Basil White

Nowadays, when a woman behaves in a hysterical and disagreeable fashion, we say, 'Poor dear, it's probably PMS.' Whereas, if a man behaves in a hysterical and disagreeable fashion, we say, 'What an asshole.'   Molly Ivins

Men can't help it. They're trained to be bastards. We're trained to be angels so they can be bastards.   Marilyn French, *The Women's Room*

When men and women agree, it is only in their conclusions; their reasons are always different.   George Santayana

What he finds unbearable about women is that they are so resolutely in touch with reality.   John Osborne

The stronger women get, the more men love football.
                              Mariah Burton Nelson

It is the little questions from women about tappets that finally push men over the edge.
Philip Roth

The freedom that women were supposed to have found in the sixties largely boiled down to easy contraception and abortion; things to make life easier for men in fact.
Julie Burchill

We have terms like 'sexual harassment' and 'battered women'. A few years ago, they were just called 'life'.
Gloria Steinem

Women will never be equal with men until they can walk down the street with a bald head and a beer gut, and still think they are sexy.
Anon

Most women are one man away from welfare.
Gloria Steinem

We cannot reduce women to equality. Equality is a step down for most women.
Phyllis Schlafly

On one issue at least, men and women agree: they both distrust women.

H.L. Mencken

I can imagine nothing worse than a man-governed world – except a woman-governed world.
Nancy Astor

People would rather be led to *perdition* by a man, than to *victory* by a woman.
Rebecca West

Women and cats will do as they please and men and dogs should relax and get used to the idea.
Robert A. Heinlein

No one will ever win the Battle of the Sexes. There's just too much fraternising with the enemy.
Henry Kissinger

ATTRACTION

—I just met the most wonderful guy!
—Are you sure you didn't just lean into the doorknob again?

Karen Walker and Rosario Salazar, *Will and Grace*

—You had me at 'hello'.
—I didn't say 'hello'.

Homer Simpson and Mel Gibson, *The Simpsons*

—Do you want to come up for coffee?
—I don't drink coffee.
—I haven't got any.

Gloria and Andy, *Brassed Off*

—Your lips say no, but your shoes say yes.
—They're French. You can't trust a word they say.

Dr House and Dr Wilson, *House*

—Darling, I could live in your eyes.
—You'd be at home, there's a sty in one of them.

Les Dawson

—I know you want me.
—Like a cold sore.

Simon Cowell and Paula Abdul

—What a ladykiller!
—Acquitted!

Debbie Jellinsky and Gomez, *Addams Family Values*

—You are so much less attractive when I'm sober.
—Thank goodness it's not that often.

Anna and Walter Fielding, *The Money Pit*

—You two are just too nasty to each other not to have been…*nasty.*
—Hey, I can be a jerk to people I haven't slept with. I am *that* good.

Dr Chase and Dr House, *House*

—I can't stand you.
—I loathe you.
—I despise you.
—I hate you.
—I can get us a room.
—I can drive.   **Berg and Ashley, *Two Guys, a Girl and a Pizza Place***

In my day, I would only have sex with a man if I found him extremely
attractive. These days, girls seem to choose them in much the same way
as they might choose to suck on a boiled sweet.   **Mary Wesley**

The great tragedy of my life is that in my search for the Holy Grail
everyone calls True Love, I see myself as Zorro, a romantic and
mysterious highwayman – and the women I desire see me as Porky Pig.
Harlan Ellison

If I'd seen me at a party, I'd never have gone up and met me.
Dustin Hoffman

—When it comes to women you're hardly Omar Sharif.
—If Omar Sharif lived in Gateshead I doubt he'd be Omar Sharif.
Bob Ferris and Terry Collier, *The Likely Lads*

Give me ten minutes to talk away my ugly face and I will seduce the Queen of France.   **Voltaire**

I've gone out with some of those guys – the ones who are short, fat and
ugly – and it doesn't make any difference. They're just as unappreciative
and self-centred as the good-looking ones.   **Candace Bushnell**

Nothing is more harrowing than the cold sexual appraisal of a
woman's eyes.   **John Osborne**

Men always say the most important thing in a woman is a sense of humour. You know what that means? He's looking for someone to laugh at *his* jokes.
Sheila Wenz

The thing that men always say when they get married is, 'You know, since I've become a married man, I find I'm suddenly so much more attractive to other women.' It's only because their wife's bought them some decent clothes.
Jeremy Hardy

A woman always knows when it's her husband you like, not herself.
Mignon McLaughlin

O, she is the antidote to desire.
William Congreve

As erotic as a darning mushroom.
Duncan Fallowell, on Rowan Pelling

Where have you been all my life – and when are you going back?
Mark Lamarr, *Never Mind the Buzzcocks*

No man wanted me. Rapists would tap me on the shoulder and say, 'Seen any girls?'
Joan Rivers

She would serve after a long voyage at sea.
William Shakespeare

If I don't like a woman, if there's no chemistry, if I'm not attracted to her, then I don't lead her on. I just get out of there, every time…before she even wakes up.
Patrick Maitland, *Coupling*

I picked up a guy – not young or handsome – and he asked me if I had a place. We were on our way home when he caught sight of me – full-face under a street lamp. 'I don't think I'll bother,' he said.
Ossie Clark

What's a rotten girl like you doing in a nice place like this?
Craig Gamble, *Dr Goldfoot and the Bikini Machine*

Saffron is a virgin in a world where men will even turn to soft fruit for pleasure.
Patsy Stone, *Absolutely Fabulous*

She is chaste whom nobody has asked.

Ovid

—Say, baby, let's make like we're the last two people on earth.
—If we were, pal, we always would be.

Roger and Pam Dalrymple

COMPLIMENT

I told my wife she looks sexy with black fingernails. Now she thinks I slammed the car door on her hand on purpose.

Emo Philips

She looked a million dollars, I must admit, even if in well-used notes.

Angela Carter

—Oh, Mr Wilde, I have heard so much about you. Perhaps you have heard of me? I am the ugliest woman in Paris.
—No, Madame. You are the ugliest woman in all of the world!

Elsa Maxwell and Oscar Wilde

Penny Smith is easily my favourite presenter on GMTV, which sounds like a compliment but is a bit like saying she's my favourite member of Al-Qaeda.

Simon Amstell, *Never Mind the Buzzcocks*

Of a compliment only a third is meant.

Welsh proverb

What you say: 'What fragrant perfume!' *What you are thinking*: 'Why don't you just wear Magic Tree car air fresheners as earrings?'

Kevin Dopart

It is my invariable custom to say something flattering to begin with so that I shall be excused if by any chance I put my foot in it later on.

Prince Philip

The surest way to be hated is to be caught delivering the same compliment to two different people.
                                                    Mignon McLaughlin

Mother always said, 'If you haven't got anything nice to say, then fuck off!'
                                                    Jimmy Carr

KISS

Hey, baby, how'd you like to take a bath without ever having to step into the tub?
                                          Lewis Kiniski, *The Drew Carey Show*

Unless you're served in a frosted glass, never come within four feet of my lips.
                                          Karen Walker, *Will and Grace*

—What would I have to give you for one little kiss?
—Chloroform.
                                          Wally Fields and Loretta, *For the Boys*

She has been kissed as often as a police court Bible, and by much the same class of people.
                                                    Robertson Davies

—These lips remind you of anything?
—Yeah, I think the liver in my freezer has gone bad.
                                          Sam Malone and Rebecca Howe, *Cheers*

I married the first man I ever kissed. When I tell this to my children they just about throw up.
                                                    Barbara Bush

Yeah, you remember kissing. It used to come between saying 'Hi' and fucking. I'm an old-fashioned guy.
                                          David Lodge, *Small World*

Kissing is a means of getting two people so close together that they can't see anything wrong with each other.
                                                    Gene Yasenak

Passion: the desire to take one's cigarette out of one's mouth before kissing one's betrothed.
                                                    Gary Davies

Kissing Brad Pitt? You just pop in a mint and get on with it.

Catherine Zeta-Jones

I said I liked it; I didn't say I wanted to kiss it.

Laurel Grey, *In a Lonely Place*

SEX

I'm a celebrity. I'm on TV. There's 24-hour binge drinking. And I *still* can't get a shag.

Alan Carr

—My bedroom. At midnight.
—Perfect. Will you be there too?

Countess Alexandrovna and Boris Grushenko, *Love and Death*

Don't have sex. It leads to kissing and pretty soon you have to start talking to them.

Steve Martin

Australian foreplay: Brace yourself, Sheila.

Anon

What should one say after making love? Thank you seems like too much. I'm sorry – not enough.

Simon Munnery

—Thank you for last night.
—I wasn't with you last night.
—And don't think I'm not eternally grateful.

Carla and Nick Tortelli, *Cheers*

Poor Emily. It's so sad she mixed drugs and alcohol and spent the night with you – when most people only die.

Elaine Nardo, *Taxi*

—How was it for you?
—Very nice.
—Just 'very nice'? 'Very nice' is hardly the phrase to describe two bodies locked in heavenly transport. You wouldn't chisel 'very nice' in granite under Rodin's *The Kiss*. 'Very nice' is when you get a get well card from the butcher or TV repairman.

Steve Blackburn and Vicki Allessio, *A Touch of Class*

I'm a bad lover. I once caught a Peeping Tom booing me.

Rodney Dangerfield

'I Just Died In Your Arms Tonight' is a song about that post-coital feeling. Rejected titles include: 'I'm done, bacon sandwich, please', 'Now just finish yourself off', and 'Do you take Switch?'

Mark Lamarr, *Never Mind the Buzzcocks*

When it comes to sex, one person's always disappointed. So far, I've been lucky, it's always been the woman.   **Lewis Kiniski,** *The Drew Carey Show*

I was in bed last night with my boyfriend, Ernie, and he said to me, 'Sophie, the trouble with you is you've got no tits and a tight box.' I said, 'Ernie, get off my back!'   **Bette Midler**

Men wake up aroused in the morning. We can't help it. We just wake up and we want you. And the women are thinking, 'How can he want me the way I look in the morning?' It's because we can't see you. We have no blood anywhere near our optic nerve.   **Andy Rooney**

For guys, sex is like going to a restaurant. No matter what you order off the menu, you walk out of there going, 'Damn, that was good.' Women go to the restaurant and order something. Sometimes it's good. Sometimes you gotta send it back. Sometimes you might get food poisoning.   **Wanda Sykes**

I've had more women than most people have noses.   **Steve Martin**

—What's the difference between a clitoris and a pub?
—Most men can find a pub.   **Anon**

—Does size really make a difference? You know what women always say...
—Ouch?   **Mark and Patrick Maitland, *Coupling***

Sex is totally ludicrous to everybody except the participants.
Alan Plater

Lap dancing is the ultimate nightmare of man. It's porn that you can see.
Steve Taylor, *Coupling*

I turned down *Playboy*. I had a lot of requests to do a centrefold. But my husband Norm was opposed to it. He said if he can't see it, why should other people?   **Dame Edna Everage**

If women ran the porn industry, the climax of the movie would be when the man shouts, 'I was wrong!'   **Tom McCudden**

I met a girl in a bar and asked her if we could go to bed. She told me that she didn't like casual sex. I told her, 'Okay, I'll wear a tie.'
Rodney Dangerfield

—What was it like [with the German prostitute]?
—I'll tell you one thing, man. Sex is in its infancy in Gateshead.
Neville Hope and 'Oz' Osbourne, *Auf Wiedersehen, Pet*

Is he in need of cold, unloving, rubber-insulated sex in a seedy hotel?
Judge Bernard Caulfied, on Jeffrey Archer, during the libel case, 1987

Coquettes know how to please, not how to love, which is why men love them so much.   **Ovid**

Sleeping with prostitutes is like making your cat dance with you on its hind legs. You know it's wrong, but you try to convince yourself that they're enjoying it as well.   **Scott Capurro**

Blanche, not all of us are classified by the navy as a friendly port.
Dorothy Zbornak, The Golden Girls

She only said 'no' once and then she didn't hear the question.
Andy Lee, 42nd Street

—I marvel at you after all these years. Still like a democratic drawbridge: going down for everybody.
—At my age there's not much traffic any more.
Henry and Eleanor, The Lion in Winter

She could be in a coma but put a man within five miles of her and she'd roll over and shave her legs. *Dorothy Zbornak, The Golden Girls*

If sex were fast food, there'd be an arch over your bed.
Julia Sugarbaker, Designing Women

Although it's true blondes have more fun, it's important to remember that they also have more venereal disease. *George Carlin*

—Mother Superior, do you know we have a case of syphilis in the convent?
—Oh good, I was getting a bit tired of the Beaujolais. *Anon*

I was very sheltered growing up. I knew nothing about sex. My mother said this: 'Sex is a dirty, disgusting thing you save for somebody you love.'
Carol Henry

The first time that she had spread her legs for him it had been like opening her jaws for the dentist. *Tom Robbins*

I told my kid about the birds and the bees. He told me about my wife and the butcher. *Rodney Dangerfield*

Jordan said Gareth Gates was very inexperienced and didn't know where to put his hands. If anyone is in that position again: round her throat and squeeze till her eyes pop. *Mark Lamarr, Never Mind the Buzzcocks*

I was reading an article that was discussing a rare medical condition in which people actually have sex while they are asleep. Now correct me if I'm wrong but isn't that called marriage?
David Letterman

When my old man wanted sex, my mother would show him a picture of me.
Rodney Dangerfield

The only reason my wife has an orgasm is so she'll have something else to moan about.
Bob Monkhouse

The total amount of undesired sex endured by women is probably greater in marriage than in prostitution.
Bertrand Russell

My girlfriend said to me in bed last night, 'You're a pervert.' I said, 'That's a big word for a girl of nine.'
Emo Philips

Never have sex with your best friend, because it's always a mistake. I did that last week. The next morning I was so embarrassed. I thought, 'Oh no, I've had sex with my best friend!' I couldn't look at him. I couldn't talk to him. I couldn't feed him. I couldn't bring him for walks...
Kevin Gildea

I've tried several varieties of sex. The conventional position makes me claustrophobic and the others give me a stiff neck or lockjaw.
Tallulah Bankhead

Sex manuals? Easier done than said.
Peter de Vries

The silliest and most unscientific book on sex that I have ever read is Vatsayana's *Kama Sutra*... It is not even good pornography... The author of the Hindu classic on sex, was, himself, impotent.
Khushwant Singh

If you don't have an erection, but you want to have one, the simple answer is to fall asleep with your flies open on a National Express coach.
Jeremy Hardy

Now I'm pushing 48 and all women seem to want is hot sex and to parade around in Agent Provocateur underwear. How I long for a Wendy Craig, once a sex kitten of suburbia, to make me a cup of tea, bring me a bourbon and tickle me under the covers.   Tim Lott

At my age I'm envious of a stiff wind.   Rodney Dangerfield

Holly Madison, 27, has got engaged to Hugh Hefner, 80. Asked what the founder of *Playboy* likes best in bed, Holly said, 'The guard rail.' Anon

I used to ask women to come upstairs and have sex, but now it has to be one or the other.   Clement Freud

His testicles were as flat and juiceless as trampled grapes.   Tom Robbins

In the United States now, there's 'Viagra Plus', which gives 36 hours of erection. So you have 90-year-old guys with their poor old dry wives – in and out, in and out, they're setting them on fire! You've heard of the fires we've been having in California? They were started by my neighbour, Harry Schwartz, 92, taking Viagra Plus.   Joan Rivers

If Marx were alive today, he would have been hard put to avoid saying that imaginary sex is the opiate of the people.   John Ralston Saul

Well, thanks to the Internet, I'm now bored of sex.   Fry, *Futurama*

No one in this life is a virgin because life has screwed us all at some point.
                      Anon

DATING

Romance is dead. So is my mother. Man, 42, inherited wealth. Box no.
7652.   **Personal ad, *London Review of Books***

Asian gentleman, tall, honest, suffers from Tourette's syndrome,
obsessive-compulsive disorder, paranoid schizophrenia, also impotent,
would like to meet attractive, professional lady for relationship with
possible view to marriage.   **Personal ad, *Wolverhampton Chronicle***

I want a man who'll commit, not a man's who's committed.
                                    Carrie Bradshaw, *Sex and the City*

I know a nice schizophrenic. Or how about a manic-depressive? At least
you know they'll be fun half the time.
                                    Robert Hartley, *The Bob Newhart Show*

I would ask you back to my place but I've got a chain-saw in soak.
                                    Graeme Garden, *I'm Sorry I Haven't a Clue*

—So, Lenny, how are things working out with that girl next door?
—It's all over. She got a window shade.
                                    Carl Carlson and Lenny Leonard, *The Simpsons*

The compulsion to find a lover and husband in a single person has
doomed more women to misery than any other illusion.   **Carolyn Heilbrun**

I met this guy in a bar. He said, 'When I make love I turn into an animal.'
Well, that's a step up.   **Judy Tenuta**

When a man says he wants to meet a girl with a sense of humour, he
means one who will laugh at everything he says while her breasts jiggle.
                                    Cheri Oteri

—Do you know the biggest turn-off on a first date?
—You?   **Jeff Murdock and Steve Taylor, *Coupling***

—How would you like it if I made your life a living hell?
—Well, I'm not really ready for a relationship right now.
                    Lois Einhorn and Ace Ventura, *Ace Ventura: Pet Detective*

—I just came out of a seven-year marriage. It's hard to think of replacing Lilith.
—Just go to the morgue and open any drawer.
                    Frasier Crane and Carla Tortelli, *Cheers*

—What are you doing Saturday night?
—Committing suicide.
—What about Friday night?
                    Allan Felix and girl in museum, *Play it Again, Sam*

I went out with an Irish Catholic. Very frustrating. You can take the girl out of Cork...   **Markus Birdman**

What you say: 'Hi, can I get you a drink?' *What you are thinking*: 'Hi, will you sleep with me in exchange for a vodka and cranberry?'
                    Michael Levy

How was dinner? Well, let's just say that when I picked my lobster out of the tank, I had no idea he was in for a better evening than I was.
                    Niles Crane, *Frasier*

I had a great time tonight, really. It was like the Nuremberg Trials.

Woody Allen

I have no luck with women. I once went on a date and asked the woman if she'd brought any protection. She pulled a switchblade on me.
                    Scott Roeben

Bartender! Two Bloody Marys, please. And there's a twenty in it for you if one of them's poisoned. I don't even care which one.
                    Roz Doyle, on a bad date, *Frasier*

If I wanted to be treated like shit, I'd get married.

Gloria Trillo, *The Sopranos*

One woman's sexual harassment is another woman's night off.

Karen Walker, *Will and Grace*

Men: they're either married or gay. And if they're not gay, they've just
broken up with the most wonderful woman in the world, or they've just
broken up with a bitch who looks exactly like me. They're in transition
from a monogamous relationship and they need more space. Or they're
tired of space, but they just can't commit. Or they want to commit, but
they're afraid to get close. They want to get close, you don't want to get
near them.

Meg Jones, *The Big Chill*

—Guys are like the subway. You miss one, another one comes along in
five minutes.
—Unless it's the end of the night, then you get on anything.

Robin Scherbatsky and Lily Aldrin, *How I Met Your Mother*

Man, what a night I've had! My inflatable girlfriend ran off with my air mattress.

Drew Carey

I had a blind date. I waited two hours on the corner. A girl walked by,
and I said, 'Are you Louise?' She said, 'Are you Rodney?' I said, 'Yeah.'
She said, 'I'm not Louise.'

Rodney Dangerfield

Let's face it, the only way you're gonna be in there with Deborah is if
you're both marooned on a deserted island and she eats a poisonous
berry or a nut which makes her temporarily deaf, dumb, stupid, forgetful
and desperate for sex.

Gary Strang, *Men Behaving Badly*

Forget her, Stanley. That girl will tear your heart out, put it in a blender
and hit 'frappé'.

Charlie Schumacher, *The Mask*

Don't give up hope. There are new women turning 18 every day.

Matchmaker, *How I Met Your Mother*

—I'll make you forget you were ever married to Lilith!
—That's never happened before without a prescription.

Madeleine and Frasier Crane, *Frasier*

There's only two reasons to date a girl you've already dated: breast implants.

Barney Stinson, *How I Met Your Mother*

—She's really got him by the balls.
—That's not so bad, is it?
—Depends on the grip.

Lester Murphy and Petra, *Rounder*

Women completely plot the course of every love affair, and are completely wrong.

Mignon McLaughlin

—I've taken myself off the dating circuit. I was getting a bit desperate.
—Well, I was a bit concerned when you called to ask if Gloria was our first or second cousin.

Niles and Frasier Crane, *Frasier*

I'd prefer a new edition of the Spanish Inquisition than to ever let a woman in my life.

Professor Henry Higgins, *My Fair Lady*

—So why a dating agency?
—Because I'm tired of wasting my time on people who aren't desperate.

Sally Harper and Jane Christie, *Coupling*

My computer dating bureau came up with a perfect gentleman. Still, I've got another three goes.

Sally Poplin

I joined a dating agency and went out on a load of dates that didn't work out. I went back to the woman who ran the agency and said, 'Have you not got somebody on your books who doesn't care about how I look or what job I have and has a nice big pair of boobs?' And she checked on her computer and said, 'Actually, we have one, but unfortunately, it's you.'

Karl Spain

Speed dating is when 12 men and 12 women get together in a room. They spend 8 minutes talking to one other and then move on to the next person after a bell rings. Basically, it's all the stress and humiliation of a blind date…times 12.

Frasier Crane, *Frasier*

Speed dating…
You: Hi.
She: Piss off.
You: Thank you for your time.

Jeff Green, *The A-Z of Being Single*

I have always been the lover – never the beloved, and I have spent much of my life waiting for trains, planes, boats, footsteps, doorbells, letters, telephones, snow, rain, thunder.

John Cheever

When you're away, I'm restless, lonely, wretched, bored, dejected; only here's the rub, my darling dear, I feel the same when you are here.

Samuel Hoffenstein

Relationships are hard. It's like a full-time job, and we should treat it like one. If your boyfriend or girlfriend wants to leave you, they should give you two weeks' notice. There should be severance pay, and before they leave you, they should have to find you a temp.

Bob Ettinger

Why do you have to break up with her? Be a man. Just stop calling.

Joey Tribbiani, *Friends*

I'll get the speech about how wonderful I am. Basic rule, isn't it? The more wonderful you are at the start of the speech, the more dumped you are at the end.

Sally Harper, *Coupling*

—Are you gonna miss me?
—Only until I go to the news-stand and buy a *Hustler*.

Lois and Peter Griffin, *Family Guy*

I think my ex-girlfriend has weekly lessons with the devil on how to be more evil. I don't know what she charges him.

Emo Philips

—I'm getting back with Sonia.
—I thought it was only dogs that returned to their own vomit.

Martin and Pauline Fowler, *EastEnders*

These days, I favour older men. They don't have such awful taste in music.

Jerry Hall

—What do women and cowpats have in common?
—The older they get, the easier they are to pick up.

Anon

If you're 48 and you haven't seen people in 30 years, don't do it. They're 48. They look like parents.

Bill Cosby

ROMANCE

Today is Valentine's Day – or, as men like to call it, Extortion Day.

Jay Leno

I wanted to make it really special on Valentine's Day, so I tied my boyfriend up. And for three solid hours I watched whatever I wanted to on TV.

Tracy Smith

Nothing spoils a romance so much as a sense of humour in the woman.

Oscar Wilde

The historical St Valentine was clubbed to death, you know.   Lynne Truss

Screw The Roses, Send Me Thorns: The Romance and Sexual Sorcery of Sadomasochism

Philip Miller, book title

I live in New York City. I think it's romantic when someone offers me a seat on the subway.

Carrie Bradshaw, *Sex and the City*

You've forgotten those June nights at the Riviera…the night I drank champagne from your slipper – two quarts. It would have been more but you were wearing inner soles.
Groucho Marx

Remember those magical nights, Cynthia…we'd dance cheek to cheek. I'd rub my stubble against yours.
Milton Berle

Romance. I gave the bitch romance! I've never once come back from that chip shop without saving her the skin off my fish supper.
Rab C. Nesbitt, *Rab C. Nesbitt*

Alan Sugar, *The Apprentice* star, once sent his wife a birthday card with the message 'from Alan Sugar'.
Fiona Phillips

I wanted a Heathcliff to my Cathy; I've found a Ken Barlow to my Deidre.
Janet, *The Smoking Room*

And what, for instance, would have happened had Romeo and Juliet lived to middle age, their silhouettes broadened by pasta.
Anita Loos

Like all good romantics, Shakespeare realised love was a lot more likely to end with a bunch of dead Danish people than with a kiss.
Dawson Leery, *Dawson's Creek*

LOVE

They had the perfect love affair. Until they fell in love.
Tagline, *A Touch of Class*

—Tell me you love me, Al.
—I love football, I love beer, let's not cheapen the meaning of the word.
Peggy and Al Bundy, *Married With Children*

You don't know what love means. To you it's just another four-letter word.
Brick Pollitt, *Cat on a Hot Tin Roof*

Your picture's in my wallet and I'm sitting on it. And if that isn't love, I don't know what is.   Frank Burns, *M*A*S*H*

Love is in the air – run for cover.   Tagline, *Four Weddings and a Funeral*

Love is the desire to prostitute oneself. There is, indeed, no exalted pleasure that cannot be related to prostitution.

Charles Baudelaire

What is irritating about love is that it is a crime that requires an accomplice.   Charles Baudelaire

Love: looks and sounds like murder.   Theodore Roethke

If you've never wanted to kill your mate, you've never been in love. If you've never held a box of rat poison in your hand and stared at it for a good long while, you've never been in love.   Chris Rock

One often falls in love with a woman out of boredom; one does not know what else to do with her.   Jean Paul Richter

No one has ever loved anyone the way everyone wants to be loved.
Mignon McLaughlin

Love is an agreement on the part of two people to overestimate each other.   E.M. Cioran

I never loved a man I liked, and I never liked a man I loved.   Fanny Brice

We all like someone because. We love someone although.
Henri de Montherlant

You say stupid things to the person you're in love with, like, 'Here's all my money.'   Sean Hughes

If I ever really love it will be like Mary, Queen of Scots, who said of her Bothwell that she could follow him round the world in her nightie.

J.M. Barrie

The more serious your love affair, the more people will find it ridiculous.

Mignon McLaughlin

Love is the fart
Of every heart:
It pains a man when 'tis kept close
And others doth offend when 'tis let loose.

Sir John Suckling

Love is an exploding cigar we all willingly smoke.

Lynda Barry

—What's the difference between love, true love, and showing off?
—Spitting, swallowing, and gargling.

Anon

There's nothing like unrequited love to take all the flavour out of a peanut butter sandwich.

Charlie Brown

He loves me not, he loves me not, he loves me not, he loves me not, he loves me not.

Anna Burns

—He said he loved me.
—Men say that. They all say that. Then they come.

Julie Hawkes and Helen Bowman, *Parenthood*

The way to a man's heart isn't through his stomach; it's through his hankie-pocket with a bread knife.

Jo Brand

I love Mickey Mouse more than any woman I've ever known.

Walt Disney

MARRIAGE

—How are tornadoes and marriage alike?
—They both begin with a lot of blowing and sucking, and in the end you lose your house.
Anon

I have always thought that every woman should marry, and no man.
Benjamin Disraeli

There is one woman whom fate has destined for each of us. If we miss her we are saved.
Anon

Why the hell should I get a wife when the man next door's got one?
Furry Lewis

I can dimly understand why people get married because if it wasn't for marriage men and women would have to fight with strangers.
Les Dawson

I always wanted a beautiful, loving wife. And she always wanted to be a citizen.
Emo Philips

Will you marry me? It's risky, but you'd get fucked regularly.
John Osborne, proposing to Penelope Gilliatt (she became his third wife)

—Please marry me, Bev. Because I'm shit without you.
—Oh, how romantic – a marriage proposal that contains the word 'shit'.
Raymond and Bev, *Riding in Cars With Boys*

There's something you ought to know. When Alan J. Lerner asks a girl to marry him, it's his way of saying goodbye.
Bud Whitney

As soon as I got married I knew I was in trouble. My in-laws sent me a thank-you note.
Rodney Dangerfield

No man should marry until he has studied anatomy and dissected at least one woman.
Honoré de Balzac

A man should marry only a very pretty woman in case he ever wants some other man to take her off his hands. Sacha Guitry

Once a woman passes a certain point in intelligence, it is almost impossible to get a husband: she simply cannot go on listening to men without snickering. H.L. Mencken

Never marry a man you wouldn't want to be divorced from. Nora Ephron

I proposed to Neil. It wasn't a question. It was an order. Christine Hamilton

Men don't settle down. Men surrender. Chris Rock

Wow, let's have a look at that engagement ring. It's beautiful. When is the stone being put in? Will Truman, *Will and Grace*

A wedding invitation is a beautiful and formal notification of the desire to share a solemn and joyous occasion sent by people who have been saying, 'Do we have to ask them?' to people whose first response is, 'How much do you think we have to spend on them?' Judith Martin

It's too bad that in most marriage ceremonies they don't use the word 'obey' any more. It used to lend a little humour to the occasion.
Lloyd Cory

The bride was dressed in white and with the sheer size of her, it looked as though someone was towing a sight screen to Lord's. Les Dawson

The kneeling was rather tedious, the cushions were stuffed with peach stones I believe and made me make a face which passed for piety. I got a wife and a cold on the same day. Lord Byron

At the age of 20, Bob Monkhouse was disowned by his parents after marrying his first wife, Elizabeth. His mother turned up at the wedding in mourning black. BBC news website

Marriage: a gift a man gives to a woman for which she never forgives him.
                                                                    Thomas Szasz

In every marriage more than a week old there are grounds for divorce.
                                                            Robert Anderson

The problem is many terrific women have made themselves overqualified for the job of wife, because many men are looking for a woman with receptionist-level wife skills, not CEO-level wife skills.
        Karen Salmansohn, *How to Succeed in Business Without a Penis*

—What are the disadvantages of life with a professional wife?
—Nobody takes any interest in whether you have any socks or, indeed, pants.   Interviewer and Boris Johnson

Marriage entitles women to the protection of a strong man who will steady the stepladder while they paint the kitchen ceiling.   Fran Lebowitz

—You don't work. You're unemployed.
—Loving you is my job, Larry.
                        Larry and Cheryl David, *Curb Your Enthusiasm*

—I do have my own opinions. I'm not just a trophy wife.
—Trophy wife? What contest in hell did I win?
                        Marie and Frank Barone, *Everybody Loves Raymond*

I used to think of marriage as a plate-glass window just begging for a brick. The self-exhibition, the self-satisfaction, smarminess, tightness, tight-arsedness. The way married couples go out in fours like a pantomime horse, the men walking together at the front, the women trailing a little way behind. The men fetching the gin and tonics from the bar while the women take their handbags to the toilet. It doesn't have to be like that but mostly it is.   Jeanette Winterson, *Written on the Body*

Marriage has teeth, and him bite very hot.   Jamaican proverb

My marriage with Bill Arnold was like a close-up of tooth decay.
                                                                    Roseanne

At times her marriage seemed like a saint, guillotined and still walking for miles through the city, carrying its head.　　Lorrie Moore, *Like Life*

Matrimony is the union of meanness and martyrdom.　　Karl Kraus

Marriage is wonderful. It's my wife I can't stand.　　Frank Carson

There's a curious statistic I came across recently. The average married couple converse for twenty minutes every week. What do they find to talk about?　　Dave Allen

If they like your little jokes before you're married, afterwards they ask why you're always trying to be funny.　　J.B. Priestley

I have come to terms with the fact that my dinner is in the oven and always will be.　　Jeffrey Bernard

The other night I said to my wife Ruth, 'Do you feel that the sex and excitement has gone out of our marriage?' She said, 'I'll discuss it with you during the next commercial.'　　Milton Berle

No one had thought fit to reveal to me the great secret of married sexual love, which is that it comes to an end.　　Kathleen Tynan

My wife doesn't. Understand me?　　William Cole

It's tough having sex during marriage because you're always walking that tightrope between 'This again?' and 'Where did you learn that?'　　Emo Philips

I suppose this is what it's all about when it comes to it, marriage – reaching 60 and spraying each other with Ralgex.　　Victor Meldrew, *One Foot in the Grave*

Without allotments, golf courses, pubs, and fishing trips, the divorce (and murder) figures in the UK would undoubtedly soar, because it's a sad truth that many couples can only manage to stay together by living apart.　　Victor Lewis-Smith

I gave him the best years of my thighs.   **Dorothy Zbornak, *The Golden Girls***

I was very fond of him before we were married, and even *after* we were married. It was the bit in between which got so difficult.
Elizabeth Harris, ex-wife of Rex Harrison

It seems a shame that marriage can't be saved as a retirement plan for sensible grown-ups after the children have left home.   **Irma Kurtz**

REMARRIAGE

—So, Sir Paul McCartney, do you think that you will ever go down on one knee again?
—Oi! Her name's Heather.   **Anon**

I got married the second time in the way that, when a murder is committed, crackpots turn up at the police station to confess the crime.
Delmore Schwartz

She had exercised a mysterious attraction and then an unmysterious repulsion on two former husbands, the second of whom had to resort to a fatal coronary to get away from her.   **Kingsley Amis**

If their husbands died, most middle-aged women would immediately look ten years younger.   **Mignon McLaughlin**

One woman friend of mine told me she hated her husband so much that when he died she had him cremated, blended him with marijuana, and smoked him. She said, 'That's the best he's made me feel in years.'
Maureen Murphy

For her fifth wedding, the bride wore black and carried a Scotch and soda.   **Phyllis Battelle, on Barbara Hutton's marriage to Porfirio Rubirosa**

Love and marriage is like a horse and carriage – obsolete for a hundred years.
Ivor Dembina

Marriage has been replaced by the mortgage. It's harder to get out of a mutual mortgage than it is a marriage.
Germaine Greer

CHEATING

You're wearing the wrong shade of lipstick, Mister.
Johnny Morrison, *The Blue Dahlia*

The chains of marriage are so heavy that it takes two to carry them, and sometimes three.
Alexander Dumas

A football referee is facing divorce proceedings after he pulled a pair of knickers out of his pocket instead of a red card during a match. Carlos Jose Figueira Ferro was so embarrassed that he ended the game with 20 minutes still to go, as his wife, watching, called lawyers.
Terra, *Observer*

When will I understand that what's astonishing about the number of men who remain faithful is not that it's so small but that there are any of them at all?
Nora Ephron

If you marry a man who cheats on his wife, you'll be married to a man who cheats on his wife.
Ann Landers

Men cheat for the same reason dogs lick their balls...because they can.
Samantha Jones, *Sex and the City*

She blamed me for cruelty and flagrant infidelity. I spent a whole weekend in Brighton with a lady called Vera Williams. She had the nastiest-looking hairbrush I have ever seen.
Noël Coward, *Private Lives*

You've got to believe me, Edith, nothing was ever constipated.

Archie Bunker, *All in the Family*

A man never forgives a woman who forces him to tell lies.

Georges Simenon

Gone but not forgiven.   **Epitaph for an adulterous husband, Georgia**

DIVORCE

Dear Mrs McCartney, oh what a mess! You must be kicking yourself.

I'm Sorry I Haven't a Clue

Don't get mad. Get everything!   **Ivana Trump**

I wanted to keep it simple, but she wanted a big divorce with reporters, photographers, witnesses...   **Bill Hoest**

—And you better get yourself a damn good lawyer!
—Best your money can buy!

Oliver and Barbara Rose, *The War of the Roses*

My wife left me, which was very painful. Then she came back to me, which was excruciating.   **Frasier Crane, *Frasier***

Excruciate: the ligament that attaches your ex-wife to your paycheck.

Kevin Cuddihy

Judges, as a class, display, in the matter of arranging alimony, that reckless generosity which is found only in men who are giving away someone else's cash.   **P.G. Wodehouse**

Alimony: the ransom that the happy pay to the devil.   **H.L. Mencken**

I always pay my alimony on time, because if I ever fall behind, I'm afraid my ex-wife might try to repossess me.   **Henry Youngman**

My husband and I had our best sex during the divorce. It was like cheating on our lawyers.   **Theresa**, *Cheaper to Keep Her*

—What's the difference between getting a divorce and getting circumcised?
—When you get a divorce, you get rid of the whole prick.   **Anon**

I've been divorced for seven years now. Each year I celebrate the anniversary of my divorce by watching my wedding video, backwards. It's very therapeutic. First, you see the bouquet flying into my hands, we take the rings off, we look at each other and say, 'Do I?' and march back up the aisle.   **Ellen Orchid**

If you made a list of the reasons why any couple got married, and another list of the reasons for their divorce, you'd have a hell of a lot of overlapping.   **Mignon McLaughlin**

My first wife divorced me on grounds of incompatibility and, besides, I think she hated me.   **Oscar Levant**

The ideal divorce becomes relatively simple, as long as you have gone through all the groundwork of having a really miserable marriage.
                                      Artie Shaw (married 8 times)

Divorce is just nature's way of recycling.   **Jasmine Birtles**

GRUMPY
HOME
& FAMILY

FAMILY-PLANNING & CHILDREN

The other night, the President gave a speech. He said, 'Children are our most precious natural resource.' I thought, 'Let's hope it never comes to that.'
Emo Philips

My wife wants to have a kid. I say, 'Why bring strangers into the house?'
Anon

Of course I want to have kids, Claire – just not all the time.   **David Sipress**

How to avoid becoming broody: get up every hour throughout the night and burn two hundred quid.
Jeff Green, The A-Z of Having a Baby

Slogans for the New Male Birth Control Pill...
Safe, effective way to avoid male pregnancy.
Recommended by 4 out of 5 doctors who cheat on their wives.
He shoots, he doesn't score!
David Letterman

We don't think our 17-year-old daughter is ready for the pill, so we've been slipping her a placebo.
Jonathan Katz

You wake up one day and say, 'You know what, I don't think I ever need to sleep or have sex again.' Congratulations, you're ready to have children.
Ray Romano

I was sued by a woman who claimed that she became pregnant because she watched me on television and I bent her contraceptive coil.
Uri Geller

She was really surprised to find out that she was pregnant. 'When did you have your last check up?' the doctor asked her. 'Never! An Italian, a Frenchman and a Yank, but never a Czech!'   **Anon**

I'm going to have a baby! A bad noisy thing with eyes is going to crawl out of my genitals and destroy my life. And my mother is going to side with it!   **Sally Harper, *Coupling***

—What's it like, being pregnant?
—Everything's twice the size it was nine months ago, and I'm growing another head inside me.
                    Dorothy and Gary Strang, *Men Behaving Badly*

—Can we please talk about this pregnancy without bringing up John Hurt?
—No man can do that.   **Susan Walker and Steve Taylor, *Coupling***

You should never say anything to a woman that even remotely suggests that you think she's pregnant unless you can see an actual baby emerging from her at that moment.   **Dave Barry**

The little girl who was notified that a baby brother or sister was on the way listened in thoughtful silence, then raised her gaze from her mother's belly to her eyes and said, 'Yes, but who will be the new baby's mummy?'
                                                            Judith Viorst

By far the most common craving of pregnant women is not to be pregnant.   **Phyllis Diller**

'Delivery' is the wrong word to describe the childbearing process. Delivery is, 'Here's your pizza.' Takes thirty minutes or less. 'Exorcism' is more apt.   **Jeff Stilson**

As Diana Ross once told me, 'Giving birth is like shitting a fridge.'
                                                            Trisha Goddard

—Aww, it's a boy. And *what* a boy!
—Ah, no. That's the umbilical cord. It's a girl.
                            Homer Simpson and Dr Hibbert, *The Simpsons*

Michael Jackson and the doctor are walking out of the delivery room after his wife gives birth to their son. Michael says, 'How long before we can have sex?' The doctor says, 'At least wait until he's walking.'   **Anon**

Madonna's figure looks fantastic considering it's only eight weeks since she bought a baby.   **Graham Norton**

Women are now waiting till they're about 63 to have children, which isn't a bad idea because you don't have to push, it just falls out. Also, you can breast-feed standing up.   **Dr Phil Hammond**

Kids. They're not easy. But there has to be some penalty for sex.
     Bill Maher

Having a baby is a big responsibility. It's like being in charge of sanitation at a Haitian jail.   **Frank Drebin, *Naked Gun 33½***

A baby, if you really break it down, is just a tiny, shirtless, bald human being with a bag of its own crap tied around its waist.   **Patton Oswalt**

Most men cannot change a diaper without subsequently renting an airplane that trails a banner that says, 'I CHANGED A DIAPER.'
     Anna Quindlen

If you were to open up a baby's head – and I'm not for a moment suggesting that you should – you would find nothing but an enormous drool gland.   **Dave Barry**

—He has my father's eyes.
—Gomez, take those out of his mouth!
     Gomez and Morticia Addams, *Addams Family Values*

I would play peek-a-boo with babies if the game had an official ending.

     Jason Love

—I just got the baby to sleep.
—Do you sing to him?
—Only if he's been bad.

Miranda Hobbes and Robert Leeds, *Sex and the City*

What mother would sing death threats to her baby? Yet how many moms – night after night, in deceptively soothing tones – threaten to stick their infants in a tree, and then casually hint of the impending doom from the dangerously overloaded bough? It's no wonder that the lyricist wishes to remain anonymous.

Jeffrey Martin

Parenting is like your Aunt Edna's ass. It goes on for ever and it's just as frightening.

Frank Buckman, *Parenthood*

There's so much crap talked about bringing up a child. A fucking moron could do it. Morons do bring up their children. It's just endless love, endless patience, that's it.

Bob Geldof

You don't know what love is till you become a parent. You don't know what love is till you fish a turd out of the bath tub for someone. And then have to act positive about it: 'Good job!'

Margaret Smith

—How can I ensure an accurate aim when my little boy goes to the toilet?
—Rest the barrel on the edge.

Humphrey Lyttleton and Tim Brooke-Taylor, *I'm Sorry I Haven't a Clue*

You need a lot of money to raise a modern child. Hair gel alone will run you thousands of dollars.

Dave Barry

On a bus the other day a woman with a baby sat opposite, the baby bawled, and the woman at once began to unlace herself, exposing a large, red udder, which she swung into the baby's face. The infant, however, continued to cry and the woman said, 'Come on, there's a good boy – if you don't, I shall give it to the gentleman opposite.' Do I look ill-nourished?

W.N.P. Barbellion

When Baby's cries grew hard to bear
I popped him in the Frigidaire.
I never would have done so if
I'd known that he'd be frozen stiff.
My wife said: 'George, I'm so unhappé!
Our darling's now completely *frappé*!'   **Harry Graham, *'L'Enfant Glacé'***

I don't understand what children are for, except to eat, shit and sweep chimneys.   **Jackie Clune**

Every minute in the presence of a child takes seven minutes off your life.   **Barbara Kingsolver**

Alligators have the right idea. They eat their young.   **Ida Corwin, *Mildred Pierce***

Toddlers are more likely to eat healthy food if they find it on the floor.   **Jan Blaustone**

Have you seen the cost of children's shoes? Sixty pounds! That's a wrap of coke. In some countries you can get a whole child for sixty pounds. Fully dressed.   **Jackie Clune**

Entertainers at children's birthday parties are a) cheating b) too expensive and c) all booked up by the time you really get in a panic, anyway. Spend the money on gin: for you, beforehand; for you, afterwards; and for the mothers who collect so that they'll think the kids had a good party.   **Katharine Whitehorn**

Insecure Yuppie parents even have 'play dates', for Christ's sake! Playing is now done by appointment! Whatever happened to 'You show me your wee-wee, and I'll show you mine'? You never hear that any more.   **George Carlin**

Let's face it, there's a lot of spoilt kids out there – because you can't spank Grandma.   **Janet Anderson**

Of all the things I dislike, there is nothing so abhorrent to me as a spoilt child. I have pinched several, and never had the slightest qualm of conscience afterwards; and though I am a man of peace, I hope to pinch many more before I die.   H.L.R. Shepherd

Billy, in one of his nice new sashes,
Fell in the fire and was burnt to ashes;
Now, although the room grows chilly,
I haven't the heart to poke poor Billy.   Harry Graham, 'Tender Heartedness'

It's no wonder people are so horrible when they start life as children. Kingsley Amis

Some people do not make good children. They should spring upon the world fully grown, preferably with a gin and tonic in hand, and conversation in full swing.   Margaret Morley

When other children misbehaved I gather they were threatened with me as a playmate.   Peter Ustinov

One of the reasons children are such duds socially is that they say things like, 'When do you think you're going to be dead, Grandma?'   Jean Kerr

Babysitters are expensive. They charge $8 an hour. When I was a teenager, I'd charge 75 cents. Course, I drank all the booze in the house.
                                                      Margaret Smith

I don't have a baby, but I still book a babysitter. I tell her to check on the kid after half an hour or so. Then when I return I say, 'Escaped?! Well, give me £50 and we'll call it even.'   Harry Hill

If you have never been hated by a child, you have never been a parent.
                                                        Bette Davis

I can do one of two things. I can be president of the United States or I can control Alice. I cannot possibly do both.   Theodore Roosevelt

—My son's rather highly strung.
—Highly strung...he should be.

Mrs Heath and Basil Fawlty, *Fawlty Towers*

Should you smack? Everybody smacks; all that varies is the amount of guilt you feel about it.　　　　　　　**Katharine Whitehorn**

My parents are from Glasgow which means they're incredibly hard, but I was never smacked as a child – well, maybe one or two grams to get me to sleep at night.　　　　　　　**Susan Murray**

My father only hit me once – but he used a Volvo.　　**Bob Monkhouse**

Son, I'm going to punish you so hard that they'll throw a benefit concert for you.　　　　　　　**Dan Conner,** *Roseanne*

Honey! Bring down my copy of my will...and an eraser.
　　　　　　　Bob Dandridge, *Everyone Says I Love You*

My parents put a live teddy bear in my crib.　　　　**Woody Allen**

When I was a kid I asked my mother for a bubble bath, so she brought the water to a boil.　　　　　　　**Rodney Dangerfield**

My mother tried to kill me when I was a baby. She denied it. She said she thought the plastic bag would keep me fresh.　　　**Bob Monkhouse**

—How do you stop your kid from wetting the bed?
—Give him an electric blanket.　　　　　　　**Anon**

My childhood was so bleak, I wanted to stick my head in my Easy Bake oven.　　**Mary O'Halloran**

I got kicked out of Scouts for eating a brownie.　　**Ross Noble**

When my parents got divorced there was a custody fight over me and no one showed up.

Rodney Dangerfield

Sometimes I wish I'd had a terrible childhood, so that at least I'd have an excuse.

Jimmy Fallon

Am I the only person in Britain who was not sexually abused as a child? Every day, I hear adults blaming their dysfunctional personalities on unwanted advances during childhood, yet the bitter truth is that I was a plain boy, and nobody really fancied me.

Victor Lewis-Smith

My parents neglected to abuse me. They're gone now, alas... I've thought about asking my wife's parents to abuse me, but it seems too little, too late.

P.J. O'Rourke, planning his memoirs

There was abuse in my family, but it was mostly musical in nature.

Terry Bohner, *A Mighty Wind*

Your children vividly remember every unkind thing you ever did to them, plus a few you really didn't.

Mignon McLaughlin

Mother Nature is wonderful. She gives us twelve years to develop a love for our children before turning them into teenagers.

Eugene Bertin

Enquiring about her twin 16-year-old daughters, my American friend replied, 'They are ranting, self-absorbed, hormonal bags of protoplasm. Procreation sucks.'

Chris Green

As a teenager in the early 1970s I wore long, straight, home-made frocks; had long, straight, home-made hair; listened to folk music without laughing; kept going to see *Elvira Madigan*; and wrote 'irony' in the margins of most of my books.

Lynne Truss

When I was a kid I had acne. Was it bad? Oh, it was bad. I fell asleep once in the library and woke up with a blind kid reading my face.

Rodney Dangerfield

Too many young people are beginning to regard home as a filling station by day and a parking place for the night.   **Revd William Joyce**

—Darlene, you're grounded till menopause.
—Yours or mine?
—Your father's.   **Roseanne and Darlene Conner,** *Roseanne*

The true nightmare of the empty nest is that the kids were the only people in the house who knew how to use the remote control.
                    Nora Ephron

It bothers me that the world revolves around married people with children, so I've come up with a politically correct term for Single With No Kids: Happy.   **Danielle Broussard**

People have been marrying and bringing up children for centuries now. Nothing has ever come of it.   **Celia Green**

There are enough people in the world. I did my part by raising dogs.
                    Anita O'Day

FAMILY

Some men have a Dream. Louie has a Family.   **Tagline,** *Lucky Louie*

I come from a very big family so you would very rarely find us all at the same time in the same place. There's only three occasions in life when you'd find the whole family together: a family wedding, a family funeral, or if I brought home a bag of chips.   **Ardal O'Hanlon**

Eight kids? Jiminy Christmas, someone should tell her it's a vagina not a clown car.   **Jackson Harrison,** *Gary the Rat*

When I remember my family, I always remember their backs. They were always indignantly leaving places.   **John Cheever**

When I was ten my family moved to Illinois. When I was twelve, I found them.
                                                                    Emo Philips

Families! I hate you! Enclosed hallways, shut doors, jealous possessors of happiness.
                                                                    André Gide

Any bar-room brawl is better than the persistent pinpricks of the happy little family.
                                                                    Dawn Powell

If Mr Vincent Price were to be co-starred with Miss Bette Davis in a story by Mr Edgar Allan Poe directed by Mr Roger Corman, it could not fully express the pent-up violence and depravity of a single day in the life of the average family.
                                                                    Quentin Crisp

There was a lot of drinking and a lot of violence in my family. My mom has home movies you have to be 18 to get into.
                                                                    Margaret Smith

What a family! They make the Borgias look like the Archers.
                                                   Harold Steptoe, *Steptoe and Son*

I had four children – one was abducted by a koala bear under tragic circumstances – and it has been difficult. For a long time I blamed myself, but Megastars Anonymous taught me the secret of happiness: put your family last.
                                                                    Dame Edna Everage

Ah, now to spend some quality time away from my family.
                                                                    Homer Simpson

I don't do family.   **Darren Day, walking out on his girlfriend and child**

MOTHER

Every morning I start out as Mary Poppins, and end up like Cruella de Vil.
                                                           Robin, *Mum's the Word*

It serves me right for putting all my eggs in one bastard.   **Dorothy Parker**

Oh, honey, you're not the world's worst mother. What about the freezer lady in Georgia?   **Homer Simpson**

Motherhood changes you so that you forget you ever had time for small things like despising the colour pink.   **Barbara Kingsolver**

I call my daughter every single day. And she always says the same thing: 'How the hell did you get this number?'   **Joan Rivers**

Instead of saying hello, my mother gets on the phone and says, 'Guess who died?'   **Dom Irrera**

Mother and Hitler's birthday. Worked a bit and lay in the sun.   Noël Coward, diary entry

In our society mothers take the place elsewhere occupied by the Fates, the System, Negroes, Communism or Reactionary Imperial Plots. Mothers go on getting blamed until they're 80, but shouldn't take it personally.   **Katharine Whitehorn**

Mama does everything for the first baby, who responds by saying Dada first.   **Mignon McLaughlin**

I asked my mother if I was adopted. She said, 'Not yet, but we've placed an ad.'   **Dana Snow**

Hyperactive kid for sale, good at vacuuming, not great at washing dishes because he's too short. Guaranteed to annoy. £5 or nearest offer.
**Alex Wilson, ad placed online to tease his seven-year-old son,
Liam, later removed on police orders**

[*On the phone*] No, Mother, I can't come and see you tonight. Well, accidental amputations happen all the time. Deal with it.
Gary Andrews, *Gary the Rat*

FATHER

—God, I hope you're not inviting that bloody, bollocky, selfish, two-faced chicken bastard, pig-dog man, are you?
—You could just say 'Dad'.　　**Edina and Saffie Monsoon, *Absolutely Fabulous***

There are all these new things I have to do now I'm a father: I have to provide, I have to plan for the future, and I have to drive without using the 'F' word.　　**Jeremy Hardy**

Things a Father Should Know: How to change a nappy – *and* dispose of the old one; how to cook a meal the children will eat; how to say 'That's final' and not go back on it as soon as his wife's out of sight; that Elizabethandthechildren is actually four words, not one.
Katharine Whitehorn

My idea of fatherhood is sending a telegram from Abyssinia saying, 'Have you had your child yet, and what have you called it?'
Evelyn Waugh

You know when you're young, you think your dad is Superman. Then you grow up and you realise he's just a regular guy who wears a cape.
Dave Attell

My father wore the trousers in the family – at least, after the court order.
Vernon Chapman

Make me proud, son…or, at least, less ashamed.
Grampa and Homer Simpson, *The Simpsons*

I wouldn't say my father hated me, but at my christening, he tipped the vicar a fiver to hold me under.　　**Bob Monkhouse**

I never used to get along with my dad. Kids used to come up to me and say, 'My dad can beat up your dad,' and I'd say, 'Yeah? When?'
Bill Hicks

My father went out for cigarettes when I was four years old, and we're still waiting for him to come back. Guess they must have been an obscure brand.

Stephen King

My dad used to wash my mouth out with soap, but that was just to remove any traces of his DNA.

Doug Stanhope

The games Daddy and me played! Blind man's bluff. On Beachy Head.

Les Dawson

When I was a kid, my dad would say, 'Emo, do you believe in the Lord?' I'd say, 'Yes!' He'd say, 'Then stand up and shout Hallelujah!' So I would. And then I'd fall out of the rollercoaster.

Emo Philips

I always used to hate it when my father carried me on his shoulders. Especially when we were in the car.

Ardal O'Hanlon

My father took me fishing once. He marched me to the riverbank and snapped a picture of me with a fishing rod in my hand, then we went home.

Andrei Codrescu

I became a barrister because I hated my father; my father hated lawyers.

Clarissa Dickson Wright

—Don't worry, son. You don't have to follow in my footsteps.
—I don't even like to use the bathroom after you.

Homer and Bart Simpson, *The Simpsons*

—I wanted to be a doctor, but you wouldn't let me.
—Well, that saved a few lives, didn't it?

Harold and Albert Steptoe, *Steptoe and Son*

My daughter's boyfriends? I figure if I kill the first one, word will get out.

Charles Barkley

I am the father of three daughters, who are not yet of marriageable age but have no prospect of being able to afford grey topper and champagne occasions when the time comes. My solution is to provide a stout ladder suitable for elopement.   **W.E.G. Manning**

I grew up to have my father's looks, my father's speech patterns, my father's posture, my father's opinions and my mother's contempt for my father.   **Jules Feiffer**

My kids hate me. Every Father's Day they give a 'World's Greatest Dad' mug to the milkman.   **Rodney Dangerfield**

[*Picture of Sigmund Freud on greeting card*] I'd wish you a Happy Father's Day... [*Inside*] ...if only I didn't want to kill you and sleep with Mom.   **David Kleinbard**

RELATIVES

If a man's character is to be abused, say what you will, there's nobody like a relation to do the business.   **William Makepeace Thackeray**

My uncle's dying wish was that I sit in his lap. He was in the electric chair.   **Rodney Dangerfield**

She was looking more and more like an aunt than anything human.   **P.G. Wodehouse**

It is no use telling me that there are bad aunts and good aunts. At the core they are all alike. Sooner or later, out pops the cloven hoof.   **P.G. Wodehouse**

Becoming a grandmother is great fun because you can use the kid to get back at your daughter.   **Roseanne**

New Guinea Tapeworms and Jewish Grandmothers
                               Robert S. Desowitz, book title

Grandmotherf***er!   **Pat Candaras, title of Edinburgh show**

My grandfather used to make home movies and edit out the joy.

                   Richard Lewis

Grandpapa fell down a drain;
Couldn't scramble out again.
Now he's floating down the sewer
There's one grandpapa the fewer.   **Harry Graham, 'Grandpapa'**

I played with my grandfather a lot when I was a kid. He was dead, but
my parents had him cremated and put his ashes in my Etch-a-Sketch.

                   Alan Hawey

MOTHER-IN-LAW

Just then there was a tap at the door, I opened the portal, and the wife's
mother was stood there in the pouring rain. I said, 'Don't stand there
getting wet. Go home.'   **Les Dawson**

Mussolini in knickers.   **Les Dawson**

My brother said, 'The last time I saw my mother-in-law she was climbing
up the Empire State Building with King Kong in her mouth.'   **Eve Arnold**

If your mother lived in India she'd be sacred.

           Jack Duckworth, *Coronation Street*

Never rely on the glory of the morning or the smiles of your mother-
in-law.   **Japanese proverb**

The day my mother-in-law called, the mice threw themselves on the traps.

                 Les Dawson

I bought my mother-in-law a chair for Christmas. But she won't plug
it in.   **Henny Youngman**

I bought the mother-in-law a jaguar. It bit her leg off.   Chic Murray

The wife's mother said, 'When you're dead, I'll dance on your grave.'
I said, 'Good. I'm being buried at sea.'   Les Dawson

I just got back from a pleasure trip. Drove my mother-in-law to the
airport.   Rodney Dangerfield

My mother-in-law broke up my marriage: my wife came home from work
one day and found me in bed with her.   Lenny Bruce

HOME

—Well, the place looks lived in.
—Yeah, but by *what*?   Delong and Rocky Mulloy, *Cry Danger*

—It's quite spacious, though.
—Did you say 'quite spacious'? If you were coming out of a phone booth
wearing a parka jacket, it might be considered spacious.
          Real estate agent and Conan O'Brien

Always live in the ugliest house in the street, then you don't have to look
at it.   David Hockney

Our house is semi-detached. The walls are so thin you can hear the
neighbours changing their minds.   Anon

There's only one thing worse than an estate agent but at least that can be safely lanced, drained and surgically dressed.   Stephen Fry

I've no objection to people owning a second home in Cornwall provided they allow the homeless to live there from Monday to Friday, and in Staines from Saturday to Monday. **Correspondent,** *Saturday Live*

[*Couple talking to building contractor*] Would it be possible to totally exaggerate how much it will cost and how long it will take, so we'll be pleasantly surprised at the end? **David Sipress**

Our dream is to live long enough to see the end of our renovations.

David Sipress

When we were finishing our house, we found we had a little cash left over, on account of the plumber not knowing it. **Mark Twain**

A house is a big responsibility. You got lawns to mow, you got plumbing to fix, you got gutters to clean, then every couple of years you gotta paint the entire thing from top to bottom. Honestly, I don't know where Vera gets the energy. **Norm Peterson,** *Cheers*

My greatest claim to fame outside soccer? I once put together an MFI wardrobe in less than four days. **Terry Gibson**

What in the name of God's arse is pot pourri? Looks like breakfast. Smells like your auntie. **Steve Taylor,** *Coupling*

HOUSEWORK

A fellow gets married and the morning after the wedding night, goes to the bathroom and finds a dead horse in the bathtub. He runs out and says, 'Darling, there's a dead horse in the bathtub!' And his wife replies, 'Well, I never said I was neat.' **Walter Matthau**

Women are sluts when it comes to housework. I've got a pilot TV show ready that will show the truth of women's domestic capabilities. It's called *Fuck It, That'll Do*.   Jo Brand

There's a TV show called *Clean Sweep* where these women invade your home and make you throw away what you don't need. Their motto is, 'If you haven't used it in six months, throw it out.' By that logic, I have three weeks to get laid.   Basil White

One man's pet-stained carpet is another man's Twister game.   Emo Philips

Now they show you how detergents take out bloodstains. I think if you've got a T-shirt with a bloodstain all over it, maybe laundry isn't your biggest problem. Maybe you should get rid of the body before you do the wash.   Jerry Seinfeld

Do you know that we all shed skin? Something like 90 per cent of the dust in the world is made up of dead human skin. You think you're dusting your house. You're not. You're just moving your grandmother around.   Dave Allen

Home is the place where, no matter where you're sitting, you're looking at something you should be doing.   Anon

I can't relax here. These people have no pubic hair anywhere in their house. In our house we have pubic hair on the ceiling.   Dylan Moran

I was never much good at domestic work. My mother had a theory that if you didn't know how to do it you wouldn't have to.

Muriel Spark

Pre-Maid Clean-up Service: they tidy up your house just enough so you're not embarrassed when the maid comes the next day.   Joel Ross

Housework is like bad sex. Every time I do it I swear I'll never do it again. Until the next time company comes.

Lulu Brecht, *Can't Stop the Music*

No one knows what her life expectancy is, but I have a horror of leaving this world and not having anyone in the entire family know how to replace a toilet tissue spindle.   Erma Bombeck

—Maybe tidying is true love.
—Nah, oral sex.

Jane Christie and Sally Harper, *Coupling*

GRUMPY
WORK
& MONEY

WORK

I went to the Job Centre for an interview. I said: 'I ain't got no qualifications, no skills and as for my customer service, sod off!' She said: 'You're exactly what they're after at Dixons.' Simon Brodkin

I have the most corny CV possible. It goes: Eton, Oxford, Conservative Research Department, Treasury, Home Office, Carlton TV and then Conservative MP. David Cameron

Trahey's Simple Rule: Would you hire you? Jane Trahey

[*Interviewer to interviewee*] This resumé appears to cover only the last 45 minutes. David Sipress

Never wear a backwards baseball cap to an interview unless applying for the job of umpire. Dan Zevin

101 Job Interview Tips. Tip no. 102: Ask for the name of the interviewer's cosmetic surgeon. Marjorie Streeter

All jobs fall into four categories: 1. Stimulating, but not financially rewarding; 2. Secure, but soul-destroyingly dull; 3. Financially rewarding, but very stressful without being stimulating; and, 4. Somebody else's. Douglas Frank

Our experts describe you as an appallingly dull fellow, unimaginative, timid, lacking in initiative, spineless, easily dominated, no sense of humour, tedious company, and irrepressibly drab and awful; and whereas in most professions, these would be considerable drawbacks, in chartered accountancy, they're a positive boon. *Monty Python's Flying Circus*

My first ambition was to be an orphan. Tom Baker, *Who on Earth is Tom Baker?*

When I grow up I want to be a school principal or a caterpillar. Ralph Wiggum, *The Simpsons*

When I finished school, I took one of the career aptitude tests, and based on my verbal ability score, they suggested I become a mime.

Tim Cavanagh

If you cannot – in the long run – tell everyone what you have been doing, your doing has been worthless. Erwin Schrödinger

—So what does a fashion director do, anyway?
—She gets 15 per cent off at Harvey Nicks.

Saffron and Edina Monsoon, *Absolutely Fabulous*

Don't trust anyone whose job was created after 1990. Anon

I think PR is a ridiculous job.
They are the headlice of civilisation.

A.A. Gill

—Oh, what a day! One sad person after another.
—Rose, you're a grief counsellor.

Dorothy Zbornak and Rose Nylund, *The Golden Girls*

I was Princess Anne's assistant for a while, but I chucked that in because it was obvious they were never going to make me Princess Anne no matter how well I did the job. It was a question of who you were, rather than how well you did, and I hate that.

Hugh Laurie, *A Bit of Fry and Laurie*

Plumbers, as you know, have to go back to fetch their tools, and what is fascinating is that in spite of thousands of jokes about them having to go back and fetch their tools, they still have to go back and fetch their tools.

Virginia Graham

I warned poor Mary of her fate,
But she *would* wed a plumber's mate!
For hours the choir was forced to sing
While he went back to fetch the ring.

Harry Graham, 'Obstinacy'

A trade unionist is someone who hates his job and is afraid someone will take it from him.   Richard Needham

Veterinarian/Taxidermist – Either Way You Get Your Dog Back.   Sign

Sign You Have a Bad Job: The sign outside your door reads 'Jim's Office/ Men's Room'.   David Letterman

I think that clocking into a factory would be the worst thing in the world. All you could say to the man next to you is, 'What's in your sandwich, Charlie?'   Rodney Marsh

My job consists of basically masking my contempt for the assholes in charge, and, at least once a day, retiring to the men's room so I can jerk off while I fantasise about a life that doesn't so closely resemble hell.
                                                    Lester Burnham, *American Beauty*

Nobody goes right to work. I mean, screw the company, those first twenty minutes belong to you.   George Carlin

The fact is, Mr Wetherby, we're looking for someone who can take it. We're already well supplied with those who can dish it out.   Riana Duncan

I hated my last boss. He said, 'Why are you two hours late?' I said, 'I fell downstairs.' He said, 'That doesn't take two hours.'   Johnny Carson

Accomplishing the impossible means only that the boss will add it to your regular duties.   Doug Larson

In Japan, employees occasionally work themselves to death. It's called Karoshi. I don't want that to happen to anybody in my department. The trick is to take a break as soon as you see a bright light and hear dead relatives beckon.   Scott Adams

All I ever wanted was an honest week's pay for an honest day's work.
                                                    Sergeant Bilko, *Sergeant Bilko*

Office Hours: 2:00 to 2:15, every other Wednesday.   George S. Kaufman

There is no romance or dignity in manual labour. If there was, the Duke of Westminster would be digging his own garden. **Jeffrey Bernard**

Some people say my sister's lazy. The only job she's ever had is a boob job. **Mickey Miller, *EastEnders***

All I want to do is sit on my arse and fart and think of Dante. **Samuel Beckett**

A lot of fellows nowadays have a B.A., M.D., or Ph.D. Unfortunately, they don't have a J.O.B. **Fats Domino**

I have been unemployed for many years. In all the time I have attended the Labour Exchange, I have only been offered one job. Apart from that they've shown me nothing but kindness. **Les Dawson**

Many people quit looking for work when they find a job. **Steven Wright**

—Peter, are you sleeping on the job?
—Uh…no. There's uh…a bug in my eye and I'm trying to suffocate him. **Mr Weed and Peter Griffin, *Family Guy***

BUSINESS

I'll keep it short and sweet – Family, Religion, Friendship. These are the three demons you must slay if you wish to succeed in business. **Mr Burns, *The Simpsons***

I was in a public toilet and I saw a piece of graffiti that said, 'I fuck UR wife while U watch. Interested? Call this number…' Didn't give any prices, though. Not sure if that's quite going to work as a business plan. But I'd like to see them pitch it on *Dragons' Den*. **Ricky Gervais**

Try as I might, I could not look at an overhead projection of a growth profit matrix, and stay conscious.

Boris Johnson, on leaving his job as a management consultant after only a week

I thought it would be better than sex. It wasn't very good and it was a lot more expensive than sex.

Ted Turner, on the AOL Time Warner merger, which cost him £8 billion

When you are skinning your customers you should leave some skin on to grow, so that you can skin them again.

Nikita Khrushchev, speech to British industrialists

What a lot of people don't realise is that if you look at things globally, from a strictly economic perspective, that makes you a wanker.

Simon Munnery

When a man hires a new secretary, he should sleep with her at once; until he does, they won't get any work done.

Anon

—Hayley, I need three thousand copies of my rugby club brochure.
—Do I look like a photocopier?
—If you must know, you've got bigger hips.

Hayley the Secretary and John Weak, *Weak at the Top*

Meetings are an addictive, highly self-indulgent activity that corporations and other large organisations engage in only because they cannot masturbate.

Dave Barry

When I die, I hope it's in a meeting. The transition from life to death will be barely perceptible.

Anon

Meetings are places where nothing happens and nothing gets done…
A biggish woman – and it's always a woman – says, 'Well, we're outside the box here with a new kind of hybrid venture and we can't know what the result will be until we've run it up the flagpole and seen which way the wind's blowing. It's mission critical that we use blue-sky thinking and that we're proactive, not reactive, if we're to come up with a ballpark figure that we can bring to the table.'

Jeremy Clarkson

[*At a meeting*] *What you say*: 'That's a great question.' *What you are thinking*: '…because for once I actually have an answer.'   Kevin Dopart

I can tell more about how someone is likely to react in a business situation from one round of golf than I can from a hundred hours of meetings.   Mark McCormack

You say it's win-win, but what if you're wrong-wrong and it all goes bad-bad?   David Sipress

If you don't know what to do, walk fast and look worried.   Scott Adams

It's my LBW file – Let the Buggers Wait.   David Cooper

1-2-3-4, make him sweat outside the door, 5-6-7-8, always pays to make them wait, 9-10-11-12…come!   C.J., *The Fall and Rise of Reginald Perrin*

[*Businessman on the phone with his desk diary open in front of him*] No, Thursday's out. How about never – is never good for you?   Robert Mankoff

Consultants have credibility because they are not dumb enough to work at your company.   Scott Adams

I always say to executives that they should go and see *King Lear* because they'll be out there one day, wandering on the heath without a company car.   Charles Handy

—Alan Sugar does everyone a great disservice by doing *The Apprentice*. Young people will be turned off business because they think that they will be shouted at by a horrible, fat, old, rich bloke.
—I'm the one that's worth 800 million quid, mate.
    Sir Digby Jones and Sir Alan Sugar

—You're fired!
—But, my lord, I've been in your family since 1532.
—So has syphilis. Now get out!   Blackadder and Baldrick, *Blackadder II*

Why did I fire him? Well, sometimes you just don't like somebody.
Henry Ford, on Lee Iacocca

ADVERTISING

'Just Do It' is a good slogan for Nike but a bad slogan for a suicide relief centre.
Jeff Keenan

I want an ad that sells kit. I don't want an ad that wins the Montreux Prize for advertising tossers.
Sir Alan Sugar

See all your best work go unnoticed.
Advert for staff for MI5

Sure I eat what I advertise. Sure I eat Wheaties for breakfast. A good bowl of Wheaties with Bourbon can't be beat.
Jay 'Dizzy' Dean

Advertising has us chasing cars and clothes, working jobs we hate, so we can buy shit we don't need.
Chuck Palahniuk

It is pretty obvious that the debasement of the human mind caused by a constant flow of fraudulent advertising is not a trivial thing. There is more than one way to conquer a country.
Raymond Chandler

MONEY

Life is a shit sandwich. But if you've got enough bread, you don't taste the shit.
Jonathan Winters

Money frees you from doing things you dislike. Since I dislike doing nearly everything, money is handy.
Groucho Marx

One day I saw an ad in the paper that said, 'Send me a dollar and I'll tell you how I make money.' I sent the guy a dollar. I got a postcard back that said, 'Thanks for the dollar. This is how I make money.'

Jackie Vernon

At my lemonade stand I used to give the first glass of lemonade away free and charge 5 dollars for the second glass – it contained the antidote.

Emo Philips

I make money the old-fashioned way: I inherit it.
Clayton Runnymede Endicott III, *Benson*

Kenneth Tynan liked bank notes and hated loose change. At Oxford, he would stand at the top of St Giles's by the taxi rank, pull the pennies out of his pocket and throw them down the street because he couldn't bear the rattle of money.

Kathleen Tynan

People argue in a committee over whether or not to spend an extra $5,000, but they vote to spend a million without much debate. That's because they understand $5,000. They don't understand a million.

Gary North

Economics sprouted from the same intellectual roots as weather forecasting – rarely accurate but devoid of memory, thus cheerful about being wrong.

John Ralson Saul

I don't want money. It is only people who pay their bills who want that, and I never pay mine.

Oscar Wilde

TAX

Maybe death and taxes are inevitable, but death doesn't get any worse every time Congress meets.

Joan I. Welsh

Every time I look at what I have to pay in taxes, it scares me shirtless.

Robert Orben

Why, oh why, do we pay taxes? I mean, just to have bloody parking restrictions and buggery-ugly traffic wardens, and bollocky-pedestrian-bloody-crossings and those bastard railings outside shops windows, making it so difficult you can't even get in them! I mean, I know they're there to stop stupid people running into the street and killing themselves but we're not *all* stupid! We don't all need nurse-maiding. I mean, why not just have a Stupidity Tax? Just tax the stupid people!

Edina Monsoon, *Absolutely Fabulous*

The creed of the Inland Revenue is simple: if we can bring one little smile to one little face today – then somebody's slipped up somewhere.

David Frost

There was a fire at the main Inland Revenue office in London today, but it was put out before any serious good was done.

Ronnie Corbett

Pelicans, penguins and the Inland Revenue all have one thing in common: they can all shove their bills up their arse.

'Oz' Osbourne, *Auf Wiedersehen, Pet*

RICH

A billion here, and a billion there, and pretty soon we're talking real money.

Everett Dirksen, 1974

A billion dollars isn't what it used to be.

Bunker Hunter, 1980

According to the latest figures, Madonna is worth 50 million pounds, and if you include Guy Richie's earnings…that's 50 million pounds.

Graham Norton

—Gee, Mr Burns, you're the richest man I know.
—Yes, but I'd trade it all for a little more.
Homer Simpson and Mr Burns, *The Simpsons*

People of privilege will always risk their complete destruction rather than surrender any material part of their advantage.
J.K. Galbraith

Perhaps I am too cynical, but I believe there is a separate class of people in America called Too Rich To Go To Prison.
Molly Ivins

In America, you're guilty until proven wealthy.
Bill Maher

Plato told Aristotle no one should make more than five times the pay of the lowest member of society. J.P. Morgan said twenty times. Jesus advocated a negative differential – that's why they killed him.
Graef Crystal

When the doctor was there, Alfred refused to believe that he'd had a stroke. 'I can't have had a stroke,' he grated, in a terrible rage, 'I've got £93,000 in my current account.'
Tom Baker, *Who on Earth is Tom Baker?*

Nature still obstinately refuses to co-operate by making the rich people innately superior to the poor people.
Sydney and Beatrice Webb

As a general rule, nobody has money who ought to have it.
Benjamin Disraeli

I hate almost all rich people, but I think I'd be darling at it.
Dorothy Parker

Of the billionaires I have known, money just brings out the basic traits in them. If they were jerks before they had money, they are simply jerks with a billion dollars.
Warren Buffet

Sometimes wealth seems to me as amazing as genius.
Jean Cocteau

When I was young I used to believe that wealth and power would bring me happiness. I was right.
Gahan Wilson

Maybe it is better to weep in a Rolls-Royce than on the bus.

Sven-Göran Eriksson

People will swim through shit if you put a few bob in it.   Peter Sellers

CREDIT & DEBT

The rich are different from you and me: they have more credit.

John Leonard

Money was invented so we could know exactly how much we owe.

Cullen Hightower

It's funny to me that I have to prove to the banks that *I'm* honest.

Scott Adams

Banks used to promote this self-image, 'The Open Bank', 'The Bank That Likes To Say Yes'. That's all gone now. Now the banks are, 'The Piss Off Bank', 'The You're Out of Your Mind Bank', 'The Get Out of Here You Arsehole Bank', 'The We Don't Give a Shit Bank'.   Dave Allen

The listening bank refused to listen and the bank which likes to say yes said no.   Garry Gibson

Lend me twenty dollars or I'll call your wife and tell her you're in Central Park wearing a dress.   Oscar Madison, *The Odd Couple*

Sure, I'll lend you all the money you need, but since you have no collateral I'm going to have to break your legs in advance.

Moe Szyslak, *The Simpsons*

I borrowed that money to pay for my boob job. If they want to repossess them, they know where to find them.   Big Larry

Teenage borrowing – a polite form of theft.   Rick Spleen, *Lead Balloon*

If you ever have to steal money from your kid, and later on he discovers it's gone, I think a good thing to do is to blame it on Santa Claus.

Jack Handey

Credit buying is much like being drunk. The buzz happens immediately, and it gives you a lift… The hangover comes the day after.   **Joyce Brothers**

Capitalism without bankruptcy is like Christianity without hell.

Frank Borman

POOR

Poor people have more fun than rich people, they say, and I notice it's the rich people who keep saying it.   **Jack Parr**

I know a fellow who's as broke as the Ten Commandments.

John P. Marquand

We have minus fifty dollars in our account. We have to raise fifty dollars just to be broke!   **Louie, *Lucky Louie***

I'm so broke I can't even redeem my clothes from the dry cleaner's. It's like the clothes are in jail. I go in every so often and say, 'Could I just see the pants?'   **Paula Poundstone**

At one point, I was eating dog food, dividing the cans between my dog and myself. It didn't taste that bad when you heated it up.

Andy Williams, veteran crooner

When I was born, I owed twelve dollars.   **George S. Kaufman**

I'm not saying things are bad, but I've been evicted from my flat so often for non-payment of rent, I've had the loose covers made to match the pavements.   **Les Dawson**

When shit becomes valuable, the poor will be born without assholes.

Brazilian proverb

101 Ways to Save Money. No. 102: Spit your mouthwash back into the bottle to be used again. The alcohol kills all the germs, so one bottle can last for years.

Stephen Greene

We're too poor to economise.

F. Scott Fitzgerald

The poor do not know that their function in life is to exercise our generosity.

Jean-Paul Sartre

CHARITY

There was a man begging in the street with a card that said 'Homeless'. When I passed him he shouted after me, 'I know you! I've seen you on TV!' I said to him, 'Excuse me, but exactly *how* homeless are you?'

Graham Norton

Times have sure changed. Yesterday a bum asked me if I could spare a few dollars for a double cappuccino with no foam.

Bill Jones

I am shameless now. I've got a whole routine. When I spot those guys with clipboards, those 'charity zombies', in the distance, straight away I get my phone out and pretend to have a phone call. I'm always talking to my friend 'Paul'... 'Oh, I dunno, mate. You try and tell her that, mate.' I always continue the conversation and hang up – do the whole fake call.

Stephen Merchant

Socially prominent people are very fond of disease, because it gives them a chance to have these really elaborate charity functions, and the newspaper headlines say EVENING IN PARIS BALL RAISES MONEY TO FIGHT GOUT instead of RICH PEOPLE AMUSE THEMSELVES.

Dave Barry

I've been doing lots of charity gigs lately – just in case I catch anything in the future.   **Noel Gallagher**

—It doesn't matter to me how the auction goes. I'm doing this for charity.
—You know Vera has that carved on our headboard.
                                                    Rebecca Howe and Norm Peterson, *Cheers*

Richard Branson often visits London's homeless and hands out free promotional copies of Mike Oldfield's 'Tubular Bells'.   **Mrs Merton**

It's too bad they don't have a telethon for Fuckface-itis. They find a cure yet?   **Tony Soprano, *The Sopranos***

It's one thing to want to save lives in Ethiopia, but it's another thing to inflict so much torture on the British public.
                            Morrissey, on the Band Aid record, 'Do They Know It's Christmas?'

Geldof disease has spread through television faster than Aids through Africa over the past 20 years, and still there is no cure... Apart from watching Siamese twins who are joined at the mouth when one of them is vomiting, I cannot conceive of a more revolting spectacle than what I saw.   **Victor Lewis-Smith, on 'Children In Need'**

I'm not ringing in to Comic Relief to send a load of glue-sniffers yachting.
                            Stingy woman played by Catherine Tate, Comic Relief, 2005

Do I really need Dawn French and Robbie Coltrane telling me there's not enough food: why is that?   **Ricky Gervais**

The urge to save humanity is almost always only a false-face for the urge to rule it.   **H.L. Mencken**

—Will you be attending any of the Live Earth concerts?
—I would rather cut my buttocks off, varnish them and sell them in a
provincial gift shop.   Fi Glover and Will Self, *Saturday Live*

—If you could change the world in one way, what would you do?
—I'd clothe the hungry.   David Genser

I wonder if it isn't just cowardice instead of generosity that makes us
give tips.   Will Rogers

Many men in Packy's position would have shrunk from diving into the
rescue, fully clad. Packy was one of them.   P.G. Wodehouse

I gave that man directions, even though I didn't know the way, because
that's the kind of man I am this week.   Homer Simpson

Some people are so full of the milk of human kindness that it slops over
and messes everything.   Winifred Holtby

When the milk of human kindness turns sour, it is a singularly
unpalatable draught.   Agnes Repplier

There is no one nastier than a recovering people-pleaser.   Howard Ogden

When I see someone coming towards me with the obvious intention of
doing me good, I run a mile.   Henry David Thoreau

Kindness. The most unkind thing of all.   Edna O'Brien

—I don't need your pity! Or your
money! [*He pockets the money*]
—Usually when people say that, they
give the money back.

Homer Simpson and Ron Howard, *The Simpsons*

GIFT

Hi! Welcome back from your coma!   **Rejected Hallmark greeting card**

It's Going to be a Great First Marriage   **e-greeting card**

You say I'm afraid of commitment, but maybe it's you who's afraid of total uncertainty.   **Greeting card, cyranet.com**

Greeting cards are for people who mean every word that someone else said.   **Jason Love**

My breasts were a present for my husband on his 40th. I figured he'd appreciate them more than a sweater.   **Samantha Campbell,** *House*

The cat brings a rat or mouse into the house and people say, 'Oh, it's a present!' I've had better gifts from godparents.   **Jeremy Hardy**

A truly appreciative child will break, lose, spoil, or fondle to death any really successful gift within a matter of minutes.   **Russell Lynes**

Just last week, I was given a present. As I opened it, a woman mentioned, with an intense but guarded horror, that I was good at getting gifts. 'You don't like them?' I enquired. 'No,' she shuddered, 'I can't bear the attention. I don't know how to arrange my face. I sound so insincere. I am insincere and embarrassed. Thanking people is hell.'   **A.A. Gill**

I don't like 'Thank You' cards because I don't know what else to say. What do I put on the inside? '…man!' or 'See front'?   **Demetri Martin**

People who pay for things never complain. It's the guy you give something to that you can't please.   **Will Rogers**

I've got something for you, Victor – a little retirement present… It's a gravestone. You haven't got one already, have you? Obviously I haven't filled in the second date on it yet.   **Vince,** *One Foot in the Grave*

My father is now 76, my mother 68. Two years ago she finally gave
herself a present she had been wanting for 45 years: a divorce.

Phillip Lopate

MEANNESS

My grandfather's always complaining about how much things cost.
'£1.50 for a cup of tea? £2.25 for three custard creams?' I said, 'Look,
Granddad, you just popped round. I didn't *invite* you.' **Milton Jones**

Eighty-five pence for a plastic bottle of Coke? I thought they'd stopped
using cocaine as one of the ingredients. **Jeremy Clarkson**

When Jack Benny has a party, you not only bring your own Scotch, you
bring your own rocks. **George Burns**

Tight as a gnat's chuff he was. He was the only man I know who used
to bring his hair home from the barber's. He used to stuff his cushions
with it. **Albert Steptoe, *Steptoe and Son***

He's that mean that when a fly lands in the sugar he shakes its feet before
he kills it. **Bill Wannan**

I had written to Aunt Maud,
Who was on a trip abroad,
When I heard she'd died of cramp,
Just too late to save the stamp. **Harry Graham, 'Waste'**

When they asked Jack Benny to do something for the Actors' Orphanage
he shot both his parents and moved in. **Bob Hope**

GRUMPY TRANSPORT & TRAVEL

TRANSPORT
– GENERAL

I don't get no respect. Every time I get in an elevator, the operator says the same thing to me: 'Basement?'
Rodney Dangerfield

—Going down!
—Why, you cut right to the chase!
Karen Walker and man in elevator, Will and Grace

There's nothing about an elevator I like. It's filled with people I did not invite. And often these people are wearing conflicting perfumes.
Fran Lebowitz

Structurally an elevator car resembles both a jail cell and a burial vault; in order to deny these resemblances, we make ourselves deaf, dumb, and blind.
Tad Tuleja

If I have to move up in a building, I choose the elevator over the escalator. Because one time I was riding the escalator and I tripped. I fell down the stairs for an hour and a half.
Demetri Martin

Peter's Bicycling Law: No matter which direction you go, it's uphill and against the wind.
Laurence J. Peter

Unfortunately for you lot, we are now stuck behind a broken train. We'll be here for quite a while but I don't care, I'm now on overtime.
London tube train announcement

Londoners are apologetic about their underground, which they believe has become filthy and noisy and dangerous, but which is in fact far more civilised than the average American wedding reception.
Dave Barry

I was hitchhiking the other day and a hearse stopped. I said, 'No thanks, I'm not going that far.'
Steven Wright

I picked up a hitchhiker once. Well, you gotta when you hit 'em.

Emo Philips

Waiting for a 136 bus from Highgate station to Muswell Hill Broadway on a misty evening in February is a bit like lurking outside the gates of purgatory. I stood there once; at the bus stop, I mean, one nineteenth of a grey-faced crocodile of the depressed...

Tom Baker, *Who on Earth is Tom Baker?*

Lady Wolverton, thinking the time had come to economise, got into a bus. She sat beside a woman who kept loudly sniffing and she asked her aggressively if she hadn't got a handkerchief. The woman replied: 'Yes, but I never lend it in a bus.'

Lady Cynthia Asquith

You have your own company, your own temperature control, your own music – and don't have to put up with dreadful human beings sitting alongside you.

Steven Norris, Minister for Public Transport, on why people prefer private cars

Public transportation is for jerks and lesbians.

Homer Simpson

If you anticipate a bus trip in Latin America, go through the following checklist prior to boarding... Does the bus have a least one windshield wiper? Good. If it's on the driver's side, so much the better. Try to avoid buses whose windshields are crowded with decals, statues, and pictures... Shrines to saints, pious homilies, boastful bumper stickers, and religious trinkets do not reflect the safety of a bus.

Tom Miller

What would be a road hazard anywhere else, in the Third World is probably the road.

P.J. O'Rourke

CAR

A drunk staggers down the road and sees a man tinkering under the bonnet of his car. 'What's up?' asks the drunk. 'Piston broke,' says the man. 'So am I,' says the drunk.

Anon

My car broke down. I called the Automobile Association. They towed *me*.

Rodney Dangerfield

Start! Start, you vicious bastard! Oh my God! I'm warning you, if you don't start... I'll count to three: one, two, three – right, that does it! I'm going to give you a damn good thrashing!

Basil Fawlty, to his car, *Fawlty Towers*

Nissan QX. It exists. So does dog dirt but I don't want any outside my house.

Jeremy Clarkson

As soon as I get behind the wheel of a car, I'm like anybody else: a bastard. I'm sure everybody's the same: no man is a man any more, he's not a chap or a fellow, he's a bastard – a hairy bastard, a fat bastard, a thin bastard, a small bastard or a big bastard, but definitely a bastard.

Dave Allen

The worst drivers on the roads are women in people carriers, men in white vans and anyone in a baseball cap. That's just about everyone.

Paul O'Grady

I'll never forget the time my wife, Ida, went for her driver's test. She got three tickets – just for the written part.

Eddie Cantor

So I'm not the best behind the wheel. But if you don't like the way I drive, stay off the sidewalk!

Joan Rivers

Telling people at a dinner party you drive a Nissan Almera is like telling them you've got the Ebola virus and you're about to sneeze.

Jeremy Clarkson

This is a Renault Espace, probably the best of the people carriers. Not that's much to shout about. That's like saying, 'Ooh good, I've got syphilis, the best of the sexually transmitted diseases.'

Jeremy Clarkson

Whether driven by some ridiculous Yummy Mummy ferrying little Josh between violin lessons and Junior Masterchef classes in town, or by some ex-Londoner in a faux farmer's jacket who spends his weekends second-homing and playing at being a country dweller, 4x4s are always badly driven, under occupied and just too bloody big. They've got the carbon-footprint of a Yeti.
Jackie Clune, *The Jeremy Vine Show*

The only time 4x4 drivers go off-road is when they hit the kerb on their way to pick their children up from school.
Mark Restorick

If people want to drive their kids to school in a Hummer, which is an armoured vehicle, as a *quid pro quo* pedestrians ought to be allowed to shoot at them. It's only fair.   Hugh Punt and Steve Dennis, *The Now Show*

A car company is coming out with a supersize truck that is 4 feet longer, 2 feet taller, and twice as heavy as a Hummer. You know, it's a lot cheaper to buy a hat that says, 'I have a small penis.'   Conan O'Brien

I would rather have a vasectomy than buy a Ford Galaxy.   Jeremy Clarkson

Why is it that when a car is causing an obstruction, they bloody clamp it and *leave* it there?   Dave Allen

You do not just avoid the Suzuki Wagon R. You avoid it like you would avoid unprotected sex with an Ethiopian transvestite.   Jeremy Clarkson

—[*In a traffic jam*] Oh God AL...MIGHTY!
—Want a sucky sweet?
—Sucky sweet? I'll be sucking on that exhaust pipe in a minute if there's much more of this. I always say that for a really super Bank Holiday treat you've got to go a long way to beat four and a half hours staring up a horse's bottom... It's like watching a party political broadcast.
Victor and Margaret Meldrew, *One Foot in the Grave*

Now you're stuck behind a caravan...a great ugly fridge on wheels...
At the core of your irrational rage is the feeling that these smug bugs
swaying from side to side across the road though never quite enough to
allow you space to pass on either side are causing you all this grief just
because they felt it would be nice to take their house with them on
holiday.

Jonathan Margolis

101 Fun Activities for Family Car Trips. No. 102: Blindfold Dad and see
if he can steer just from your directions.

Wayne Rodgers

Oh my God, I'm getting pulled over. Everyone, just...pretend to be normal.

Richard, to his family in the back of the car, *Little Miss Sunshine*

I was pulled over in Massachusetts for reckless driving. When brought
before the judge, I was asked if I knew what the punishment was for
drink-driving in that state. I said, 'I don't know – re-election to the
Senate?'

Emo Philips

One way to solve all the traffic problems would be to keep all the cars
that aren't paid for off the roads.

Will Rogers

We should build cars so that if they are moving and the turn signal is on,
the car automatically turns that way after three minutes.

Douglas Frank

We should equip every car with a razor-sharp spear protruding from the
steering wheel towards the driver. Such a device would make every driver
wish to avoid any sudden stop, and thus all drivers would be inclined to
drive much less recklessly.

Steve Shapiro

Dead slow or dead. Please yourself.

Road sign in Nigeria, approaching a 100-foot drop

They drive so crazy in Chicago that anything moving slower than 65mph
is considered a house.

J. Joshua

You can't possibly hear the last movement of Beethoven's Seventh and go slow.

Oscar Levant, justifying a speeding ticket

In Miami…it is customary for everyone to drive according to the laws of his or her own country of origin.

Dave Barry

In Milan, traffic lights are instructions. In Rome, they are suggestions. In Naples, they are Christmas decorations.

Antonio Martino, Italian Defence Minister

I read that one of those speed cameras earned £80,000 in a year. *I'd* like that job. For £80,000 I'd be painted fluorescent-yellow and hide in a hedge with a speed gun.

Andy Parsons

Cab drivers tend to confuse knowledge with The Knowledge.

Al Murray, the Pub Landlord

Dying is easy. Parking is impossible.

Art Buchwald

TRAIN

Does anyone have any nuts or bolts?

Virgin train driver, request to passengers, after the windscreen wiper broke

Conductors declaim over the PA with the prolixity of Olivier doing Shakespeare, until something goes wrong and they suddenly turn into Buster Keaton doing Pinter, all mysterious pauses and menacing silences.

Stuart Maconie, *Pies and Prejudice*

Trekking through the Amazon pales into insignificance beside the train journey from Dorset to London. It was the worst journey I've ever done.

John Blashford-Snell, explorer

Dear Sir…in the matter of the late arrival of trains at Waterloo…
This morning my train arrived, as always, 11 minutes late. It is rapidly
becoming apparent to me that not only are you not competent to hold
your job, you could not even run a game of strip poker in a Turkish
brothel. It should be obvious, even to a retarded hamster, that all your
trains should be retimed to take 11 minutes longer. Yours faithfully,
Reginald Iolanthe Perrin P.S. Why don't you divide your carriages into
sneezers and non-sneezers?

> Reginald Perrin, letter to British Rail, Southern Region,
> *The Fall and Rise of Reginald Perrin*

They will only encourage the common people to move about needlessly.

> The Duke of Wellington, on early steam railways

I got the 9.15 train to London on Saturday and sat next to two revolting
creatures who entered carrying 12 cans of beer each. She had straggly
blonde hair and a mirthless giggle, he had black stubble everywhere and
a T-shirt promoting some football team. I changed my seat at Doncaster.
It seems odd to find so many of the great unwashed in First Class. One
never saw such filth in the old days. It's democracy gone mad.

> Kenneth Williams

The most common of all antagonisms arises from a man's taking a seat
beside you on the train, a seat to which he is completely entitled.

> Robert Benchley

I was on an increasingly packed train where people were removing bags
and coats from seats to free them for new passengers. One young man
determinedly kept the seat alongside him piled with his belongings while
reading *How to Win Friends and Influence People*.   Andrew Billington

If someone starts talking loudly on their mobile phone on the train, what
I like to do is to answer them as if they're talking to me. This not only
amuses me but usually annoys them sufficiently to shut up.   Caroline Blake

The Croydon Bends: An irrational feeling that one is on the wrong train, usually accompanied by a feeling that even if one is on the right train, it won't stop at the right station.   **Miles Kington**

'Do you, Reginald Iolanthe Perrin, take British Rail's Southern Region for all your dreaded life? For better, for worse, for fuller, for dirtier, in lateness and in cancellation to retirement or phased redundancy do you part?' 'I do. I have to.' 'Place this ring of dirt around your neck, it will be there every day.'   **Reginald Perrin, *The Fall and Rise of Reginald Perrin***

It was then that we heard the words that strike fear into the heart of every God-fearing commuter: 'Replacement bus service.'   **David Lewis**

CRUISE

Cruising: If you thought you didn't like people on land...   **Carol Leifer**

The advert says, 'Spacious suites to enjoy as you cruise the Norwegian fjords.' This is accompanied by a picture of a woman in an evening dress sitting at a small table while her husband in a tuxedo pours her a glass of champagne. What the picture doesn't indicate is that they have to hoist the table on the sofa before they can open the door, he is sitting on the toilet-seat lid, the room is below the water line, the curtains cover a wall, and they are both trolls.   **Erma Bombeck**

There are a lot of mysterious things about boats, such as why anyone would get on one voluntarily.   P.J. O'Rourke

I have met cruise staff with the monikers 'Mojo Mike', 'Cocopuff' and 'Dave the Bingo Boy'. I have, in one week, been the object of over 1,500 professional smiles.   **David Foster Wallace**

I have seen every type of erythema, pre-melanomic lesion, liver spot, eczema, wart, papular cyst, pot belly, femoral cellulite, varicosity, collagen and silicone enhancement, bad tint, hair transplants that have not taken – i.e. I have seen nearly naked a lot of people I would prefer not to have seen nearly naked.   David Foster Wallace

Boats are wretched. You see little water, feel miserable and are condemned to whoever else was foolish enough to embark on one – generally the senile and very rich. It is no mystery to me at all why so many people commit suicide on boats. There's nothing preferable to do.
                                                                            Colin Thubron

When does this place get to England?   Bea Lillie, aboard the *Queen Mary*

AEROPLANE

The Devil himself had probably redesigned Hell in the light of information he had gained from observing airport layouts.   Anthony Price

At the airport they asked me if anybody I didn't know gave me anything. Even the people I know don't give me anything.   George Wallace

Air fares are now assigned by a machine called the Random Air Fare Generator, which is programmed to ensure that on any given flight (1) no two people will pay the same fare, and (2) everybody will pay less than you. People are flying across the country for less than you paid for your six-week-old muffin at the airport snack bar.   Dave Barry

Never board a commercial aircraft if the pilot is wearing a tank top.
                                                                            Dave Barry

On a flight to Belfast, I was upgraded to business class. I was a bit scared. I thought, 'Will I have to play golf?'   Jeremy Hardy

There are only two emotions in a plane: boredom and terror. Orson Welles

He hated to fly. He felt imprisoned in an airplane. In an airplane there was absolutely no place in the world to go except to another part of the airplane.   **Joseph Heller**

Sit Back. Relax. Enjoy the Fright.   **Tagline, *Snakes on a Plane***

Ladies and gentlemen, we'd like to recognise some special groups we have on the flight today: The 'Fat and Proud of It' Club of Burke; the panel of judges returning home from the Fourth Annual Cooking With Garlic Competition; and the National Association of Families With Colic-Prone Twins. Welcome aboard!   **Russell Beland**

I was flying to Atlanta, Georgia, and the pilot came on and said, 'In the event of sudden loss of cabin pressure, an oxygen mask will fall in front of you. Pull it towards you and place it over your nose and mouth. If you have a small child travelling with you, secure your own mask before you secure theirs. If you are travelling with two small children decide now which one you love best.'   **Sandi Toksvig**

No airline, unfortunately, has yet advertised a crated freight service for sending children.   **Katharine Whitehorn**

It is not only children who provide torment and anxiety. We need to take this a step further by establishing any annoying habits that adults may have. I suggest a questionnaire as part of the boarding process…
1)Are you a nail-biter? 2) Do you fiddle with things when unoccupied? 3) Do you engage in superficial small talk for periods in excess of two minutes? 4) Do you understand that a person reading a book or newspaper is signalling an intention not to be disturbed? 5) Do you crunch sweets, crisps or nuts? 6) Do you have a Walkman or MP3 player? 7) Do you have a drink problem? 8) Do you fit into a single seat? 9) Have you now or ever had a beard? 10) Are you a vegan? (I have an aversion to ponchos.)   **Shaun Carter**

There are only two reasons to sit in the back row of an airplane: either you have diarrhoea or you're anxious to meet people who do.
                    Henry Kissinger

I'm always seated next to somebody who feels that just because we're seated next to each other we should form some sort of bond with each other. But the thing is, no matter how friendly they are up there, when the plane is down, the relationship is over. They could have been chatting with you the entire time, suddenly the plane's on the ground and it's 'Outta the way! Fuck you! Where are my bags?!' Ellen DeGeneres

Your attention, please: as a cost-cutting measure, this flight will be remotely piloted from India. Tom Witte

Do not accept any food from an airline that you would not accept from a vendor in Calcutta. If it's bottled or if you peel it yourself, it may be all right. Otherwise it may stay with you for the rest of your life.
Roy Blount, Jr

I ate a chicken breast so tepid that the cooking process could only have consisted of a stewardess breathing on it. Mark Lawson

I don't know why they don't just serve lunch in a sick bag – save time.
Bill, *Weak at the Top*

I took one of those cheap flights, no frills. I finished eating, and had to do the dishes. Rodney Dangerfield

The pilot says, 'We're hurtling through the air at 500 miles per hour. Please feel free to move about the cabin.' Then you land. You're rolling to the gate at one mile per hour and you hear, 'You must remain seated for your own safety! Sit down!' I'm wondering, could we take off again?
Carol Leifer

I hate to fly. Every time I get off a plane, I view it as a failed suicide attempt. Barry Sonnenfeld

You define a good flight by negatives: you didn't get hijacked, you didn't crash, you didn't throw up, you weren't late, you weren't nauseated by the food. So you are grateful. Paul Theroux

Experts say you're more likely to get hurt crossing the street than you are flying, but that doesn't make me any less frightened of flying. If anything, it makes me more afraid of crossing the street. **Ellen DeGeneres**

—How was your flight, sir?
—Have you ever flown in a plane?
—Oh, yes, often.
—Well, it was just like that. **Official and Prince Philip**

Airplane travel is nature's way of making you look like your passport photograph. **Al Gore**

Immediately after Orville Wright's historic 12-second flight, his luggage could not be located. **Sidney Harris**

The first piece of luggage on the carousel belongs to no one. It's just a dummy suitcase to give everyone hope. **Erma Bombeck**

The devil-airplane is responsible for, among other things, cultural defilement (by taking certain people to places they were never meant to be), loss of feeling for the true and awesome dimensions of the country, and angel impersonation. **Andrei Codrescu**

TRAVEL & TOURISM

I consider myself a well-seasoned traveller. I can say 'diarrhoea' in 30 different languages. **Victor Lewis-Smith**

Cahill's Expedition Rule Number One: Absolutely no one is interested in the nature, quality or content of your last bowel movement. **Tim Cahill**

The first condition of understanding a foreign country is to smell it. **Rudyard Kipling**

One of the things I always look out for, when trying to get to grips with a new place, is graffiti. It tells you more than headlines or editorials.

Toby Litt

Whenever I travel I like to keep the seat next to me empty. I found a great way to do it. When someone walks down the aisle and says to you, 'Is someone sitting there?' just say, 'No one – except the Lord.'

Carol Leifer

To travel is to discover everyone is wrong about other countries.

Aldous Huxley

People travel to faraway places to watch, in fascination, the kind of people they ignore at home.

Dagobert D. Runes

A journey of a thousand miles begins with a cash advance.

Anon

Pack the one bag. Unpack it, pack it, unpack it, pack it: passport, ticket, book, taxi, airport, check-in, beer, announcement, stairs, airplane, fasten seat-belt, airborne, flight, rocking, sun, stars, space, hips of strolling stewardesses, read, sleep, clouds, falling engine speed, descent, circling, touch down, earth, unfasten seat-belt, stairs, airport, immunisation book, visa, customs, questions, taxi, streets, houses, people, hotel, key, room, stuffiness, thirst, otherness, foreignness, loneliness, fatigue, life.

Ryszard Kapuscinski

I am a traveller. *You* are a sightseer. *He* is a tourist.

Craig Brown

Tourists are terrorists with cameras.

Andrei Codrescu

Years ago, climbing the marble steps of the Acropolis, a companion raised his camera to his eye and when the Parthenon came into view he snapped it, before, as it were, he had seen it. This seemed to me the placing of a barrier between himself and experience.

P.J. Kavanagh

A tourist could be anywhere. The place doesn't matter. It's just another TV channel.
Jeanette Winterson

The tourist in Ireland has only to ask and he will be directed to something; whether or not it is what he thinks he is looking for is another matter.
Ciarán Carson

Next morning we visited sixty-three more Cambridge colleges and after lunch I said I was going to my room to lie down.
P.G. Wodehouse

The Pyramids, whose function as a public latrine no guide book mentions...
V.S. Naipaul

I don't want to see any more rubble.
Kingsley Amis, visiting classical sites in Greece

Those who write about the Grand Canyon generally begin by saying that it is indescribable, then they undertake to describe it.
Joseph Wood Krutch

I doubt whether I ever read any description of scenery which gave me an idea of the place described.
Anthony Trollope

Everest is relatively easy to climb, given an experienced guide, porters, equipment and good weather. The result is that many inexperienced, well-heeled people climb it each year, a certain percentage die, and the mountain has become a leisure resort, albeit one dotted with corpses, turds and oxygen cylinders, none of which decay at that altitude.
Sean French

Polar exploration is at once the cleanest and most isolated way of having a bad time which has been devised.
Apsley Cherry-Gerard

Utah's Great Salt Lake, the largest inland body of salt water in the world, is of no use, even for suicide.
Cecil Roberts

Crossing what the egocentric British like to call the English Channel is, as everyone knows, a sickening experience, unrelieved by the sight of the white cliffs of Dover which, in the pale moonlight, greet the nauseated traveller like huge piles of slightly off cottage cheese.   **Alberto Manguel**

Walking down Princes Street in Edinburgh, soaking up the atmosphere, I saw a big sign that said: 'Bus Tours, £10.' So I thought I'd give it a try. What a rip-off. Ten quid to have a look round a bus!   **Seymour Mace**

He knew he'd have to go to Disney World eventually. It's middle-class American's version of a pilgrimage to Mecca... With frayed nerves and tattered wallets the faithful stream through the turnstiles of the Magic Kingdom, intent on giving every child his or her birthright: the opportunity to gawk at a six-foot duck in a blue jacket.   **Caryl Rivers**

Visitors who care about real food will discover that gourmet dining is as much a fantasy as everything else in the Magic Kingdom.
Fodor's Travel Guide

I find the theme in most theme parks is, 'Wait in line, Fatty.'
Demetri Martin

Americans are rather like bad Bulgarian wine: they don't travel well.
Bernard Falk

Americans who travel abroad for the first time are often shocked to discover that, despite all the progress that has been made in the last thirty years, many foreign people still speak in foreign languages.   **Dave Barry**

Everything in Europe is lukewarm except the radiators. You could use the radiators to make party ice.   **P.J. O'Rourke**

Tourists in Hawaii are easily identifiable because they're the only people wearing Hawaiian shirts.   **Dave Barry**

In India, the first sign of a problem is when your guide says, 'No problem!'

Lynn Ferrin

Phuket, it is generally agreed, is a tourist shithole – best served for anthropological studies of fat German men who wear Speedos.   Rolf Potts

The four Rs of tropical travel: rats, roaches, rain, and rip-off.

Barbara Ann Curcio

Night night, sleep tight, don't let the bed bugs paralyse.

African tour guide, *The Simpsons*

Travel is glamorous only in retrospect.

Paul Theroux

On your return from an excursion to North Wales, the Lakes, etc, the first friend you meet asks whether you saw X, the most celebrated spot of the whole tour – the only place, however, by some villainous mischance, you did *not* see.

James Beresford

No one wants to see your slides. Get that through your head. Not your parents who gave you life. Not your kids who are insecure and need your approval. Not your priest, minister, or rabbi who are paid to be kind and forgiving. Not even someone whose life you saved in the war and who owes you big.

Erma Bombeck

However far you travel, you will never find the girl who smiles out at you from the travel brochure.

Anon

HOTEL

You ponce in here expecting to be waited on hand and foot while I'm trying to run a hotel here!

Basil Fawlty, *Fawlty Towers*

Boy, what a hotel that was. They stole my towel.

Rodney Dangerfield

You can imagine how big my room was – when I closed the door, the doorknob got in bed with me.   Henny Youngman

It used to be a good hotel, but that proves nothing – I used to be a good boy.
                                                                  Mark Twain

The hotel I'm in has a lovely closet. A nail.   Henny Youngman

A satisfied customer. We should have him stuffed.
                                                      Basil Fawlty, *Fawlty Towers*

'Boutique' hotels whose lobbies are masses of flickering candles, whose staff resemble surly rock stars and whose bathrooms contain little but a tin washbasin and an orchid…   Philip Norman

There was a gold-wrapped chocolate on each pillow, it being a peculiar assumption of expensive hotels that the kind of people who can afford to pay a labourer's weekly wage for one night's accommodation will suddenly go ape-shit with gratitude for a free piece of confectionery.
                                                                 Mark Lawson

A hotel mini-bar allows you to see into the future at what a can of Pepsi will cost in 2020.   Rich Hall

Twenty-four-hour room service generally refers to the length of time that it takes for the club sandwich to arrive. This is indeed disheartening, particularly when you've ordered scrambled eggs.   Fran Lebowitz

Room service gives you the chance to pay 42 dollars for a 4-dollar egg. There's no profit-margin on any product in the history of the world like room service. An egg in the coffee shop on the ground floor costs 4 dollars. Why is it that when that egg goes up one floor in an elevator it becomes a 42-dollar egg?   Jackie Mason

I spent the night at the Downtowner Inn, a motel intriguingly reminiscent of a mobile home. It was one of those establishments in which, as protection against theft or absentmindedness, the key was attached to a vast slab of aluminium so cumbersome that only guests with a tin leg or a permanent erection could plausibly forget they had it in their pocket.

Mark Lawson

—This place is the crummiest, shoddiest, worst-run hotel in the whole of Western Europe.
—No, no, I won't have that. There's a place in Eastbourne.

Mr Hamilton and Major Gowen, *Fawlty Towers*

COUNTRIES
– GENERAL

Every nation ridicules other nations, and all are right.

Arthur Schopenhauer

Life in Africa is nasty, British, and short.

Paul Theroux

Alaska represents the ultimate time-activity ratio nightmare: nothing to do and 22 hours of daylight in which not to do it.

Mark Lawson

Antarctica? I thought the oldest, coldest object on earth was Faye Dunaway.

David Letterman

There are many non-intellectual countries; Australia is one of the few anti-intellectual ones.

George Mikes

Australia is like Britain on Prozac.

Rob Brydon

Melbourne is the perfect place for making a film about the end of the world.

Ava Gardner, star of *On the Beach*

Canada: nothing like stepping off a ten-hour flight and bumping into
French people.   Craig Campbell

Hello, moose-fuckers!   Jerry Sadowitz, on Canada

I've been to Canada, and I've always gotten the impression that I could
take the country over in about two days.   Jon Stewart

Canada? Why would I want to leave America just to visit America Jr?
                                                            Homer Simpson

A Canadian is just like an American. Only without the gun.   Dave Foley

Very big, China.   Noël Coward

I wouldn't mind seeing China if I could come back the same day.
                                                            Philip Larkin

If you stay here much longer, you will go home with slitty eyes.
                               Prince Philip, to Simon Kirby, studying in China

France: ever want to slap an entire country?   Steve Landesberg

I would have loved France. Without the French.   D.H. Lawrence

The French remind me a little bit of an ageing actress of the 1940s who is
still trying to dine out on her looks but doesn't have the face for it.
                                                       Senator John McCain

You know how unpredictable the French are. One minute they're kissing
a woman's hand, the next they're chopping her head off.
                                              Marge Simpson, *The Simpsons*

I would rather be eating cheese and reading Sartre on the banks of the
River Seine than eating popcorn with a born-again Bible-belt
fundamentalist Republican administration in Crawford, Texas, execution
capital of the world.   George Galloway

There's just something about Germans. You can listen to a nice, young, affable German fellow and he'll be saying things like, 'Vell, ya, dis is eine critical time for Germany now, economically we are good, but ve have been better. Ve are investing a lot in ze arts, and emerging globally....' and you'll be there listening, thinking, 'Mmm, yeah, mmm... Hitler... mmm...yeah, Hitler, Hitler, Hitler, Hitler, Hitler, Hitler...' **Dylan Moran**

One thing I will say for the Germans, they are always perfectly willing to give somebody else's land to somebody else. **Will Rogers**

—Don't knock the Greeks. They invented civilisation.
—Yeah, ass-fucking too.
Jimmy McNulty and William Moreland, *The Wire*

From the moment you set foot in India, you realise there's something different, something special in the air. Some say it's spiritual, others say it's cultural. I think it's a wicked combination of curry, cow shit, and breath-taking body odour; India has 900 million people, 200 million cows, and enough curry to turn the Pacific Ocean into a giant seafood stir-fry. **Doug Lansky**

India: It is a curious people. With them, all life seems to be sacred except human life. Mark Twain

Two key rules of Third World Travel: 1) Never run out of whiskey; 2) Never run out of whiskey. **P.J. O'Rourke**

The Irish: Charming, soft-voiced, quarrelsome, priest-ridden, feckless, and happily devoid of the slightest integrity in our stodgy English sense of the word. **Noël Coward**

Being Irish is, no matter how real, a pose. **Mignon McLaughlin**

Italy: anarchy tempered by bureaucracy. **George F. Will**

Rome, Italy, is an example of what happens when the buildings in a city last too long.   Andy Warhol

There are two things a Sicilian won't do: lie about pizza, and file a tax return.   Sophia Petrillo, *The Golden Girls*

—How is it possible to get pregnant in Sicily just by crossing the street?
—Cheap Chianti and narrow streets.
                              Rose Nylund and Sophia Petrillo, *The Golden Girls*

[*Working on a crossword puzzle*] A four-letter Italian word for 'goodbye'... Bang. B-A-N-G.   Archie Bunker, *All in the Family*

Is there a Japanese smile that does not seem like an expression of pain? Paul Theroux

The Middle Eastern states aren't nations, they're quarrels with borders.
                                                            P.J. O'Rourke

Pakistan is the sort of place every man should send his mother-in-law, for a month, with all expenses paid.   Ian Botham

In the past few centuries, Poland has become known as 'the airplane lavatory of Europe' – dirty, subject to turbulence, and almost constantly occupied.   Chris Harris

Singapore: Disneyland with the death penalty.   Eve Jones

Long before I visited Sweden for the first time, I had built up a composite portrait of the average Swede. He was withdrawn and spasmodic, reserved on the surface but explosive beneath it, veering between troughs of depression and fits of abandon. He was a pacifist, a socialist, an alcoholic and a hiker. He swam nude and tended to commit suicide during the long winters. Like many popular misconceptions (e.g. that the French are greedy and the Spanish stoical), this turned out to be fairly close to the truth.   Kenneth Tynan

The only nation I've ever been tempted to feel really racist about are the Swiss – a whole country of phobic handwashers living in a giant Barclays Bank.

Jonathan Raban

Switzerland is a country to be in for two hours, to two and a half if the weather is fine, and no more. Ennui comes in the third hour, and suicide attacks you before the night.

Lord Brougham

Turkey is aptly named.

Howard Odgen

—I used to serve in the Third Monmouthshire Regiment.
—What do you want to go to Wales for?

Jack Spencer and Prince Philip

Wales is a Third World country.

Sir Paul McCartney

Wales is a country where Sunday starts early, and lasts several years.

Peg Bracken

Growing up in Wales is tough. It's always wet. I was eight before I realised you could take a cagoule off.

Rhod Gilbert

Apart from the phone boxes and the people, everything is pebbledashed in Holyhead.

Byron Rogers

I'm Welsh and a lot of people do make fun of the Welsh accent. A friend of mine said, 'I can never do the Welsh accent. If I try, it comes out Pakistani.' I said, 'Well, you've to try harder to master it – Ahmed.'

Mark Watson

ENGLAND

If countries were named after the words you first hear when you go there, England would have to be called *Damn It*.

Georg Christoph Lichtenberg

An Englishman can be defined as someone who lives on an island in the North Sea governed by Scots.

Jeremy Paxman

England is a horrible place with horrible people, horrible food, horrible climate, horrible class system, horrible cities and horrible countryside (Gloucestershire is now one big car park).   **Stephen Pile**

We're not really a nation of zinc kitchen surfaces and brushed aluminium; we're more a nation of Weatherspoons, and *Heat* magazine, and chlamydia.   **Jeremy Clarkson**

We take more illegal drugs than any other nation in Europe, we take more Prozac than any other nation, we are the most obese nation in Europe. We have more childhood asthma, we have the highest rate of teenage pregnancy. We're just a bunch of stoned, illiterate, wheezing, shagging, lardy bastards.   **Bill Bailey**

A truism holds that not all people are best suited to the countries they inhabit. I have always thought the Indians would make a better fist of England than the English. The best Germans are from Austria and the best Americans are from Ireland.   **Simon Jenkins**

We have exported so many great things around the world – slavery, hooliganism and *Starlight Express*.   **Narrator, *Little Britain***

What's the matter, Ozzy? You haven't looked this depressed since you remembered you were from Birmingham.   **Sharon Osbourne, *Dead Ringers***

My mum and dad are Scottish but they moved down to Wolverhampton when I was two 'cause they wanted me to sound like a twat.
                                                                            Susan Murray

I really don't like the north of England. It's always raining, it's very cold and I don't like all those little houses.   **Frederick Kanoute, French footballer**

Blackpool is the *end of the line*. It is the English Siberia. It is pure TORTURE. Hateful, tasteless, witless, bleak, boring, dirty, tat – IT HAS NOTHING. I loathe every disgusting minute of it.   **Kenneth Williams**

Too full of drugs, obesity, underachievement and labour MPs.
                                                          Boris Johnson, on Portsmouth

The man who is tired of London is tired of looking for a parking space.

Paul Theroux

Crowds without company, and dissipation without pleasure.

Edward Gibbon, on London

I've loved seeing the sights in London. But I was really pissed off to find out that Big Ben was a clock.

Ron Allen

Pretend you don't live in Tottenham by walking around Tottenham with an *A-Z* guide, asking people for directions.

Simone Glover

I'm leaving because the weather is too good. I hate London when it's not raining.

Groucho Marx

I was born in the town of Erith, Kent. It's not twinned with anywhere, but it does have a suicide pact with Dagenham.

Linda Smith

—We could lose all our money and the house...
—Jerry, I will stand by you no matter what – even if it means moving to Esher.

Margot and Jerry Leadbetter, *The Good Life*

SCOTLAND

The awful Lowland Scot face – the long-jawed face which looks as tho' the owner were holding an egg concealed in his mouth – it is what spoils R.L. Stevenson's face.

A.C. Benson

It is never difficult to distinguish between a Scotsman with a grievance and a ray of sunshine.

P.G. Wodehouse

A typical Scot has bad teeth, a good chance of cancer, a liver under severe stress, and a heart attack pending. He smokes like a chimney, drinks like a fish, and regularly makes an exhibition of himself.

Alan Bond

The most Scottish thing I've ever seen: there was a man leaning against a front door and pissing inside. He then took out his keys and went inside.

Frankie Boyle

We did find evidence of the Mediterranean diet in Scotland – albeit in the form of deep-fried pizza.   **Dr Mark Petticrew, Medical Research Council**

The name Govan was formed by joining two Gaelic words, 'Go' meaning 'stop' and 'Van', 'to be without tax or insurance'.

Rab C. Nesbitt, *A Stranger Here Myself*

Edinburgh...a dignified spinster with syphilis.   **Charles Higham**

Angus was stripping his wallpaper when Archie called round. 'Och, Angus,' he said, 'I see you're decorating.' 'No,' replied Angus, 'moving.'

Anon

Dunoon... What a gaff that is... Even saying the name makes yi feel as if it's started drizzling on the roof of your mouth. Dun-oon!'

Rab C. Nesbitt, *Rab C. Nesbitt*

How do you keep the natives off the booze long enough to get them past the test?   **Prince Philip, to Robert Drummond, a Scottish driving instructor**

In Scotland, you cannae smoke or smack your kids, but in England you can smoke and sort of smack them. So I run a bus to Carlisle every Sunday and get off over the Border for a good fag and wee slap at a cheeky toddler.

Will Smith

AMERICA
– GENERAL

As an American, I'd like to apologise – for everything. Rich Hall

America…just a nation of 200 million used car salesmen with all the money we need to buy guns and no qualms about killing anybody else in the world who tries to make us uncomfortable. Hunter S. Thompson

The land of the dull and the home of the literal. Gore Vidal

A country founded by people so uptight that the British kicked them out.
Aaron Ludensky

They're the experts where personality is concerned, the Americans; they've got it down to a fine art. Alan Bennett

We Americans are like guys in beer commercials – loud, gross, fun-loving and we think that if we can just get drunk enough we can get chicks to do anything we want – except in America's case, other countries are the chicks. Harry Shearer

I don't know why we have this 'special relationship' with America. We're like the nerdy kid hanging round with the big bully. America's like the bully of the world going up to countries and going, 'Give us your sweets or I'll smash your face in.' And Britain leans round the back and goes, 'Yeah.' Bill Bailey

—I'm in favour of kissing Franklin D. Roosevelt on both cheeks.
—Yes, but not on all four.
Edward Marsh and Winston Churchill, *attrib*.

Gratitude, like love, is never a dependable international emotion.
Joseph Alsop

—Why do we have a 'special relationship' with the United States?
—Because we can't be bothered to learn French.

Steve Punt and Hugh Dennis, *The Now Show*

The First Wives Club had strong American values: divorce, alcoholism, plastic surgery and revenge.

Bette Midler

...as American as pizza pie, unwed mothers and cheating on your income tax.

Mike Royko

America is a vast conspiracy to make you happy.

John Updike

—You know we're the only country where the pursuit of happiness is guaranteed in writing? Do you believe that? A bunch of fucking spoiled brats. Where's my happiness then?
—It's the *pursuit* that's guaranteed.
—Yeah, always a fucking loophole.

Tony Soprano and Dr Melfi, *The Sopranos*

What the United States does best is to understand itself. What it does worst is understand others.

Carlos Fuentes

America is a country no one should go to for the first time.

Jawaharlal Nehru

It only takes a room of Americans for the English and Australians to realise how much we have in common.

Stephen Fry

In America, through pressure of conformity, there is freedom of choice, but nothing to choose from.

Peter Ustinov

Americans are the only people in the world known to me whose status-anxiety prompts them to advertise their college and university affiliations in the rear window of their automobiles.

Paul Fussell

The men the American people admire most extravagantly are the most daring liars; the men they detest most violently are those who try to tell them the truth. **H.L. Mencken**

This is how Americans think. You believe that if something happens to someone, they must have deserved it. **Barbara Kingsolver**

We live in a country where John Lennon takes eight bullets, Yoko Ono is walking right beside him and no one hits her. Explain that to me.
Denis Leary

America's in love with two big ideas: its own innocence and the impossibility of it ever losing at anything. **Harry Shearer**

I think the greatest taboos in America are faith and failure. **Michael Malone**

I have never been able to look upon America as young and vital, but rather as prematurely old, as a fruit which rotted before it had a chance to ripen. The word which gives the key to the national vice is waste.
Henry Miller

When I was a graduate student at Harvard, I learned about showers and central heating. Ten years later, I learned about breakfast meetings. These are America's three contributions to civilisation. **Mervyn A. King**

I think there are only three things America will be known for two thousand years from now when they study this civilisation: the Constitution, jazz music, and baseball. **Gerald Early**

With enough time, American civilisation will make the Midwest of any place. **Garrison Keillor**

AMERICA – PLACES

I come from Des Moines. Somebody had to.   **Bill Bryson**

Here is the difference between Dante, Milton and me. They wrote about
hell and never saw the place. I wrote about Chicago after looking the
town over for years and years.   **Carl Sandburg**

Dallas is a city that salutes a man who can buy a piece of art, but not a
man who can create one.   **A.C. Greene**

Dallas is the kind of town that would have rooted for Goliath to beat
David.   **Molly Ivins**

New York's such a wonderful city. Although I was at the library today.
The guy was very rude. I said, 'I'd like a card.' He says, 'You have to
prove you're a citizen of New York.' So I stabbed him.   **Emo Philips**

New York: the only city where people make radio requests like, 'This is
for Tina – I'm sorry I stabbed you.'   **Carol Leifer**

I love New York City; I've got a gun.   **Charles Barkley**

The New York marathon went very well. Only 12 runners are missing.
                    David Letterman

Ken Livingstone says he feels safer in New York than London. Perhaps this is because no one knows him there.

Nicholas Lloyd

This is New York City and there's no law against being annoying.
                    William Kunstler

People say New Yorkers can't get along. Not true. I saw two New Yorkers, complete strangers, sharing a cab. One guy took the tyres and the radio; the other guy took the engine.   **David Letterman**

The faces in New York remind me of people who played a game and lost.

Murray Kempton

The main thing I like about New Yorkers is that they understand that their lives are a relentless circus of horrors, ending in death. As New Yorkers, we realise this, we resign ourselves to our fate, and we make sure that everyone else is as miserable as we are.

Kyle Baker, *Why I Hate Saturn*

In New York, there's no room for amateurs, even in crossing the streets.

George Segal

I'm bored with the Statue of Liberty. It's not like she does anything.

Ian Shoales

We stayed at Caesar's Palace in Las Vegas, a giant hotel-casino authentically decorated to look exactly the way the Roman Empire would have looked if it had consisted mainly of slot machines.   **Dave Barry**

Las Vegas was never meant to be seen by day.   **Peter S. Beagle**

L.A.: where there's never weather, and walking is a crime.   **Ian Shoales**

No one walks in Los Angeles. I didn't know this and as I was walking along this guy drove past in his car and called out, 'Hey, loser! Get a car!'
Stephen Merchant

The only people who walk in Los Angeles are hookers and the British.
Los Angeles shopkeeper

Californians invented the concept of lifestyle. This alone warrants their doom.

Don DeLillo

Los Angeles is a greedy city. It's a city devoted to pleasure, self-indulgence, prettiness, health, immortality and gracefulness. People are devoting so much time to avoiding death they haven't got much time for leading their life.

Jonathan Miller

I left Los Angeles for a while. I wasn't on business, I just wanted to smoke a cigarette.

Richard Jeni

We can see California coming, and we're scared.

James Brady

GRUMPY
SPORT & LEISURE

SPORT & GAMES
– GENERAL

The greatest dread of all, the dread of games.   John Betjeman

I have never willingly chased a ball.   Robert Morley

Why is it when men play they always play at killing each other?
          Marge Sherwood, *The Talented Mr Ripley*

I know that women throng to every sporting event, but you'll never convince me that any of them really enjoy it.   Mignon McLaughlin

The game women play is men.   Adam Smith

I'm Jewish. We don't play sport. We sell you the equipment.   Joan Rivers

Karate is a form of martial arts in which people who have had years and years of training can, using only their hands and feet, make some of the worst movies in the history of the world.   Dave Barry

Karate mystifies me. All that stuff about breaking bricks. Why don't they just pick up the brick and hit 'em over the head with it?   Pat Morita

Watching Steve Davis play snooker is like watching your stools float.
          Alex 'Hurricane' Higgins

The atmosphere at this darts match is a cross between the Munich Beer Festival and the Colosseum when the Christians were on the menu.
          Sid Waddell

I think they've gone overboard in cleaning up darts. It's about pints, fags and blokes in cardigans.   Sid Waddell

Skipping. Huge fucking boxers and very small girls are the only two social groups in the world who do skipping.   Eddie Izzard

Croquet is polo for people who are too fat to get on a horse.

Frankie Boyle

Hurling? I'm always suspicious of games when you're the only ones that play it.

Jack Charlton

I believe that professional wrestling is clean and everything else in the world is fixed.

Frank Deford

Professional wrestling's most mystifying hold is on its audience.

Luke Neely

The Oxford and Cambridge Boat Race would be much more attractive if the rules were changed to allow the boats to ram each other.

Miles Kington

Bullfighting: men in fancy dress tormenting cattle.

John Carey

Bullfights are hugely popular because you can sit comfortably with a hot dog and possibly watch a man die.

Albert Brooks

It's no use asking politicians to run an Olympic Games; they'd probably have a relay for backstabbing.

Ken Livingstone, on the 2012 London Olympics

The Winter Olympics is a celebration of amateur athletes, frostbite and unpronounceable Russian surnames. Until they include a Sumo Ski Jump competition, they'll always be a second-rate affair.

Ryan Murphy

The Winter Olympics: 40 kinds of sliding.

Dara O'Briain

How to Improve the Winter Olympics: The Die-athlon – two skiers follow parallel paths and stop to shoot at each other. No silver or bronze medals will be awarded.

Douglas Frank

We are all endowed with certain God-given talents. Mine happens to be punching people in the head. **Sugar Ray Leonard, boxer**

I don't mind the fight going out at three o'clock in the morning. Everyone in Glasgow fights at three in the morning. **Jim Watt, Scottish boxer**

All fighters are prostitutes and all promoters are pimps. **Larry Holmes**

Come on, we're all harlots – it's all a matter of price. **Kerry Packer**

—Are you still in the fight game?
—In a way. I married Benjy's mother.
Alan Swann and Rookie Carroca, *My Favorite Year*

Comparing my own athletic career with Brendan Foster's is a bit like having a shower with Errol Flynn. **Arthur Smith**

—Do you think Gareth Thomas would make a good captain of the Welsh Lions?
—The short answer is 'no' and the longer answer is also 'no'.
Reporter and Graham Henry, rugby coach

I predict that sumo wrestling will become the next big sport because it actually requires participants to be fat and it only lasts three seconds. **Bill Geist**

I don't have nightmares about my team. You gotta sleep before you have nightmares. **Bep Guidolin, coach to Kansas City Scouts**

If you ever wondered what it was like to be an Oakland Raiders fan, you are in luck because I'm about to give you some insight: first, take an ice pick and just ram it into your left testicle. If you can make it all the way through so it sticks into a table or chair, that is preferable. Next, headbutt the nearest immovable object (table, brick wall, etc.) seven times or until you draw blood, whichever comes first. After that, put your left hand on a table and smash it with a hammer three times as hard as you can, then dip it in scalding hot water. After that wears off, eat an Oreo cookie, because they actually look like they are going to score, but as soon as you eat the cookie wash it down with a quart of antifreeze because they found some way to screw it up. While you are still alive, slowly remove the ice pick to make sure you achieve maximum torture, and then stab yourself in the temple.   **B.J. of Syracuse**

I resigned as coach of the Denver Broncos because of illness and fatigue: the fans were sick and tired of me.   **John Ralston**

The secret of managing is to keep the guys who hate you away from the guys who are undecided.   **Casey Stengel**

I'll never make it with the Yankees. All the great Yankees are Italian. What chance do I have? My mother makes spaghetti with ketchup.
                    Eugene Jerome, *Brighton Beach Memories*

CRICKET

I can't bat, can't bowl and can't field these days. I've every chance of being picked for England.   **Ray East**

He may be good enough for England, but not for Yorkshire.
                    Brian Sellers, after Yorkshire sacked Johnny Wardle

Civil war is never far below the surface of Yorkshire cricket.
                    James P. Coldham

Can you lend me your brain 'cause I'm building an idiot?
                    Australian heckler, to Phil Tufnell

The other advantage England have got when Phil Tufnell's bowling is that he isn't fielding.   **Ian Chappell**

—Oi, Brandes, why are you so fat?
—Because every time I fuck your wife she gives me a biscuit.
                    Glenn McGrath and Eddie Brandes

I'll bowl you a fucking piano, you Pommie poof. Let's see if you can play that.

Merv Hughes, to Michael Atherton

That's rubbish, is that.

Geoffrey Boycott

At least you'll never die of a stroke, Boycs.

Fred Trueman, to Geoffrey Boycott

—So, how's your wife and my kids?
—Wife's fine. Kids are retarded.

Rod Marsh and Ian Botham

I was once offered a Foster's from someone over the fence, but it was warmer and frothier than a Foster's.

Bob Willis

Why do Australia usually beat the Poms? Whereas the Australians hate the Poms, the Poms only despise the Australians.

David Stove

We shouldn't have beaten the Australians that summer. It only made them angry.

England cricket fan, on Australia's 5-0 Test Match win, 2007

—What do you call an Englishman with a hundred runs against his name?
—A bowler.

Anon

Supporting the English cricket team is like supporting a second division football team. I support Norwich City football team and when they lose I really don't mind because I *expect* them to; but when we win I'm *so* happy – much happier than any Arsenal supporter could ever be.

Stephen Fry

A fart competing with thunder.

Graham Gooch, on England v. Australia, 1990–1

This can only help England's cause.

Ian Botham, after Geoffrey Boycott began coaching young Pakistani batsmen

Ian Botham couldn't bowl a hoop downhill.   **Fred Trueman**

There is a final drop of venom which transforms a good bowler into a great one.   **T.C.F. Prittie**

Derek Randall bats like an octopus with piles.

Anon

He went through a bad patch where he couldn't bat his eyelids.
                    Mike Selvey

—[*After letting the ball go between his legs*] I should've kept my legs together.
—Not you, son. Your mother should've!
                    Raman Subba Row and Fred Trueman

It's a catch he would have caught ninety-nine times out of a thousand.
                    Henry 'Blowers' Blofeld

I need seven wickets from this match, and you buggers had better start drawing straws to see who I don't get.   **Fred Trueman**

I'm not one to blame anyone, but it was definitely Viv Richards' fault.
                    Fred Trueman

The only acceptable form of dissent is a dirty look – and we don't like that.   **England Test umpire**

I am here to propose a toast to sports writers. It's up to you whether you stand up or not.   **Fred Trueman**

Once while he was playing cricket in Bombay, the wife of the Nawab of Pataudi rang him up. The secretary of the club replied, 'Madam, the Nawab Sahib has just gone out to bat. I will ask him to ring you back as soon as he returns to the pavilion.' 'No,' replied his wife, 'I'll wait on the line. He never stays at the wicket for very long.'   **Khushwant Singh**

If you were to ask a representative of almost any profession what were the essential qualities of their calling, they would almost certainly say honesty, integrity and a sense of humour. In a good village cricket captain these qualities would be utterly redundant.   **Robert Holles**

Dr W.G. Grace after getting out in a country game, put the bails back on the stumps and told the bowler, 'They haven't come to see you bowl, they've come to see me bat.' He then continued his innings.   **Dom Kureen**

Spectators who did not fall asleep before tea at the Saffrons yesterday were undoubtedly kept awake by the town hall clock, which, for much of the time, was striking more frequently than the Sussex batsmen.
                                                        Doug Ibbotson

Cricket needs brightening up a bit. My solution is to let the players drink at the beginning of the game, not after. It always works in our picnic matches.   **Paul Hogan**

How could they liven cricket up? They could turn the pitch into a rectangle, put goalposts at either end, give people boots and allow them to kick the ball.   **Angus Deayton**

FOOTBALL

A male MP was found dead in stockings and suspenders. He was also wearing a Manchester City scarf but the police kept that quiet so as not to embarrass the relatives.   **Bernard Manning**

Nature hating a vacuum like the average English mind, it has hastened to fill it with football: though, in truth, the English are very mediocre even at the sport they so unfortunately gave to the rest of the world.
                                                   Theodore Dalrymple

Hartlepool are bound to finish bottom unless there's a place even lower in the bloody table.   **Peter Taylor**

Every thousandth person created, God unhinges their heads, scoops out their brains and issues them to football clubs as supporters.   **Mike Bateson**

The fans all had the complexion and body-scent of a cheese-and-onion crisp, and the eyes of pit-bulls.   Martin Amis

This place is like a morgue. Most of those that did come are moaning bastards. There's no home advantage for us.

Joe Kinnear, on low attendance at matches

There is no known cure.   **John Major, on being a Chelsea fan**

The natural state of the football fan is bitter disappointment, no matter what the score.   **Nick Hornby**

The score is Sunderland nil, Leicester nil, the temperature is nil, and the entertainment value is not much above nil.   **Radio 5 Live**

They were lucky to get nil.   **Len Shackleton**

Apart from Oliver Kahn, if you put all the players in a sack and punched it, whoever you hit would deserve it.   **Franz Beckenbauer**

Our guys are getting murdered twice a week.   **Andy Roxburgh**

There are already millions of camera angles showing everything, and referees even have things in their ears now. Pretty soon they'll be going out on to the pitch with a satellite dish stuck up their arses.   **Ian Wright**

It was a game of two halves, and we were rubbish in both of them.

Brian Horton

Our passing was poor, we didn't get behind the ball, but I still blame the referee.   **Bryan Robson**

We can't win at home, we can't win away. As manager, I just can't figure out where else to play.   **Jock Brown, Celtic manager**

There's only two Andy Gorams, two Andy Gorams...
        Football chant, when Rangers' goalie was diagnosed with mild schizophrenia

I was hurt to read in Wayne Rooney's autobiography that I'm his least favourite TV celebrity. I mean, what have I ever done to the potato-headed granny-shagger?   **Jonathan Ross**

Never use sarcasm on players. It doesn't work.   **Alex Ferguson**

Perhaps it is because Arsène Wenger sees himself as passing down judgements from a moral Everest that his admirable brain sometimes seems to be starved of oxygen.   **Hugh McIlvanney**

I'll try not to apologise too much for the game but I'm glad I got in for free.   **Micky Adams, manager**

We were caviar in the first half, cabbage in the second.   **Phil Thompson**

If I wasn't the manager I'd have gone home early.   **Alex Miller**

It looked as if we'd picked eleven people off the streets of Birmingham and asked them if they wanted a game.
                                    Steve Bruce, manager of Birmingham City

When Rioch came to Millwall we were depressed and miserable. He's done a brilliant job of turning it all around. Now we're miserable and depressed.   **Danny Baker**

If that was a penalty, I'll plait sawdust.
                                    Ron Atkinson

At least we were consistent – useless in defence, useless in midfield and crap up front.   **Ron Atkinson**

The last ten years have been one long story of learning how to cope with disappointment. **Delia Smith, director of Norwich City, 2002**

[*Mobile phone goes off at a post-match press conference*] That'll be the Samaritans. They usually call me this time of day. **Gordon Strachan**

—Will you stay as Newcastle manager until they win something?
—Well, I don't know if I'm going to live to be 127.
Interviewer and Bobby Robson

I haven't felt this bad since I killed a man.
**Uri Geller, co-chairman of Exeter and former
Israeli paratrooper, on his team's relegation**

David Beckham can't kick with his left foot. He can't head a ball. He can't tackle. And he doesn't score many goals. Apart from that he's all right. **George Best**

Becks hasn't changed since I've known him. He's always been a flash Cockney git.

Ryan Giggs

Maybe David Beckham wants to go into the movies. If they are silent movies, he has a good chance.
Max Clifford, on Beckham's move to Los Angeles

People always say I shouldn't be burning the candle at both ends, maybe because they don't have a big enough candle. **George Best**

I had nothing but contempt for the so-called hard men. For hard men I always read men who couldn't play. **George Best**

As Tommy Smith went out on the pitch he handed me a piece of paper. It was the evening menu for the Liverpool Royal Infirmary. **Jimmy Greaves**

Pablo Alfaro has seen more red cards than any La Liga player and collects opponents' eyeballs on his sharpened elbows like pickled onions on a cocktail stick... But this week Alfaro surpassed even himself. By sticking his fingers up another player's back passage... Said Roberto Palomar: 'When Ronaldo faces him on Wednesday, he's going to wear shin pads – and a cork.'
                                                                    Sid Lowe

—The striker's concussed. He doesn't know who he is.
—Tell him he's Pelé and get him back on.
                              John Lambie, Partick Thistle manager, and trainer

A penalty shoot-out is like loading a bullet into the chamber of a gun and asking everyone to pull the trigger. Someone will get the bullet, you know that, and it will reduce them to nothing. Fairness is not even an issue.
                                                          Christian Karembeu

...stepping off the edge of the world into silence.
                              Chris Waddle, on missing the penalty that knocked
                              England out of the 1990 World Cup Final

The tension felt by football fans during penalty shoot-outs can trigger heart attacks and strokes in male spectators. The day Holland lost to France in Euro '96, deaths from heart attacks and strokes rose by 50 per cent.
                                                          Dr Miriam Stoppard

If you missed a penalty you had your hair hacked off and were spat on by Uday's bodyguards. For every poor pass, you got a punch, and some players were forced to kick concrete balls in a prison yard.
           Habib Jaafer, Iraqi footballer, on the 'training' from Saddam Hussein's son

A penalty is a cowardly way to score.   Pelé

Sex could never be as great as winning the World Cup. It's not that sex isn't great, just that the World Cup is only once every four years.
                                                                   Ronaldo

The World Cup – I can't wait till it's over. The whole country's decked out like a loyalist estate.
                                                               Jeremy Hardy

The manager sent me to Liverpool to see if I could spot a weakness, and I found one: the half-time tea's too milky. **Kevin Summerfield, 1996**

Liverpool – 30 Miles From Greatness.
Manchester United banner, seen at Anfield

Attilio Lombardo is starting to pick up a bit of English on the training ground. The first word he learned was 'wanker'. **Steve Coppell**

Roman Abramovich has parked his Russian tank in our front garden and is firing fifty-pound notes at us.

David Dein, Arsenal vice-chairman, on the threat posed by big-spending Chelsea, 2003

Two months ago he was over the moon, now he's asking for it.
Juventus official, on Paolo Rossi's pay demands

I'm going to have to listen for offers for all my players – and the club cat, Benny, who is pissed off because there are no mice to catch because they have all died of starvation. **John McGrath, manager of Halifax, 1992**

I'd hang myself but the club can't afford the rope. **Iain Munro**

When you look at other sports, like golf, the players earn a lot more money without running around. I wish I had that little cart to take me to the corner kicks. **Thierry Henry**

Footballers have a very short career…a few seasons in the spotlight is followed by retirement, death and then a stint on *Sky Soccer Saturday*.
Jeff Stelling

Someone asked me last week if I missed the Villa. I said, 'No, I live in one.' **David Platt, on swapping Aston Villa for Bari, Italy**

I always answer letters from supporters. It's the death threats I object to.
                                        Reg Burr, Millwall chairman, 1990

It wasn't so much the death threats or the vandalism, but when you sit with your family in the directors' box and hear a couple of thousand people chanting, 'Gilbert Blades is a wanker!' then you feel it's time to go.   **Gilbert Blades, resigning as Lincoln chairman**

Football management these days is like nuclear war: no winners, just survivors.
                                                        Tommy Docherty

As manager of the national team, you know that, apart from the Chancellor, you will probably be the most hated person in the country.
                                                        Ossie Ardiles

One of the main reasons I never became England manager was because the FA thought I would take over and run the show. They were dead right.   **Brian Clough**

Being England coach is a great job. Until a ball is kicked.   **Terry Venables**

Just make sure you don't lose.
    Graham Taylor, England manager's advice to his successor, Terry Venables, 1994

Far from being an inspiring leader, Sven-Göran Eriksson sometimes gave the impression he couldn't inspire a nun to go to mass.   **Hugh McIlvanney**

We've never really played well in colour.
                                        Willie Rushton, on the England team

Being manager of Barnet was like living with a double-decker bus on your head. When I left it was like it had been driven off.   **Barry Fry**

The only person certain of boarding the coach for the Cup Final is Albert Kershaw, and he'll be driving it.   **Brian Clough**

When I was manager of Oldham I felt like a nitro-glycerine juggler.
                                                               Joe Royle

Coaching is for kids. If a player can't trap a ball and pass it by the time he's in the team, he shouldn't be there in the first place. I told Roy McFarland to go and get his bloody hair cut – that's coaching at this level.   **Brian Clough**

When I was admitted to the heart unit, somebody sent me a 'get well' telegram that said, 'We didn't even know you had one.'
                                                            Brian Clough

Like all the great dictators, from de Gaulle to Thatcher, Brian Clough stayed on a little too long.   *Gazzetta dello Sport*

When the television people asked me if I'd like to play a football manager in a play, I asked how long it would take. They told me 'About ten days,' and I said, 'That's about par for the course.'   **Tommy Docherty**

Football hooligans? Well, there are 92 club chairmen for a start.
                                                            Brian Clough

The ideal board of directors should be made up of three men – two dead and the other dying.   **Tommy Docherty**

This game drives you either to drink or the madhouse...and I'm not going to the madhouse for anybody.   **Tommy Docherty**

I'm handing the asylum back to the lunatics.
                          Keith Harris, resigning as chairman of the Football League

GOLF

Golf is the worst damn fun anyone can have.   Cy Manier

Temporary insanity practised in a pasture.   Dave Kindred

Golf's the only sport that comes with a slave.   Gregg Rogell

My goal is to play 72 holes someday without changing expression.
                                                               Jack Renner

—What's your handicap?
—I'm a coloured, one-eyed Jew – do I need anything else?
                                        Interviewer and Sammy Davis Jr

For me, the worst part of playing golf, by far, has always been hitting
the ball.   Dave Barry

The fourth hole found him four down, and one had the feeling that he
was lucky not to be five.   P.G. Wodehouse

Dyer on missing an easy putt: 'The sun was in my eyes – and then I have
such *light* eyelashes.'   A.C. Benson

The least thing upsets him on the links. He missed short putts because of
the uproar of the butterflies in the adjoining meadows.   P.G. Wodehouse

Gimme: an agreement between two losers who can't putt.   Jim Bishop

—If you could rewrite the Rules of Golf, what new rule would you
bring in?
—You are allowed to tackle your opponent.
                                        Interviewer and David Feherty

If every golfer in the world, male and female, were laid end to end, I, for
one, would leave them there.   Michael Parkinson

This is the Weekend They Didn't Play Golf.   Tagline, *Deliverance*

TENNIS

You cannot be serious!   John McEnroe

I'm not having points taken off me by an incompetent old fool. You are the pits of the world! Vultures! Trash!

John McEnroe, to tennis judge, Edward Jones

Do you have any problems, other than that you're unemployed, a moron and a dork?   John McEnroe, to a spectator

These days I get docked 10 or 20 per cent of my appearance fee if I *don't* yell at some people and break at least one racket.   John McEnroe

Why should a player be denied the sheer pleasure and release of smashing his own expensive racket into pieces occasionally?   Peter Ustinov

—Call me *Mister* Nastase.
—Look, Nastase, we used to have a famous cricket match in this country called Gentlemen and Players. The Gentlemen were put down on the scorecard as 'Mister' because they were gentlemen. By no stretch of the imagination can anybody call *you* a gentleman.

Ilie Nastaste and Trader Horn, Wimbledon umpire

Mister Bastard to you.   Jimmy Connors, to a spectator shouting abuse

I don't know that my behaviour improved all that much with age. They just found somebody worse.   Jimmy Connors

Mary Pierce had to take out a restraining order on her father after he threw a juice can at her opponent's head and urged his daughter to 'kill the bitch!'   Marc Horne

The proper method of playing mixed doubles is to hit the ball accidentally at the woman opponent as hard and as accurately as possible. Male players must not only retain equanimity on their side of the net, but create dissension on the other.   Art Hoppe

You can almost watch a couple play mixed doubles and know whether they should stay together.   **Dr Herbert Hendin**

The most depressing thing about playing tennis is that no matter how much I play, I'll never be as good as a wall. I played a wall once. Fucking relentless.   **Mitch Hedberg**

—What's the definition of endless love?
—Stevie Wonder and Ray Charles playing tennis.   **Anon**

HOBBIES & LEISURE

I went to the zoo the other day. You know, sometimes you gotta get away, stop and smell the gorilla shit.   **Tony Soprano, *The Sopranos***

Are we having fun yet?   **Carol Burnett**

Most of the time I don't have much fun. The rest of the time I don't have any fun at all.   **Woody Allen**

In Kazakhstan we have many hobbies: disco dancing, archery, rape and table tennis.   **Borat, a.k.a. Sacha Baron Cohen**

The British have a curious notion of leisure. A leisure centre is somewhere where people do hard physical exercise for two or more hours. A leisure centre ought to be somewhere where you can sit around in your pants watching cartoons.   **Jeremy Hardy**

You bought a Frankenstein doll on the Internet? Why would anyone spend three hundred dollars on a doll you can't fuck?   **Rich, *Lucky Louie***

This summer I'm going to go to the beach and bury metal objects that say 'Get a life' on them.   **Demetri Martin**

Only a man could think that getting a miniature plane off the ground was time well spent.   Lucy Ellmann

My wife made me join a bridge club. I jump off next Tuesday.
                                                    Rodney Dangerfield

Recreations: Smoking.   Jeremy Clarkson, *Who's Who*

—What is your favourite colour?
—I hate colours.   Interviewer and Ian Shoales

—I'm going out and have myself a wild time.
—Don't forget your library card.
                                    Gretchen Kraus and Benson DuBois, *Benson*

English country gents often hunt birds and no one objected when Sheikh Zaid Ben Sultan, ruler of Abu Dhabi, decided to try his hand at the sport at his luxurious English mansion in the shire. What distressed neighbours was that he used a machine gun.   *Newsweek*

The real objection to hunting by those who oppose it is that people enjoy it. It's a kind of modern Puritanism.
                                                    Roger Scruton

My father didn't enjoy enjoying himself.   Simon Raven

Deprivation is for me what daffodils were for Wordsworth.   Philip Larkin

Once at the country club, coming out of the showers in the nude and sitting down on the nearest bench to dry himself, Mr Cobbold's attention had been drawn to the fact that a fellow member had left a lighted cigar there, and until tonight he had always regarded that as the high spot of his emotional life.   P.G. Wodehouse

Perhaps all pleasure is only relief.   William S. Burroughs

CLUB

Clubs are places where men spend all their time thinking angrily about nothing.
Viscount Castlerosse

A club is a kind of transport café for the upper classes. *The Times Diary*

A crusty roll, whizzing like a meteor out of the unknown, shot past the Crumpet and the elderly relative whom he was entertaining to luncheon, and shattered itself against the wall… 'Just someone being civil,' he explained.
P.G. Wodehouse

Most clubs have the atmosphere of a Duke's house with the Duke lying dead upstairs.
Douglas Sutherland

One MP said, 'Tony Blair is notoriously clubbable.' He'll have to join the queue.
Chris Tarrant, Have I Got News for You

GAMBLING

The likelihood of winning the lottery is the same as Elvis landing a UFO on top of the Loch Ness Monster.
Ladbrokes, bookmakers

I think of lotteries as a tax on the mathematically challenged. **Roger Jones**

—If you won the lottery tomorrow, what would you spend it on?
—Hiring a lawyer. Winning the lottery without entering is bound to cause legal problems.
Interviewer and Simon Munnery

Americans spend $300 billion every year on games of chance, and that doesn't even include weddings and elections.
Argus Hamilton

Slot machines are like crack for old people.
Keenan Ivory Wayans

—Your mother has this crazy idea that gambling is wrong. Even though they say it's okay in the Bible.
—Really? Where?
—Uh…somewhere in the back.   **Homer and Lisa Simpson, *The Simpsons***

I only gamble with my life, never my money.   **Rick O'Connell, *The Mummy***

If you remove the gambling, where is the fun in watching a bunch of horses being whipped by midgets?   **Ian O'Doherty**

There's only one 'system': bet, lose, borrow, steal, lose, take drugs, lose, prison…*death*.   **Manny Bianco, *Black Books***

I used to be a heavy gambler. But now I just make mental bets. That's how I lost my mind.   **Steve Allen**

SHOPPING

FOR SALE: Pine coffin, lightly used.   **Stephen Dudzik**

I went shopping for feminine protection. I decided on a .38 revolver.
     Karen Ripley

I like to go into the Body Shop and shout out really loud, 'I've already got one!'   **Ahmed Ahmed**

Going to Primark is a bit like being bisexual – nobody admits to going there but everybody has a dabble.   **Kevin McAleer**

Lidl makes Somerfield look like Waitrose. It sells things like 'wine-flavoured drink'.   **Jeremy Hardy**

Lidl stores are mainly situated in the types of places only normally seen in Ken Loach films… When I looked, it was offering a pink velour two-piece of the type favoured by *Little Britain*'s Vicky Pollard at an amazing £5.99.   **Chris Leach**

You're never more indignant in life than when you're shopping in a store that you feel is beneath you and one of the other customers mistakes you for an employee of that store.   Dennis Miller

I like Ann Taylor clothing stores. But the assistants in there are a little pushy and over-attentive... I'm in the dressing room for 10 or 15 minutes and they come knocking at the door: 'You've been in there a while, are you okay?' I open the door a crack and say, 'No. Could you get me some toilet paper?'   Margaret Smith

What you say: Oh, I'll think about it and come back. *What you mean*: Two hundred and eighty pounds for a pair of underpants?! You must be joking!!   Jeremy Hardy

Trying on pants is one of the most humiliating things a man can suffer that doesn't involve a woman.   Larry David

—[*Whispering*] Got any condoms?
—[*Shouting*] Rubbers? Lucky you! Aisle three, between the Kotex and the flea spray.   Bill Decker and shop assistant, *Cheaper to Keep Her*

Unattended Children Will be Sold as Slaves   Sign in a pet shop, Idaho

—I'd like to return this toaster. It's broken.
—Have you got the guarantee or the receipt?
—Er, no.
—Did you keep the box?
—Keep the box? No, I did not keep the box. D'you think I'm going to put it away again after breakfast?
                                     Rick Spleen and salesman, *Lead Balloon*

—I bought this book for a friend, and they didn't want it, so I was wondering if I could exchange it, preferably for the money.
—Aha! There's sand inside the book! Sardinia...Porto Scuzo...the little beach by the monastery... Take your book and get out!
                           Bookshop customer and Bernard Black, *Black Books*

—Did you pick up your shoes from the menders?
—Can you believe it? They've lost the left shoe. Lost it! He said he'd only charge me half price! He said he couldn't say any fairer than that!
Margaret and Victor Meldrew, *One Foot in the Grave*

How about we refund your money, send you a new one at no charge, close the store and have the manager shot. Would that be satisfactory?
Sign in a New York launderette

HOLIDAYS

This summer one-third of the nation will be ill-housed, ill-nourished, and ill-clad. Only they call it a vacation.
Joseph Salak

Where do you want to worry that we're spending too much money this year?
David Sipress

'They have smashing beaches in Spain,' my friend said. 'The missus and I have a marvellous time burying each other in the sand.' 'Sounds like a great holiday,' I agreed. 'It was,' he said. 'Next year, I think I'll go back and dig her up.'
Les Dawson

During the summer I like to go to the beach and make sandcastles out of cement. And wait for kids to run by and try to kick them over.
James Leemer

I went to the beach with my sister. I said, 'You've got to go in the water.' She said, 'I can't. I've got my period.' She takes all the fun out of shark-fishing.
Emo Philips

When I go to a nude beach, I always take a ruler with me. Just in case I have to prove something.
Rodney Dangerfield

I'm sick of this island. I'm sick of having more sand in my ass than Libya.
Will Truman, *Will and Grace*

Coach holidays are divided into three roughly equal parts: motorways, seeing sights, and waiting for Colin to find the coach.   Guy Browning

We've gone on holiday by mistake.

Withnail, *Withnail and I*

Sometimes my mother, brother and I went to Saltburn, to stay in Auntie Mary's caravan. The weather was wet and windy. We endured days of torment in Pacamacs. The sea spray felt like a handful of stinging rice on your face. There were terrible shows at the end of the pier. I remember watching a pianist who literally played the piano with his nose on the keys. Arriving home to the dog, who was mad with joy at seeing us, was the best part of the holiday.   Craig Raine

We had tacky caravan holidays at Bognor when I was a child, and I didn't like roughing it. I hated how the bacon would fall on the grass when you cooked bacon sandwiches.   Richard Briers

From the age of seven to twelve, I went on holiday in a two-berth caravan in Bognor with my mum and my nan. Paaarty! You have not known pleasure till you wake up in the middle of the night to the sound of your nan pissing in a bucket.   Ricky Gervais

We took the caravan down to Dorset this year. And pushed it off a cliff.

Hugh Laurie, *A Bit of Fry and Laurie*

As kids we used to go camping at Cromer and King's Lynn, and I got so bored I used to enjoy this game where I'd jump across a field going from one cowpat to another. I mean, any holiday that makes you want to jump in faeces for fun can't be a good one.   Ross Noble

We spend grotesque amounts of money renting mansions in Tuscany and then sit there moaning that it's too hot, wondering if the children are getting skin cancer, fretting about wasps, mosquitoes and the heart-stopping expense of the whole enterprise – and, of course, going to bed nice and early with the latest must-read-even-if-I-die-of-boredom tome.

India Knight

On a Family Vacation, No One Can Hear You Scream.   **Tagline, *RV***

Vacations sometimes provide the leisure to realise unpleasant things you haven't had time to notice before... The vacation I remember most was the one during which I realised I wanted to kill my husband. He was standing with his back to me, gazing into a magnificent and deep canyon in Utah, and it came to me that if I were to hurl myself at him with all my force, precipitating him thousands of feet into the chasm, my troubles would be over.   **Diane Johnson**

And that's the wonderful thing about family travel: it provides you with experiences that will remain locked forever in the scar tissue of your mind.   **Dave Barry**

As my mother says, it's nice to get back to your own toilet.
                                    Deirdre Barlow, *Coronation Street*

CHRISTMAS

Oh, joy, Christmas Eve. By this time tomorrow, millions of people, knee-deep in tinsel and wrapping paper, will utter those heartfelt words: 'Is this all I got?'   **Frasier Crane, *Frasier***

—Merry Christmas!
—Whatever.   **Keith Charles and Claire Fisher, *Six Feet Under***

—[*Signing Christmas cards*] Who the hell is this guy and why would I care if he has a Merry Christmas?
—Just sign the damn thing.
                          Leo McGarry and Margaret Hooper, *The West Wing*

—[*Signing Christmas cards*] Who's Sarah?
—Your sister.   **Leo McGarry and Margaret Hooper, *The West Wing***

[*Front of Christmas card*] Spread some holiday cheer. [*Inside*] Or drink alone. Who am I to judge?   **Rejected Hallmark Christmas card**

May all my enemies go to hell, Noel, Noel, Noel, Noel.

Hilaire Belloc, lines for a Christmas card

A survey this week revealed that 45 per cent of people have had it away at the works Christmas do. Why? You sit opposite the plump girl for 48 weeks and it never once occurs to you that she is interesting. So how come, after one warm wine, she only needs to put on a paper hat to become Jordan?

Jeremy Clarkson

On the fourth day of Christmas my true love gave to me: genital herpes, syphilis, chlamydia, and a discharge that is hourly.

Lines from 'The 12 STDs Of Christmas',
written for the Department of Health to raise awareness of STDs

Christmas and New Year seem to get longer annually, and indeed do so. Eventually the whole bloody fucking arseholing country will be on its back from Guy Fawkes night to St Valentine's Day is my guess.

Philip Larkin

The time between one Christmas and the next is about two months now. They'll be draping tinsel over the Easter eggs before long.

Victor Meldrew, *One Foot in the Grave*

Three whole days locked in a tiled cell with a dead turkey.

Ria Parkinson, *Butterflies*

463 Ways to Make Christmas Simple.

Headline, *Prima* magazine

Holiday gift-giving is a tradition that dates back to when the Three Wise Men went to Bethlehem with gifts of gold, frankincense and myrrh for the Baby Jesus. Of course, the next day the Virgin Mary returned these items for store credit.

Dave Barry

I wrapped my Christmas presents early this year, but I used the wrong paper. The paper I used said 'Happy Birthday' on it. I didn't want to waste it so I just wrote 'Jesus' on it.

Demetri Martin

The most loathsome of all this year's crass Yuletide innovations is surely the 'ethical Christmas gift'. Instead of the DVD or handsome pair of socks you'd been hoping to receive, an ecologically crazed friend posts you a charity card informing you that 'the money I would have spent on your present has been used to buy six chickens for an African farmer' or 'a camel for a Bedouin tribesperson', and you're supposed to look pleased that he's given you precisely nothing, while he basks in a nauseating glow of self-satisfied eleemosynary.

Victor Lewis-Smith

Christmas used to be terrible at our house, not like now when kids get everything. One year, my sister got a miniature set of perfumes called 'ample'. They were tiny, and even I could see where my dad had scraped off the 's'.

Doug Stanhope

My worst Christmas? One Christmas morning, I woke up, I ran into the living room and my mother said, 'I just forgot.'

Rob Burton

A puppy isn't just for Christmas. If you're lucky, there should be enough left over for Boxing Day dinner as well.

Anon

The one thing women don't want to find in their stockings Christmas morning is their husband.

Joan Rivers

A year, two years, from now, that Booker Prize-winning novel will still lie, unopened, by our beds. Those shaving lotions will still stand, virgin, in our bathrooms. That little blue ceramic pot of Stilton will still be in the larder, back among the petrified garlic and half-crumbled stock cubes.

Philip Norman

Santa is *Satan* spelled inside out.

George Carlin

I was bought up a communist. It was Lenin who came down our chimney at Christmas.

Alexei Sayle

My husband is so cheap. On Christmas Eve he fires one shot and tells the kids Santa committed suicide.

Phyllis Diller

Always plan on a traditional family Christmas dinner, and a traditional family fight afterward.   **Mignon McLaughlin**

Everyone's gonna fight, call each other bastards, and go to bed early.
                                                                Sharon Osbourne

What shall we hang – the holly, or each other?   Henry, *The Lion in Winter*

A great psychiatric paper could be written on parental remarks at the Christmas lunch table that drive their children to the edge of the abyss, unnoticed by anyone else present.   **Philip Norman**

Christmas Day was awful. Terrible people all sitting round overeating and farting surreptitiously.   **Kenneth Williams**

Christmas stank, to quote my favourite sentence in John O'Hara.
                                                                   Philip Larkin

We go through the same ritual every year. I sit there for three solid days with a daft paper hat stuck on my head, watching you sat in front of the goggle box, walnut shells, tangerine skins and fag ash piling up all round your boots. If it wasn't for occasional calls of nature I'll swear blind you'd be buried alive by Boxing Day.   **Harold Steptoe, *Steptoe and Son***

Short of hiring a line of chorus girls and calling it 'The Queen Show', what more can you do?   **Prince Philip, on the Queen's Speech**

You ask your relatives if they'd like tea or coffee, and they say, 'Whichever's easiest.' *None* of them's easiest. What would be easiest is if you went home. NOW.   **Jack Dee**

While shepherds watched their flocks by night,
All shitting on the ground,
An angel of the Lord came down
And handed paper round.   **Anon**

Suggestion for a Non-sappy Christmas Film: 'The Bipolar Express' – a young boy finds that the exhilaration of candy canes and sugar plums can come crashing down in disappointment and loneliness.   **Peter Metrinko**

But in the end, it is all an illusion: George Bailey isn't saved; his inevitable end is only delayed. For where is George now? Dead. Mary? Dead. Uncle Billy? Dead. Mr Potter? Dead. Harry? Dead. The men on the ship Harry saved? Dead. Marty, Bert, Ernie? Dead, dead, dead. Violet Bick, dead, too. Life is only a brief spark that separates two dark abysses. Merry Christmas. There's the bridge, right over there.

Phil Battey, on It's A Wonderful Life

I come from a very traditional family. When I was seven, my Uncle Terry hanged himself on Christmas Eve. My family didn't take his body down until the sixth of January.

Nick Doody

We both hated Christmas. We only did it for the children.

Mrs Irving Berlin

NEW YEAR

—Hey, how was your New Year's Eve?
—Oh, sublime. Scott, Zelda and I shared a cab over to the Stork Club where we drank pink champagne out of Zelda's slipper.
—You know, a simple 'I stayed in' would have sufficed.

Caroline Duffy and Richard Karinsky, Caroline in the City

The etiquette question that troubles so many people on New Year's Day is: how am I ever going to face those people again?

Judith Martin

Howard Potter, a chartered accountant and folk dancer, has taken out an advertisement in the Cardiff-based Western Mail to apologise to anybody he might have offended on New Year's Eve. Potter, 51, explained: 'I don't know what happened, but you could say I was right-royally bladdered and went around being offensive to anyone and anything.' The advert states: 'Howard Potter would like to say sorry to the entire staff of the Cardiff Hilton hotel, several city centre landlords, the residents of Prospect Drive, a man called Toni at a fish bar, two passing police constables and the council cleansing department.'

The Times

New Year's Resolution: find nice sensible boyfriend to go out with and
do not continue to form romantic attachments to any of the following:
alcoholics, workaholics, commitment-phobics, peeping Toms,
megalomaniacs, emotional fuckwits or perverts.   **Bridget Jones**

Signs You're Already Having a Bad Year...
Your New Year's kiss was swiftly followed by a restraining order.
Your wife had the first baby of the year, but you haven't had sex in
two years.   **David Letterman**

PARTY

—Why didn't you tell me it was your birthday? I'd have thrown you a
birthday party.
—Question asked, question answered.

Frasier Crane and Roz Doyle, *Frasier*

What is your host's purpose in having a party? Surely not for you to
enjoy yourself; if that were their sole purpose they'd have simply sent
champagne and women over to your place by taxi.   **P.J. O'Rourke**

Last year, George Michael invited a number of celebrities to his house for
a birthday bash. Hasn't he learned yet not to do it in front of people?

Mark Lamarr, *Never Mind the Buzzcocks*

I've only been to one birthday party in fourteen years. And that was
because they trapped me. I had to gnaw off a leg to escape.   **David Gerrold**

—Who are you?
—I'm the editor-in-chief of the *Independent*, sir.
—What are you doing here?
—You invited me.
—Well, you didn't have to come!

Prince Philip and Simon Kelner, at a press reception in Windsor Castle

Like other parties of the kind, it was first silent, then talky, then argumentative, then disputatious, then unintelligible, then altogethery, then inarticulate, and then drunk.

Lord Byron

I once went to one of those parties where everybody throws their car keys into the middle of the room. I don't know who got my moped, but I drove that Peugeot for years.

Victoria Wood

Tupperware parties: *Sucker*ware parties.

Erma Bombeck

I hate cocktail parties, where everyone is looking over everyone else's shoulder, in case someone more important has arrived.

Barbara Cartland

I just wanted to thank you for inviting me. I know we've had our differences in the past, but when you get right down to it – oh, look, better people!

Karen Walker, *Will and Grace*

What you say: Do you two know each other? *What you mean*: I have forgotten both your names.

Jeremy Hardy

Bugger the table plan, give me my dinner!

Prince Philip, at a dinner party at Broadlands

One of the miseries of social life is telling, at much length, a scarce and curious anecdote, with considerable marks of self-complacency at having it to tell, then being quietly reminded by the person you have been so kindly instructing, that you had heard it first – *from himself*!

James Beresford

For some unexplained reason, it's always the other end of the table that's wild and raucous, with screaming laughter and a fella who plays 'Holiday For Springs' on water glasses.

Erma Bombeck

Parties are always full of people who hate parties.

Lillian Day

My wife spends dinner parties in the bedroom asleep under the guests' coats. She exhausts easily under the pressure to be interesting.

Niles Crane, *Frasier*

I seem to play the role of undertaker at most parties.

Dave Allen

Gee, what a terrific party. Later on we'll get some fluid and embalm each other.

Neil Simon

It is a widespread and firm belief among guests that their departure is always a matter of distress to their hosts, and that in order to indicate that they have been pleasantly entertained, they must demonstrate an extreme unwillingness to allow the entertainment to conclude. This is not necessarily true.

Judith Martin

Gentlemen, will you all now leave quietly, or must I ask Miss Cutler to pass among you with a baseball bat?

Sheridan Whiteside, *The Man Who Came to Dinner*

Every guest hates the others, and the host hates them all. Albanian proverb

It's said, 'Fish and visitors smell after three days,' but old friends from college usually smell already.

P.J. O'Rourke

A small boy, who was a stickler for the literal truth, once said to me that it was wrong to say, 'Good-bye' when you had not enjoyed yourself at a party. I enquired what should be substituted for it. He suggested, 'Bad-bye.' I have not tried this.

Arthur Ponsonby

Only the bravest of stay-at-homes asks the ticklish question: 'Did anybody ask where I was?'

Henry Haskins

GRUMPY
NATURE

ANIMALS
– GENERAL

A zoo is a place where your child asks loud questions about the private parts of large mammals.   Joyce Armor

—What's a shiatsu?
—A zoo with no animals.   Anon

Here is a rhinoceros, an animal with a hide two feet thick, and no apparent interest in politics. What a waste.   James C. Wright

—What's the collective name for a group of baboons?
—The Pentagon.   Stephen Fry and Rich Hall, *QI*

—What's the difference between a dog and a fox?
—About five drinks.   Anon

Two cows in a field, one says to the other, 'Are you worried about this mad cow disease?' 'Nope,' the other replies, 'cos I'm a goat.'   Anon

'Guk,' he said reservedly. A man has to answer snakes when they speak to him, but he is under no obligation to be sunny.   P.G. Wodehouse

Chimpanzees – why the centre parting? They're stuck in the 1920s.
                                                            Harry Hill

I don't kill flies, but I like to mess with their minds. I hold them above globes. They freak out and yell, 'Whoaa, I'm *way* too high.'   Bruce Baum

Somehow, it's hard to picture butterflies fucking.   George Carlin

The male gypsy moth can smell the female gypsy moth up to seven miles away – and that fact also works if you remove the word 'moth'.
                                                            Jimmy Carr

Growing up, my mom would always feel bad when a bird would sometimes slam head first into our living-room window. If she *really* felt bad, though, she'd have moved the bird-feeder outside.   **Rich Johnson**

Ah, to be a bird. To fly the skies, sing my song, and best of all occasionally peck someone's eyes out.   **George Carlin**

—Can anyone tell me what the national bird of England is?
—I can tell you what it is for men: cock.
—I can tell you what it is for women: thrush.
          Stephen Fry, Alan Davies, Jo Brand, *QI*

Oh, God, I knew it wouldn't be long before that bloody sparrow started. What's it got me up so early for? Shaddup! One of these days, when he's asleep, I'm going to sneak up to his nest with a Welsh Male Voice Choir. Three choruses of 'Men Of Harlech' would have him laughing out of the other side of his beak.   **Victor Meldrew, *One Foot in the Grave***

—[*In a vet's waiting room*] Oh, what a lovely parrot!
—Sod off!   **Sean Tully and parrot, *Coronation Street***

That special bond you think you have with your pet is imaginary. As long as it has food and water, you could get hit by a train tomorrow, and your pet wouldn't think anything of it.   **Scott Dikkers**

DOG

That indefatigable and unsavoury engine of pollution, the dog.
          John Sparrow

Turd-droppers.   **John Betjeman**

How can people love something so much that they're willing to walk behind it and retrieve its faeces with their own hands every day? I have yet to meet a woman for whom I'd do that.   **Joel Stein**

Dogs are the leaders of the planet. If you see two life forms, one of them's making a poop, the other one's carrying it for him, who would you assume is in charge?   Jerry Seinfeld

I live in a street in London, it's bloody Turd Terrace! Why don't dogs just come in my house and shit inside and cut out the middle man? Dave Allen

Does anyone else share my revulsion at the sight of an animal that spends large parts of the day with its face buried in its own or other dogs' nether regions licking the faces of children?   Martin Newland

I've heard that dogs are man's best friend. That explains where men are getting their hygiene tips.   Kelly Maguire

The poor dog had a distressing malady. Mrs Dorothy Parker issued bulletins about his health. Confidential bulletins, tinged with scepticism. 'He *says* he got it from a lamp post.'   Alexander Woollcott

Two old men are watching a Great Dane lick his balls. One turns to the other and says, 'All my life, I've wished that I could do that.' The second one says, 'Better pet him first, he looks mean as hell.'   Billy Crystal

You know why dogs hate mailmen? They just wanna be like everyone else.

Norm Peterson, *Cheers*

How I envy you, Eddie. The biggest questions you face are, 'Who's going to walk me? Who's going to feed me?' I won't know that kind of joy for another forty years.   Frasier Crane, *Frasier*

It is said that over time, owners come to resemble their dogs. But does that excuse Aunt Hilda from shitting in your garden?   Simon Munnery

My dog is not a child substitute. At least, that's what his piano teacher says.   Rita Rudner

We had to get rid of the kids – one of the dogs was allergic.   **Annie Lewis**

Dogs – I don't need reinforcement ten times a day that I'm an okay
person.   **John Waters**

Be thankful that dogs don't know everyone else hates you.   **Dave Prevar**

My dog needed training, so I brought him into the bedroom at night.
From me he learned how to beg. My wife taught him how to roll over
and play dead.   **Rodney Dangerfield**

CAT

Cats are the fascists of the animal world.   **Brian Behan**

A dog will sit beside you while you work. A cat will sit on the work.
                                                                 Pam Brown

I like cats too. Let's exchange recipes.   **Bumper sticker**

Cats have nine lives. Which makes them ideal for experimentation.
                                                                 Jimmy Carr

When the cat's away...chances are he's been run over.   **Michael Sanders**

The trouble with cats is that they've got no tact.   **P.G. Wodehouse**

If cats had slime or scales instead of fur there would be no gainsaying
their utter nastiness.   **Germaine Greer**

—What do you do if a cat spits at you?
—Turn the grill down.   **Anon**

After scolding one's cat, one looks into its face and is seized by the
suspicion that it understood every word. And has filed it for reference.
                                                               Charlotte Gray

It's difficult to respect a creature whose chief selling point is that it shits in a box. Let's face it, you know something sucks when people routinely give it away for free.   Ryan Murphy

People that hate cats will come back as mice in their next life. Faith Resnick

My husband takes the cat to bed with us every night. It's not even alive – he had it stuffed two years ago. I wouldn't mind but it's the only thing in our bed that's stiff.   *Loose Women*

NATURE

What's going on here? Are we...outside?

Karen Walker, *Will and Grace*

I don't like being outdoors. There are too many fat children.

Mr Burns, *The Simpsons*

Nature is by and large to be found out of doors, a location where, it cannot be argued, there are never enough comfortable chairs.

Fran Lebowitz

What you hate is walking. This is *hiking* – hiking is different from walking.   David Sipress

I like a view but I like to sit with my back to it.   Alice B. Toklas

Daylight – harsh overhead lighting that is so unflattering to the heavy smoker.   Fran Lebowitz

Ah, Nature. People love Nature, don't they? Except when it's growing out of cups.   Simon Munnery

Nature is that lovely lady to whom we owe polio, leprosy, smallpox, syphilis, tuberculosis, cancer.
                                                    Stanley N. Cohen

I hate allergy season. Mother Nature's way of telling me flowers get more sex than I do.
                                                    Basil White

There is nothing good to be had in the country, or if there is, they will not let you have it.
                                                    William Hazlitt

So, we just sit here?   Earl Hickey, on a picnic, *My Name is Earl*

Marge, can we go home? All this fresh air is making my hair move and I don't know how long I can complain.
                                                    Homer Simpson

He was a man of the great indoors.   P.G. Wodehouse

One thing that's certain about going outdoors: when you come back inside, you'll be scratching.
                                                    P.J. O'Rourke

I think it pisses God off if you walk by the colour purple in a field somewhere and don't notice it. What it do when it pissed off? I ast. Oh, it makes something else. People think pleasing God is all God care about. But any fool living in the world can see it always trying to please us back. Yeah? I say.
                                                    Alice Walker, *The Color Purple*

GARDEN

If you water it and it dies, it's a plant. If you pull it out and it grows back, it's a weed.
                                                    Gallagher

Our gardens are symbols of home rather than seduction. Young people with fire in their blood are seldom found in them. The garden is the scene of middle age, of the slow passage from sexual excitement to domestic routine.
                                                    Roger Scruton

Are you aware of a new phenomenon: garden rage? A quarter of us, apparently, have been in confrontations with our neighbours over the state of their, or our, gardens.

Charles Nevin

It was Bovril-flavour today, the empty crisp packet on the front lawn. I was expecting prawn cocktail. I'm thinking of compiling a special reference guide: *The Observer's Book of Crap on Your Front Lawn.*

Victor Meldrew, *One Foot in the Grave*

—He's got gnomes.
—Ay, he bloody would have.

Dave and Gaz, *The Full Monty*

To a gardener there is nothing more exasperating than a hose that just isn't long enough.

Cecil Roberts

Men can't be trusted with pruning shears any more than they can be trusted with the grocery money in a delicatessen... They are little boys with new pocket knives who will not stop whittling.

Phyllis McGinley

You must remember garden catalogues are as big liars as house-agents.

Rumer Godden

Seven chocolate wrappers on the lawn today... Makes you wonder why they bother with funerals any more... 'Grandma's dead, shall we bury her?' 'No, I can't be bothered. Just sling her over that bloke's fence, he'll clean it up.'

Victor Meldrew, *One Foot in the Grave*

I've had enough of gardening. I'm about ready to throw in the trowel.

Anon

I have no interest in gardening. If I did I would probably plant my flowers in a 4-4-2 formation.

Tommy Docherty, football manager

WEATHER

Another fucking perfect day!   **Lady Diana Broughton**, *White Mischief*

It is worse even than you expected, stepping out into the morning. The glare is like a mother's reproach.   **Jay McInerney**

The heat was like a hand on the face all day and night.
      Josephine W. Johnson

I was sweating like a *Star Wars* fan trying to talk to a girl.   **Conan O'Brien**

Temperatures were uterine.   **David Foster Wallace**

It's so hot Republican Congressmen are going into gay bars just for the cold stares.   **Bill Maher**

Thank heavens, the sun has gone in, and I don't have to go out and enjoy it.   **Logan Pearsall Smith**

It is one of the secrets of Nature in its mood of mockery that fine weather lays a heavier weight on the mind and hearts of the depressed and the inwardly tormented than does a really bad day with dark rain snivelling continuously and sympathetically from a dark sky.   **Muriel Spark**

That night it rained like a bitch with a charge account.   **Kinky Friedman**

If I were running the world I would have it rain only between 2 and 5am – anyone who was out then ought to get wet.   **William Lyon Phelps**

The thing about topless weather forecasters is, you can't remember what they're saying but you can tell whether it's going to be cold or not.
      Paul Merton

[*To the piano-player*] Right, Mr Braithwaite, 'The Sun'll Come Out Tomorrow'. Fat chance.   **Mrs Wilkinson**, *Billy Elliot*

THE
ENVIRONMENT

Remember when you were considered an environmentalist if you didn't throw junk out the car window? I sure do miss that simpler, happy time.

Paula Poundstone

I remember when there was no damn environment.

David Sipress

His idea of recycling is to use his beer can as an ashtray.

Gail Burton

—In today's society, if something doesn't work, you throw it out.
—Well, you don't work. Maybe we'd better throw you out.

Mike Evans and Archie Bunker, *All in the Family*

Recycling idea: little paper circles from office hole-punchers could be tossed at newlywed bureaucrats.

Jay Shuck

Hoop earrings could be recycled into hula hoops for mice. They'd appreciate the change of pace from running on that wheel all night.

Lucy Brennan-Levine

The council has put a microchip in my bin to see how much rubbish I'm throwing away. Whatever next? Are they going to put a chip in my lavatory to check that I'm eating organic food?

Liz Ryder

American gas prices are so high because first we have to kill the people who live on top of it, then we have to extract it, refine it, and ship it.

Bill Maher

Is fuel efficiency really what we need most desperately? I say what we really need is a car that can be shot when it breaks down.

Russell Baker

I prefer a vehicle that doesn't hurt Mother Earth: it's a go-cart powered by my own sense of self-satisfaction.

Ed Begley Jr, *The Simpsons*

Toyota Prius? Toyota Pious!   Anon

We all know that small cars are good for us. But so is cod liver oil. And
jogging. I want to drive around in a Terminator, not the heroine in an
E.M. Forster novel.   Jeremy Clarkson

A Range Rover, doing ten thousand miles a year, produces less pollution
a day than a cow farting.   Jeremy Clarkson

What can we do to improve our everyday lives? Home heating costs so
much, and we use so much energy on it, and the homeless sometimes
freeze to death. So what we need is a simple way to warm the earth up a
few degrees. But *how*?   Russell Beland

New York City is hosting a four-day global warming summit. But you
know, today was such a nice day, they cancelled it.   David Letterman

Plenty of people believe in energy conservation – mainly their own.
                                                      MAD magazine

I've been thinking, what can I do for energy conservation? Then it struck
me! I can have my husband, Norm, taken off his life-support system!
                                                  Dame Edna Everage

When you die there's a light at the end of the tunnel. When my father
dies, he'll see the light, make his way towards it, and then flip it off to
save electricity.   Harland Williams

If sunbeams were weapons of war, we'd have had solar energy centuries ago.

Sir George Porter

How come every time I make a speech on global warming, I have to
trudge through snow to make it?   Tony Blair, at the Davos conference

Don't for a moment imagine that the bicycle-riding, organic-hedgerow-grazing, self-denying, 40-watt miserablists are in fact selfless crusaders for the common good. Never underestimate the sustaining pleasure of a hair shirt. Just look at George Monbiot, and witness a man who couldn't be happier about the imminent demise of life as we know it. It has given him purpose, prestige and celebrity: without global warming he'd be a geography teacher.

A.A. Gill

Visits to Mars by space probes detect global warming there – but have not yet discovered the 4x4s causing it.

John Redwood

Don't tell me global warming is a myth. I don't know a great deal about CO_2 concentrations or sunspot cycles, but I do know that I don't expect to see wasps on my Christmas cake.

Steve Punt and Hugh Dennis, *The Now Show*

I don't think people give a damn whether the planet goes on or not. It seems to me as if everyone is living as members of Alcoholics Anonymous do, day by day. And a few more days will be enough.

Kurt Vonnegut

The condition of man is already close to satiety and arrogance, and there is danger of destruction of everything in existence.

A brahmin quoted in Strabo's *Geography*, 327 BC

Save the earth. It's the only planet with chocolate.

Bumper sticker

GRUMPY
ARTS &
ENTERTAINMENT

ART & CULTURE

Who among us has not gazed at a painting of Jackson Pollock's and thought: 'What a piece of crap.'   **Rob Long**

Pollocks!   **Anon**

A portrait of Prince Philip with a bluebottle fly resting on his shoulder was unveiled in 2004. Acclaimed artist Stuart Pearson Wright said he aimed to remind the viewer of the 82-year-old prince's mortality by featuring the fly, which breeds on decaying organic matter.   **A.P. Photo**

—Do you think the artist has caught your likeness?
—I bloody well hope not!
                    Interviewer and Prince Philip, on his portrait by Stuart Pearson Wright

—It's a very good likeness. It does you justice.
—It's not justice I want, it's mercy.   **Interviewer and Malcolm Gibbs**

Graham Sutherland's portrait of Lord Beaverbrook makes him look like a diseased toad bottled in methylated spirit.   **Quentin Bell**

I've posed nude for a photographer in the manner of Rodin's *Thinker*, but I looked merely constipated.   **George Bernard Shaw**

I have seen, and heard, much of Cockney impudence before now, but never expected to hear a coxcomb ask 200 guineas for flinging a pot of paint in the public's face.   **John Ruskin, on James Whistler's Nocturnes**

Painting is easy when you don't know how, but very difficult when you do.   **Edgar Degas**

If the old masters had labelled their fruit, one wouldn't be so likely to mistake pears for turnips.   **Mark Twain**

I would rather see the portrait of a dog that I know, than all the allegorical paintings they can show me in the world.   **Samuel Johnson**

If a picture wasn't going very well I'd put a puppy dog in it, always a mongrel, you know, never one of the full-bred puppies. And then I'd put a bandage on its foot.
                                                                    Norman Rockwell

Rolf Harris: a name that is to the art world what woodworm is to an antique shop.
                                                                    A.A. Gill

The philistine provides the best definition of art. Anything that makes him rage is first class.
                                                                    Louis Dudek

Anyone who has shuffled through a gallery will know the look of bafflement and boredom worn like a mask on the faces of the visitors. They should be getting something out of this, but they're not. Fortunately there is a café.
                                                                    Jeanette Winterson

—How many art gallery visitors does it take to screw in a light bulb?
—Two: one to do it and one to say, 'My four-year-old could do that.'
                                                                    Anon

The Art Snob will stand back from a picture at some distance, his head cocked slightly to one side. After a long period of gazing (during which he may occasionally squint his eyes), he will approach to within a few inches of the picture and examine the brushwork; he will then return to his former distant position, give the picture another glance and walk away.
                                                                    Russell Lynes

Edith Evans bought an incredibly expensive Renoir and, when a friend asked her why she had hung it so low on the wall, out of the light behind the curtain, she replied curtly, 'Because there was a hook.'   **Stephen Fry**

The Art Snob can be recognised in the home by the quick look he gives the pictures on your walls, quick but penetrating, as though he were undressing them. This is followed either by complete and pained silence or a comment such as, 'That's really a very pleasant little watercolour you have there.'
                                                                    Russell Lynes

Happiness is rarely painted now.
                                                                    Jeffrey Camp

Why is it that among the great artists of the world, whether male or female, we find so few blondes?   George Jean Nathan

I just went to an art museum where all of the art was done by children. All the paintings were hung on refrigerators.   Steven Wright

It may be a point of pride to have a Van Gogh on the living-room wall, but the prospect of having Van Gogh himself in the living room would put a great many devoted art lovers to rout.   Ben Shahn

Beware of artists: they mix with all classes of society and are therefore extremely dangerous.   Queen Victoria

Wyndham Lewis is the nastiest man I have ever seen... Under the black hat, when I had first seen them, the eyes had been those of an unsuccessful rapist.   Ernest Hemingway

Since my earliest years I have always resented the idea of some git breathing down my neck while I draw. All they ever say is, 'Let's have a look' and 'I don't think much of that', or worse, 'Who's that supposed to be?' So I deploy my sketchbook in such a way that a casual observer might think that I am scratching my armpit, or possibly my testicles.   Steve Bell

Every artist should be ahead of his time and behind in his rent.   Kinky Friedman

I always suspect an artist who is successful before he is dead. John Murray Gibbon

Most of those who call themselves artists are, in reality, picture dealers, only they make the pictures themselves.   Samuel Butler

Skill without imagination is craftsmanship and gives us many useful objects such as wickerwork and picnic baskets. Imagination without skill gives us modern art.   Tom Stoppard

Modern art is what happens when painters stop looking at girls and persuade themselves that they have a better idea.   John Ciardi

Gilbert and George are the Morecambe and Wise of sober-suited, straight-faced pretension.

Paul Taylor

'Jeff in the Position of Adam' by Jeff Koons is the last bit of methane left in the intestine of the dead cow that is post-modernism.   **Robert Hughes**

When I was 11, I sent two drawings of a tiger and deer to *Vision On*. They said, 'We're sorry we can't return any pictures but we give a prize for any we show.' I definitely thought I was gonna win. I watched it every week hoping mine would be on it but it never was. Does that mean they've burnt some Damien Hirsts? Maybe they're in a room somewhere at the BBC.
—They could fund the BBC for the next ten years.

Damien Hirst and Mark Lawson, *Front Row*

A work of art that contains theories is like an object on which the price tag has been left.   Marcel Proust

The goitrous, torpid and squinting husks provided by Henri Matisse in his sculpture are worthless except as tactful decoration for a mental home.   Percy Wyndham Lewis

Sculptor Henry Moore has been asked not to leave any holes in which boys could trap their heads when he carves 'Family Group' for Harlow New Town.   *News Chronicle*

—I smell a museum.
—Yeah, good things don't end with 'eum', they end with 'mania' or 'eria'.   **Bart and Homer Simpson, *The Simpsons***

'Kylie: The Exhibition' at the V&A even has a glass case containing the baggy dungarees she wore in *Neighbours* – slightly worn at the crotch, I noticed.   Mark Lawson

A children's museum sounds like a good idea, but I would imagine it's not easy to breathe inside those little glass cases.   George Carlin

It is always good to remember that people find it easier to name ten artists from any century than ten politicians.   John Heath-Stubbs

ARCHITECTURE

Warre says the Memorial Hall will have a thousand and one uses. I wish he would leave the thousand alone and tell me plainly what the one is.
E. Austen Leigh

The modern architect is, generally speaking, art's greatest enemy.
Pierre-Auguste Renoir

The Eiffel Tower: this truly tragic street lamp.   Léon Bloy

The Barbican Centre: architects seem to cry, 'When I hear the word culture I reach for my concrete mixer.'   Rodney Gradidge

Many of my building are condemned now in advance.
Richard Seifert, architect

If I ruled the world, I'd compel all architects to put a plaque bearing their name and home telephone number above the main entrance of every building they'd designed. That way, we could call them at 3.00a.m. to ask why they've erected some completely inappropriate monstrosity that jars grotesquely with the surrounding landscape.   Victor Lewis-Smith

We used to build civilisations. Now we build shopping malls.   Bill Bryson

MUSIC – GENERAL

—Anyone here keen on music?
—I am, Sarge.
—Well, bugger off over to the NAAFI and give them a hand getting the piano off the stage.   **Kingsley Amis**

—Dad, do you know why the piano's on my foot?
—You hum it, son, and I'll play it.   **PG Tips chimps, moving a piano upstairs**

It made a deafening noise, like ten honky-tonk pianos being hit by mallets.   **Penny Adie, on the sound made by a £45,000 piano
when it was accidentally dropped 14 feet by removal men**

Even before the music begins there is that bored look in people's faces. A polite form of self-imposed torture, the concert.   **Henry Miller**

If music be the food of love, this must be a vomit sandwich.   **Nick, *Beast***

Too many notes.   **Emperor Franz Josef, on a piece by Mozart**

I regard music rather in the same way as I view religion – all right so long as I have nothing to do with my fellow enthusiasts.   **Jonathan Keates**

Said Oscar Wilde: 'Each man kills the thing he loves.' For example, the amateur musician.   **H.L. Mencken**

Accordion: an instrument in harmony with the sentiments of an assassin.
Ambrose Bierce

An oboe is an ill-wind that nobody blows good.   **Bennett Cerf**

Ah, the soothing of the pipes… Whenever I find myself missing its melodious sounds, I just toss the cat in the dryer on low heat.
Jordan Montgomery

I must shut my ears. The man of sin rubbeth the hair of the horse to the bowels of the cat.
                                                                        John O'Keefe

Perhaps it was because Nero played the fiddle, they burned Rome.
                                                                        Oliver Herford

He made a trumpet of his arse.   Dante Alighieri, *The Inferno*

Oh, those jazz guys are just making that stuff up.   Homer Simpson

Jazz: it's like an act of murder; you play with intent to commit something.
                                                                        Duke Ellington

A rather bitter British musician once remarked sourly to a friend of mine, 'Oh, all *she* knows about music she learned in bed with musicians.' To that, I can only add, what better place to learn?   Val Wilmer

By and large, jazz has always been like the kind of a man you wouldn't want your daughter to associate with.   Duke Ellington

The blues is losing someone you love and not having enough money to immerse yourself in drink.   Henry Rollins

The only thing to do with a folk melody, once you have played it, is to play it louder.   Anon

—I always thought it was, 'Hey nonny no, nanny ninny no.'
—Iron-clad rule, Alan: nonny before ninny.
                                        Alan Barrows and Mark Shubb, *A Mighty Wind*

—You sing like the Spice Girls.
—Thanks.
—Unfortunately, it wasn't a compliment.
                                        Simon Cowell and *American Idol* **contestant**

—When I sing, I get heads turning.
—Yeah, which way?   **Simon Cowell and** *X Factor* **contestant**

I love to sing, and I love to drink Scotch. Most people would rather hear me drink Scotch.   **George Burns**

Only schoolchildren and spies know the second verse of the National Anthem.   **Evelyn Waugh**

POPULAR MUSIC

Here's a little song that puts the 'cunt' back into country and western...
Anon

That was the best song I've heard since – well, teatime. Mind you, I had a late tea.   **John Peel**

Now I'd like to play, 'He Almost Looks Like You' – an ode to prison rape.
Otis Lee Crenshaw, a.k.a. Rich Hall

Well, that was powerfully average.   **John Peel**

I like women and black people so I'm not a big country music fan.
Greg Proops

John Denver: cleaner than Marie Osmond's tampon.
Mark Lamarr, *Never Mind the Buzzcocks*

Shania Twain once performed at the Nobel Prize Peace Concert with Elton John and Phil Collins. You probably remember that year: they had to wrestle a Stanley knife off Nelson Mandela.
Mark Lamarr, *Never Mind the Buzzcocks*

There's more evil in the charts than there is in an Al-Qaeda suggestion box.   **Bill Bailey**

Gareth Gates: the pop equivalent of aquarium gravel.

Mark Lamarr, *Never Mind the Buzzcocks*

Barry Manilow famously wrote the words: 'I can't smile, I can't sing, I'm finding it hard to do anything.' Not only the lyrics to one of his biggest hits but also Geri Halliwell's CV. **Mark Lamarr,** *Never Mind the Buzzcocks*

The last telegram sent from the *Titanic* was recently auctioned off. It said 'Help, they won't stop playing Celine Dion's *Titanic* song!' And then everyone killed themselves. **Conan O'Brian**

—Next on *Top of the Pops*, it's David Cassidy!
—Ooh, I used to have him on my bedroom wall.
—That was very athletic of you, Janice.

John Peel and Janice Long

Pink Floyd – the highlight of Live 8, if you count mustard gas as the highlight of World War I. **Mark Lamarr,** *Never Mind the Buzzcocks*

—I wish he'd turn the microphone to one side.
—I wish he'd turn the microphone off!
The Queen and Prince Philip, watching Elton John at a Royal Variety Performance

The Depeche Mode frontman, Dave Gahan, has a pierced perineum, which is the bit between the scrotum and the arsehole. Just think Sharon Osbourne in between Louis Walsh and Simon Cowell.

Mark Lamarr, *Never Mind the Buzzcocks*

Every year on the anniversary of Elvis's death we are bombarded with Elvis films on TV and Elvis records on the radio all day. How can we be assured the same thing won't happen when Michael Ball dies?

Mrs Merton

James Blunt is so annoying he makes me want to rip my eyeballs out just to have something to plug my ears with. **Gangsta**

How fitting that the name James Blunt has now entered the Cockney rhyming slang dictionary as 'a right James'. **Chris Davis**

Carrie Grant wrote a book called *You Can Sing* which would be the cruellest gift for Westlife – something they can't read about something they can't do.   **Mark Lamarr**, *Never Mind the Buzzcocks*

Phil Collins is losing his hearing. Making him the luckiest man at a Phil Collins concert.   **Simon Amstell**, *Never Mind the Buzzcocks*

We had dinner at Madonna's. It was a lovely evening. Until Sting played the lute.   **Caroline Martin**, *Jam and Jerusalem*

Madonna has a new line of clothing. You can now pick up a Madonna dress at K-Mart. Hell, I remember when you could pick up *Madonna* at K-Mart.   **David Letterman**

The Animals were so called because they were so ugly. If you've never seen them, imagine Jimmy Carr's face on Jimmy Nail's scrotum.
Mark Lamarr, *Never Mind the Buzzcocks*

Michael Bolton has had nine hits this year. On his website.
Dame Edna Everage

Des'ree's hit song 'Life' has been voted the worst ever pop lyric according to BBC 6 Music listeners: 'I don't want to see a ghost / It's the sight that I fear most / I'd rather have a piece of toast / Watch the evening news.'
BBC News website

I love Amy Winehouse but sometimes she sounds like a duck that can't shit.
Jonathan Ross

Despite being a completely manufactured band, McFly are actually quite highly regarded by some critics. Their names are often mentioned alongside Nirvana and the Clash. Usually as the answer in odd-one-out competitions.   **Mark Lamarr**, *Never Mind the Buzzcocks*

Everybody knows that if female genitalia could speak, it would sound exactly like Enya.

Dylan Moran

Things that are better-looking than the Spice Girls: loft lagging, a bucket of slops and a waxwork model of Bill Bailey that's been left by the radiator.

Mark Lamarr, *Never Mind the Buzzcocks*

Joss Stone had to duet with Robbie Williams at the Brits. The only way I'd duet with Robbie Williams is on a tandem parachute jump. As long as I had the parachute and he had the tandem.

Mark Lamarr, *Never Mind the Buzzcocks*

I took one look at Johnny Rotten and was reminded of my time as an art teacher – I thought, I would definitely not trust that boy to hand out the scissors.

John Walters

Like old man Steptoe moaning.

Captain Sensible on Johnny Rotten's vocal style

Shut it now honey.

Anagram of Whitney Houston

Terri Walker says she fancies Robbie Williams and The Rock. I fancy Robbie and The Rock, too. The full list is Robbie, a rock, a dark alley, a saw and a double-sized coffin just in case Kelly Osbourne is first on the scene.

Mark Lamarr, *Never Mind the Buzzcocks*

Run DMC: the reason the Bronx branch of Argos has run out of jewellery.

Mark Lamarr, *Never Mind the Buzzcocks*

I was listening to some rap music this afternoon. Not that I had a choice – it was coming from a jeep four miles away.

Nick Capallo

There is simply no difference between 50 Cent, Wyclef Jean and Black Eyed Peas. Except for the amount of times each one of them has been shot.

Jeremy Clarkson

50 Cent, or as he's called over here, Approximately 29p.   Sarah Kendall

Morrissey: the Depressive's Dame Edna.
Thomas Sutcliffe

What came first, the music or the misery? People worry about kids playing with guns, or watching violent videos, that some sort of culture of violence will take them over. Nobody worries about kids listening to thousands, literally thousands of songs about heartbreak, rejection, pain, misery and loss. Did I listen to pop music because I was miserable? Or was I miserable because I listened to pop music? Rob Gordon, *High Fidelity*

I think there is a certain perversity in my music in that I continue to eat at the same ball of vomit year after year.   Nick Cave

You could dip a broom in brake fluid, shove the other end up my arse, stick me on a trampoline, in a moving lift, and I would write a better song than Rockafeller Skank on the walls.   Dylan Moran

From Mick Jagger to Marilyn Manson, the one thing that all rock antichrists have in common is that they're panto dames at heart.
Nik Cohn

The image we have would be hard for Mickey Mouse to maintain.
Karen Carpenter, the Carpenters

I don't think anybody ever made it with a girl because they had a Tom Waits album on their shelves. I've got all three, and it never helped me.
Tom Waits

That's what's cool about working with computers. They don't argue, they remember everything and they don't drink all your beer.
Paul Leary, music producer and musician

The typical rock fan is not smart enough to know when he is being dumped on.   Frank Zappa

CLASSICAL MUSIC

—Mum, we're off to the symphony.
—Haven't the Germans punished us enough?

Daphne and Mrs Moon, *Frasier*

Opera is like a husband with a foreign title: expensive to support, hard to understand, and therefore a supreme social challenge.   **Cleveland Amory**

—I think we've slept together once.
—I don't remember.
—At the opera, during 'Bérénice'.

Blanche and Adrian, *The Princess Zoubaroff*

Covent Garden audiences look as if Harrods Food Hall has yielded up its dead.   **Jonathan Miller**

When an opera singer sings her head off, she usually improves her appearance.   **Victor Borge**

The soprano couldn't hit the E flat above high C to save her life. I got so fed up I stormed out, drove home, entered my apartment, and when I saw what Dad and his girlfriend were doing in there, I hit the note myself.   **Niles Crane,** *Frasier*

Wagner's Tannhäuser is a music one must hear several times. I am not going again.   **Gioacchino Rossini**

Baroque music is muzak for the intelligentsia.   **Anon**

Show me an orchestra that likes its conductor and I'll show you a lousy orchestra.   **Goddard Lieberson**

Can't you read? The score demands *con amore*, and what are you doing? You are playing it like married men!   **Arturo Toscanini, to an orchestra**

Cadenza: the orchestra's favourite part of a solo concerto, when they can get on with reading *Playboy*, *Autocar*, etc... while the soloist sweats it out alone.   **Antony Hopkins**

The public doesn't want new music: the main thing it demands of a composer is that he be dead.   **Arthur Honegger**

The life of a classical composer: prodigy, poverty, syphilis and early death.   **Tony Robinson**

Don't bother to look, I've composed that already.
  Gustav Mahler to Bruno Walter, who paused to admire mountain scenery in Austria

I would rather have composed the melody to 'Danny Boy' than all Bach's last movements.   **Matthew Parris**

The only Bach piece I learnt made me feel I was being repeatedly hit on the head with a teaspoon.   **Dodie Smith**

Even Bach comes down to the basic suck, blow, suck, suck, blow.
                                   Larry Adler, harmonica virtuoso

Stravinsky: Bach on the wrong notes.   **Sergei Prokofiev**

My mother always said when she saw pictures of Beethoven, 'Your music is as bad-tempered as your face.'   **Carla Lane, *Instead of Diamonds***

When I play Beethoven, I always feel as if my soul were at the dry cleaner's, and that the ugly black stains caused by the impurities and nervous traumas of Wagner were being removed.   **Alma Mahler-Werfel**

I like Wagner's music better than anybody's. It is so loud that one can talk the whole time without people hearing what one says.   **Oscar Wilde**

Brahms' Requiem is patiently born only by the corpse.
                                            George Bernard Shaw

The modern composer is a madman who persists in manufacturing an article nobody wants.   **Arthur Honegger**

Twentieth-century music is like paedophilia. No matter how persuasively and persistently its champions urge their cause, it will never be accepted by the public at large, who will continue to regard it with incomprehension.   **Kingsley Amis**

The third movement of Bartok's Fourth Quartet began with a dog howling at midnight, proceeded to imitate the regurgitation of the less refined type of water-closet and concluded with the cello reproducing the screech of an ungreased wheelbarrow.   **Alan Dent**

If a young man at 23 can write a symphony like that, in five years he will be ready to commit murder.
             Walter Damrosch, on Aaron Copeland's Symphony For Organ and Orchestra

The most invigorating sound I heard during the concert of Stravinsky was a restive neighbour winding his watch.   **Mildred Norton**

Reger might be epitomised as a composer whose name is the same either forwards or backwards, and whose music, curiously, often displays the same characteristic.   **Irving Kolodin**

Debussy's 'L'Après-midi d'un Faune' was a strong example of modern ugliness. The fawn must have had a terrible afternoon, for the poor beast brayed on muted horns and whinnied on flutes, and avoided all trace of soothing melody, until the audience began to share his sorrows.
                                                                   Louis Elson, 1904

It is possible that Debussy did not intend to call it 'La Mer' but, 'Le Mal de Mer', which would at once make the tone-pictures as clear as day. It is a series of symphonic pictures of sea-sickness.
                                                        ***Boston Daily Advertiser*, 1907**

Claude Debussy played the piano with the lid down.   **Robert Bresson**

I occasionally play works by contemporary composers, and for two reasons. First, to discourage the composer from writing any more, and secondly to remind myself how much I appreciate Beethoven.
                                                                   Jascha Heifetz

My music is not modern, it is only badly played.   **Arnold Schöenberg**

It may be music in a hundred years; it is not music now.   **H.E. Krehbiel**

HOLLYWOOD & FILM

I can't talk about Hollywood. It was a horror to me when I was there and it's a horror to look back on. I can't imagine how I did it. When I got away from it I couldn't even refer to the place by name. 'Out there' I called it.   **Dorothy Parker**

Hollywood: Vomit, California.   **Montgomery Clift**

...a climate devoid of irony.   **Joan Didion**

There's a lot of nice guys walking around Hollywood but they aren't eating.   **Henry Hathaway**

Louis B. Mayer had the memory of an elephant and the hide of an elephant. The only difference is that elephants are vegetarians, and Mayer's diet was his fellow man.   **Herman J. Mankiewicz**

Louis B. Mayer seemed always, and rather belligerently, absorbed in some problem. Indeed, he usually proceeded with the air of a man on his way to give somebody hell.   **MGM story analyst**

Warren Beatty took me for lunch, and he said: 'Courtney, in the movies there are wives and there are whores. You have to learn to play a wife.'   **Courtney Love**

Not everyone who wants to make a film is crazy, but almost everyone who is crazy wants to make a film.   **Clive James**

To bring a film to the screen is to wrestle with monsters dressed as clowns.

David Thomson

Rough business, this movie business. I'm gonna have to go back to loan-sharking just to take a rest.

Chili Palmer, *Get Shorty*

There's a saying in showbiz: 'Never work with children or animals.' Never is that more true than in porn.

Video store guy, *I Want Candy*

It was reported that Guy Ritchie has cast his wife, Madonna, in a small walk-on role in his new movie. Madonna will play the part of the woman who ruins the film.

Tina Fey

I could eat a can of Kodak and puke a better movie.

Lola Brewster, *The Mirror Crack'd*

If my film makes one more person miserable, I'll feel I've done my job.

Woody Allen

If Woody Allen were taller and balder and not married to his daughter, he would be Larry David.

Nancy Banks-Smith

Richard Curtis calls me about Comic Relief every year, without fail, and says, 'Want to go to Africa? It's riddled with AIDS, poverty and war.' I say, 'No, it sounds fucking awful.' He also asked me to be in *Love Actually*. I said, 'So, tell me about that Africa trip again…'

Ricky Gervais

I was offered a small part in the fourth of the *Jaws* series of films at a tremendous fee and I took it. I have never seen the film but by all accounts it was terrible. However, I *have* seen the house that it built, and it is terrific.

Michael Caine

The only problem I have with film festivals is the films.

Duane Byrge

I don't really care for movies. They make everything seem so close up.

Macon Leary, *The Accidental Tourist*

Husband sleeps with Jeanne because Bernadette cheated on him by sleeping with Christophe. In the end they all go off to a restaurant.

Sophie Marceau, on a typical French film

I was so bored watching the foreign film, I cut the pony-tail off the guy in front of us.

Bart Simpson, *The Simpsons*

—*The Nutty Professor* is an entire movie about expelling gas.
—I think that's why people like it.

Ruth and Claire Fisher, *Six Feet Under*

The length of a film should be directly related to the endurance of the human bladder.

Alfred Hitchcock

I really detest movies like *Indecent Proposal* and *Pretty Woman* because they send a message to women that sleeping with a rich man is the ultimate goal – and really that's such a small part of it.

Laura Kightlinger

I thought *Dead Man Walking* was a documentary about Keith Richards.

Whoopi Goldberg

Helen Mirren won an Oscar for playing a stubborn, out-of-touch queen. I believe it's based on the life of Elton John.

David Letterman

MUSICAL

I never did get *Les Mis*. It's about a guy who steals a loaf of bread, and then suffers for the rest of his life. For toast! Get over it.

Darius, *Jeffrey*

You can tell how bad a musical is by how many times the chorus yells 'hooray'.

John Crosby

Casting Maureen Lipman in *Oklahoma!* was like finding Charlie Drake playing King Lear, only not funny.

A.A. Gill

Andrew Lloyd Webber, the composer who is second to none when writing musicals about cats, roller-skating trains, and falling chandeliers.

Frank Rich

Joseph and the Amazing Technicolor Dream Coat: an Old Testament version of *Up Pompeii*.

Milton Shulman

A confusing jamboree of piercing noise, routine roller-skating, misogyny and Orwellian special effects, *Starlight Express* is the perfect gift for the kid who has everything except parents.

Frank Rich

Andrew Lloyd Webber has done for music what Bomber Harris did for landscape gardening.

Miles Kington

—Fuck him! He never picks me!
—Honey, I *did* fuck him, and he never picks me either.

Two chorus girls, *All That Jazz*

THEATRE

A good many inconveniences attend play-going in any large city, but the greatest of them is usually the play itself.

Kenneth Tynan

I cannot understand people who spend hours at the theatre watching scenes between those whom in real life they would not listen to for five minutes.

Natalie Barney

Theatre must always be a golden-hearted whore, giving a kick to the complacent, a custard-pie to the pompous, and a fat-lipped snog to the vicar in the front row.

Murrough O'Brien

The structure of a play is always the story of how the birds came home to roost.

Arthur Miller

Feydeau's one rule of playwriting: Character A: My life is perfect as long as I don't see Character B. Knock Knock. Enter Character B.   **John Guare**

Most playwrights go wrong on the fifth word. When you start a play and you type 'Act one, Scene one', your writing is every bit as good as Arthur Miller or Eugene O'Neill or anyone. It's that fifth word where amateurs start to go wrong.   **Meredith Willson**

I have heard it said it took Messrs Shipman and Hymer just three and a half days to write their drama. I should like to know what they were doing during the three days.   **Dorothy Parker**

My brother, Peter Shaffer, and Tom Stoppard are close friends, and greatly admire each other's work… In 1974, after the first night of *Equus*, Stoppard was descending the stairs of the theatre as Peter was descending them. He turned briefly to Peter, pronounced the word 'Cunt!' and marched on. This, from the wittiest writer in the English language, was the most respectful accolade and was as such proudly and gleefully accepted. So what did he expect?   **Anthony Shaffer**

I like Pinter, Shaw, Kaufman and Hart, Mamet, Simon, and Chekov. I've only read their plays, because I think theatre's expensive and actors usually ruin plays.   **Kyle Baker**

There is nothing less glamorous than a West End first night. You have to fight your way through the crowds and paparazzi outside the theatre and, once inside the theatre, your route to the stalls is invariably blocked by bimbos on the make and sad celebrities past their sell-by date desperately hoping to be recognised.   **Charles Spencer**

Broadway openings – the 'first-knife' audience.
Alexander Woollcott

The New York audience, the night I went, gave the play a standing ovation. A cynical friend maintains that Broadway audiences always do this to justify to themselves the mountainous cost of the evening out.
William Goldman

Simple clapping is too altruistic for our self-absorbed times. Even when expressing approval of others, audiences have to be saying something about themselves. The ear-splitting whoops of a pack of hyenas grates with those of us who cling to the civilised round of applause. There's something so egotistical, so thick-headed about 'whoopers'.   Peter Whittell

—How did you like the show?
—I don't know. I haven't read the
reviews yet.
Alan Jay Lerner and Hollywood agent

With Val to see play *Look Back in Anger* by John Osborne. Play quite execrable – woman ironing, man yelling and snivelling, highbrow smut, 'daring' remarks... Endured play up to point where hero and heroine pretended to be squirrels.   Malcolm Muggeridge

Miss Lummins, as Madge Brindley presents her in 'A Dead Secret', is straight out of Rowlandson, and has a deadly aim with her saliva.
Roger Spate

When Mr Wilbur calls his play *Halfway to Hell* he underestimates the distance.   Brooks Atkinson

Neil Simon didn't have an idea for a play this year, but he wrote it anyway.   Walter Kerr, on *The Star-Spangled Girl*

The play opened at 8.40 sharp and closed at 10.40 dull.   Heywood Broun

The reason why Absurdist plays take place in No Man's Land with only two characters is mainly financial.   Arthur Adamov

I've never seen a play yet that can compete with a beautiful woman standing on a table in front of you. And don't tell me you'd rather hear an actor give a monologue than see a naked woman dance. Because I sure as hell wouldn't.   Mickey Rourke

I was bold enough to decline an invitation to *Hamlet* on the grounds that I already knew who won.   Quentin Crisp

With the single exception of Homer, there is no eminent writer, not even Sir Walter Scott, whom I can despise as entirely as I despise Shakespeare when I measure my mind against his. It would positively be a relief to dig him up and throw stones at him.   George Bernard Shaw

After all, all he did was string together a lot of old, well-known quotations.   H.L. Mencken, on Shakespeare

Who has not sat before his own heart's curtain? It lifts: and the scenery is falling apart.   Rainer Maria Rilke

ACTORS & ACTING

Do you remember a few years ago when Mel Gibson played a Scot in *Braveheart*? People said, 'Oh, that won't be convincing.' but look at him now – an alcoholic *and* a racist.   Frankie Boyle

Having played him twice, I do feel much affection for Tony Blair.
In much the same way that, if I played Hitler, I would probably feel affection for his character, too.   Michael Sheen

I'm no actor, and I have 64 pictures to prove it.   Victor Mature

I have more talent in my smallest fart than you have in your entire body.
                                    Walter Matthau, to Barbra Streisand

—Okay, what's my motivation for sex?
—You're a man, dear; anything short of death is a motivation for sex.
                                    Eddie Sparks and Dixie Leonhard, *For the Boys*

David Hasselhoff: more wooden than Pinocchio with a stiffie.
                                    Mark Lamarr, *Never Mind the Buzzcocks*

It's only acting, for God's sake. Kate Beckinsale can do it.

Karen Walker, Will and Grace

David Garrick begins to complain of the fatigue of the stage. Sir, a man that bawls turnips all day for his bread does twice as much.

Samuel Johnson

It's a bum's life. The money's allowed me to pay for my psychoanalysis.

Marlon Brando

—How do you manage to smile with such sincerity at the curtain call on a thin Wednesday matinée?
—It's an old trick Noël taught me and it never fails: 'Sillycunts'… 'Sillycunts'… It looks far more genuine than 'Cheese', dear boy, and you've got to hope that no one in the stalls can lip-read.

Barry Humphries and Max Oldaker, More, Please

An actor is something less than a man, while an actress is something more than a woman.

Richard Burton

Sharing other people's success is not a notable feature with actors. They generally resent it. Kenneth Williams

During *The Agony and the Ecstasy*, I played a scene with Rex Harrison in which we were walking together through a cathedral. 'Have you noticed,' said Rex, 'we're being lit by only one spotlight?' 'Yes,' I replied, 'I have noticed.' 'Well, get out of it!' he snarled.

Richard Pearson

In *First Born*, Charles Dance plays a doctor who breeds a human/gorilla baby then adopts it and rehabilitates it into the wild. Do you think a tax bill was looming when he took that part?

Jonathan Ross

Daniel Day Lewis has what every actor in Hollywood wants: talent. And what every actor in England wants: looks.

Sir John Gielgud

When American TV and movies call for a twist of limey in their cocktail, it's usually a character they're after – supervillain, emotionally constipated academic, effete eccentric, that kind of thing.   **Stephen Fry**

Daniel Radcliffe, the star of the Harry Potter movies, has made loads of money. I believe it's the most money made by a teenage boy without suing Michael Jackson.   **David Letterman**

I loved the way all the actresses smelt. I didn't realise until years after that it was gin.   **Rhys Ifans**

I do not fuck the star. That's a primary rule of mine on a picture. The stand-in, maybe...   **Billy Wilder**

FAME & CELEBRITY

Isn't it a good feeling when you read the tabloids and realise that a lot of famous people are just as fucked up as you are?   **George Carlin**

We like to know the weakness of eminent persons; it consoles us for our inferiority.   **Madame de Lambert**

Fame is a nasty Faustian bargain. Instead of selling one's soul to the Devil in order to know all things, as Faust did, one sells one's soul in order to be known. The outcome is not happy.   **Lance Morrow**

I want to be so famous that drag queens will dress like me in parades when I'm dead.   **Laura Kightlinger**

Yeah, I love being famous. It's almost like being white.   **Chris Rock**

I was once approached by a man in a shop who said, 'Here, you look just like that Andrew Marr...you poor bugger.'   **Andrew Marr**

I knew I was famous when I had to sign off the dole for fear of being recognised.   Kevin McAleer

You know who wears sunglasses inside? Blind people and assholes.
                                        Larry David, *Curb Your Enthusiasm*

I am used to being mistaken for Miriam Margolyes; *Private Eye* noticed that, and once I was even taken for Gertrude Stein. But that was at Chelsea Flower Show where uncertainty of identity is in the air.
                                        Tom Baker, *Who on Earth is Tom Baker?*

He doesn't suit daylight, does he?
Elderly lady, on seeing Michael Parkinson in real life

Becoming a celebrity hasn't made me more sympathetic to famous people. Most of them are whining little tossers.   Piers Morgan

Being a star has made it possible for me to get insulted in places where the average Negro could never hope to go and get insulted.
                                        Sammy Davis Jr

It's either vilification or sanctification, and both piss me off.   Bob Geldof

With fame I became more and more stupid, which of course is a very common phenomenon.   Albert Einstein

Of course, fame went to my head. Whereas before I had been obnoxious, I was now unbearable.   Larry Adler

Even the nose of a very modest idol cannot remain entirely untickled by the smell of incense.   J.R.R. Tolkein

Marlene Dietrich invited me to hear her new record. We all went and gathered round the gramophone, and when we were settled the record was put on. It was simply an audience applauding her! We sat through the entire first side and then we listened to the other side: more of the same!   Sir John Gielgud

One of my chief regrets during my years in the theatre is that I couldn't sit in the audience and watch me.   John Barrymore

When Mariah Carey wanted to get rid of her chewing gum, somebody put their hand out to take it: and that appeared to be their only job.
                    Lorraine Kelly, *GMTV presenter*

I think there's a danger in overexposure. Just think what happened to Lady Godiva: she became a chocolate.   Kenneth Jay Lane

I'm sick of Bono – and I am Bono.   Bono

I didn't throw myself off my balcony only because I knew people would photograph me lying dead.   Brigitte Bardot

Fame has sent a number of celebrities off the deep end, and in the case of Michael Jackson, to the kiddie pool.   Bill Maher

People are so obsessed with fame now. Murderers in prison get marriage proposals. People go, 'Ooh, he's famous.' Yes, but he'll wear your bowel...   Ricky Gervais

You should never meet a legend. It's always disappointing. Like the time I met Big Bird at the Ice Capades. Not so big.   Will Truman, *Will and Grace*

The social habits of famous people are like the sexual practices of porcupines, which urinate on each other to soften the quills.

P.J. O'Rourke

It's always the same. When they're taking off their clothes they say they hope I don't think they're doing it just because I'm George Best.
                    George Best

—What are Kelly Osbourne's chances of becoming a *Playboy* pin-up?
—I can't see it happening somehow. We don't airbrush to that extent.

Interviewer and Hugh Hefner

Mocking Hugh Hefner is easy to do, and in my mind should be made easier.

Clive James

Noel Edmonds has the allure of the package tour; of steak house meals and steering wheels upholstered in mock leopard skin.

Philip Norman

Noel Edmonds looks just the sort of person to chip in 'You can tell it's only ketchup' halfway through a horror movie.

Craig Brown

He's like a bloody bad smell, that Noel Edmonds. I wish someone would put *him* in one of those bloody boxes and bury it.

Jim Royle, *The Royle Family*

That oxymoronic thing, the television personality.

Will Self

I've long suspected that Richard Madeley has to whistle when he's at stool, to remind himself which end to wipe, and numerous clips confirmed that he also suffers from premature articulation (talking before thinking)...

Victor Lewis-Smith

Ant and Dec are just your average, common-or-garden multimillionaire television superstars who like nothing better than going down the local together for a pint. Only in their case they own the local.

Unnamed TV insider

Think of how entertaining it would be if all the people on TV still had their original teeth.

George Carlin

The world falls into two halves – those who worship Ruby Wax and those who get out of the bath to pee.

A.A. Gill

Heather Mills McCartney – what a fucking liar! I wouldn't be surprised if we found out she's actually got two legs.   Jonathan Ross

During Heather Mills McCartney's down and out days, she once said that a tramp urinated in her face while she slept on the Embankment. In the tramp's defence, he did say he wouldn't have pissed on her if she was on fire.   Mark Lamarr, *Never Mind the Buzzcocks*

Ann Widdecombe is a bizarre-looking woman. She looks like a choir boy with the bends.
Sean Lock

David Dickinson – a man so oleaginous that he leaves a slick of grease behind him wherever he goes.   Victor Lewis-Smith

Vanessa Feltz – a woman who always seems to be trying to talk over herself.   Anon

David Starkey: the Cheshire woman's Norman St John-Stevas.   A.A. Gill

Roberta Taylor, that corking actress from *EastEnders* and *The Bill*, looks like an eggbound pitbull terrier.   Matthew Sweet

Jan Dildo – or was it Jill Dando? How quickly we forget...
Victor Lewis-Smith

Sadie Frost has as much class as my second lavatory.
Marcelle D'Argy Smith

The most intolerable people are provincial celebrities.   Anton Chekhov

I'm the second-most-famous person from Timmins, Ontario – after Shania Twain. That's like being the second-most-famous person from Bethlehem. No one cares about Duncan of Bethlehem.   Derek Edwards

Every time I think I'm famous, I have only to go out into the world.

Virgil Thomson

Nothing in life is rolled up quicker than the red carpet.   Julian Amery

Every generation gets the celebrities it deserves.   Barbara Ellen

AWARDS

Why are we honouring this man? Have we run out of human beings?

Milton Berle

The Oscars are like pornography – enticing in prospect, then boring
as hell.   David Hare

Oscar winners' speeches should be limited to one minute, during which
they are required by law to thank their cosmetic surgeon and point out –
with visual aids – their most recent nips, tuck and enlargements.

Denis Leary

I don't think it's quite fair to blame people for thanking everyone who'd
ever helped them in a speech because if they dissed everyone who'd ever
hindered them they'd be there a lot longer, wouldn't they? 'Yes, and Mr
Frobisher, my maths teacher, who said I'd never amount to anything…
Oscar! Inyerface!'   Linda Smith

There's a lot of Brits here. Would I say too many? Not here. At home in
my pyjamas with half a box of Chardonnay in me, who knows what I
could say.   Ellen DeGeneres, compering the Oscars, 2007

No one should have a chance to see so much desire, so much need for a
prize, and so much pain when not given it.   Glenda Jackson, on the Oscars

This is all well and good but I'm still bald.

Larry David, accepting an Emmy award

I can forgive Alfred Nobel for having invented dynamite, but only a fiend in human form could have invented the Nobel Prize.   George Bernard Shaw

Not granting me the Nobel Prize has become a Scandinavian tradition; since I was born – 24 August 1899 – they have not been granting it to me.   Jorge Luis Borges

People with honorary awards are looked on with disfavour. Would you let an honorary mechanic fix your brand new Mercedes?   Neil Simon

What's with all these awards? They're always giving out awards. Best Fascist Dictator: Adolf Hitler.   Woody Allen

Like Olympic medals and tennis trophies, all they signified was that the owner had done something of no benefit to anyone more capably than everyone else.   Joseph Heller

You should always accept an award because of the pain it brings your enemies.   Maurice Bowra

I'm going to Iowa for an award. Then I'm appearing at Carnegie Hall, it's sold out. Then I'm sailing to France to be honoured by the French government. I'd give it all up for one erection.   Groucho Marx

THE MEDIA

Welcome to *All About the Media* where members of the media discuss the role of the media in media coverage of the media.   David Sipress

The media has so much bullshit that there is enough left over to start two law firms and a Christian bookstore.   George Carlin

Before you believe anything in the media, read an article on something that you know about – see how much they fuck that up.   Doug Stanhope

Diana turned on the radio. With a savage snarl the radio turned on her...
S.J. Perelman

Ears are assaulted by the manic gibberish of disc jockeys whose cerebral power wouldn't equip them to engage a chimpanzee in a game of Snap.
Mike Harding

When I listen to Classic FM, I always think I'm on hold. I keep thinking, any minute now, they'll put me through to my financial adviser.
David Baddiel

I always think when I am listening to some of those tense, gloomy plays on the wireless, Ibsen and things like that, oh, if only somebody would think of making a cup of tea!
Barbara Pym

My father hated radio and could not wait for television to be invented so he could hate that too.
Peter de Vries

TELEVISION

'It's wonderful to have you here,' cries the TV host. 'It's wonderful to *be* here,' replies the TV guest. Now, if only it were wonderful for us watching.
Mignon McLaughlin

Today, watching television often means fighting, violence and foul language – and that's just deciding who gets to hold the remote-control.
Donna Gephart

Busy, clever, multifunction media folk have all got tons of other more important, more prestigious, more stimulating things to do than watch television... Television is lumpen entertainment for cretins who eat crisps and have Dralon slip covers.
A.A. Gill

I watch about six hours of TV a day. Seven if there's something good on.
Bart Simpson, *The Simpsons*

I will never understand why they cook on TV. I can't smell it. Can't eat it. Can't taste it. The end of the show they hold it up to the camera: 'Well, here it is. You can't have any. Thanks for watching. Goodbye.'
Jerry Seinfeld

And then I flicked over to the other side and there were a bunch of nobodies sitting in a house and we're expected to watch them eat, sleep and shit and then as soon as they say anything interesting they put a load of bird noises on. I tell ya, I don't know what the world's coming to.
Tommy, *Early Doors*

This is what it's come to. Watching a reality show of people sleeping who I don't care about, will never meet, and actually despise. I might as well have been injecting myself with heroin while I'm at it. **Ariel Leve**

I was going to watch *Big Brother* but I had all this sweetcorn to glue back onto a cob. **Sean Lock**

Television is a device that permits people who haven't anything to do to watch people who can't do anything.
Fred Allen

The satanic genius credited with introducing the idea of *Big Brother* to Britain is Peter Bazalgette...who heads Endemol. He is the great-grandson of the illustrious Victorian engineer Sir Joseph Bazalgette, who built London's sewers and rid the capital of a great stink. There are those who think that the present generation has reversed the flow. **Alan Hamilton**

We can put television in its proper light by supposing that Gutenberg's great invention had been directed at printing only comic books.
Robert M. Hutchins

There is no medical evidence that television causes brain damage – at least from over five feet away. In fact, TV is probably the least physically harmful of all the narcotics known to man.　　**Christopher Lehmann-Haupt**

What is truly astounding to me is that 24-hour Cartoon Network channel carries commercials. What could you possibly sell to people who voluntarily watch *Deputy Dawg* at 2.30a.m. – bibs?　　**Bill Bryson**

A TV programme can never be worse than its viewers; for the more stupid it is, the more stupid they are to watch it.　　**Clive James**

The only time politicians switch on the television is to see themselves being interviewed so no wonder they think it's bloody awful.
Richard Curtis

Sky television? I imagine it's a bit like watching the *Sun* on video.
Prince Charles

When I was young we didn't have MTV. We had to take drugs and go to concerts.　　**Steven Pearl**

It's one of those new reality specials tonight – *Fast Animals, Slow Children*.　　**Peter Griffin, *Family Guy***

COMEDY

Got a phone call today to do a gig at a fire station. Went along. Turned out it was a bloody hoax.　　**Adrian Poynton**

People always say, 'You're a comedian, tell us a joke.' They don't say, 'You're a politician, tell us a lie.'　　**Bob Monkhouse**

The first thing any comedian does on getting an unscheduled laugh is verify the state of his buttons.　　**W.C. Fields**

I'm the only Iranian comedian. That's three more than Germany.

Omid Djalili

How lucky you English are to find the toilet so amusing. For us, it is a mundane and functional item. For you, the basis of an entire culture.

Baron Von Richthoven, *Blackadder Goes Forth*

By your inflection, I can tell that you think what you're saying is funny, but...no.

Karen Walker, *Will and Grace*

It went down as well as Bernard Manning at Peter Tatchell's birthday party.

Ted Robbins

...as funny as haemorrhoids at a rodeo.

A.A. Gill

I would laugh harder at my own autopsy.

Zoey Woodbine, *Cybill*

Maybe I left my sense of humour in my other suit.

Sidney Falco, *The Sweet Smell of Success*

You should always be ready to laugh at yourself – you might be missing out on the joke of the century.

Dame Edna Everage, to Joan Rivers

I've always believed that people who laugh loudly in restaurants are usually not very happy.

Kinky Friedman

I don't laugh out loud, hardly ever. Maybe once every five years.

Rowan Atkinson

I hasten to laugh at everything, for fear of having to cry.

Pierre de Beaumarchais

Laughter is overrated.

Ivor Dembina

HECKLES

—Hello, I'm a schizophrenic.
—Well, you can both fuck off then!

Jim Tavare, comedian, and heckler

Excuse me, I'm trying to work here. How would you like it if I stood yelling down the alley while you're giving blowjobs to transsexuals?

Paul Merton

I may be black, but I know who my parents are.

Richard Blackwood

Isn't it a shame when cousins marry?

Malcolm Hardee

Listen, hot stuff, I'm more woman than you'll ever get and more man than you'll ever be!

Divine, drag queen

If your cock's as big as your mouth, honey, I'll see you after the show.

Mae West

If you don't shut up, I'll sit on your face. But I'm not going to bother at the moment because I haven't got my period.

Jo Brand

If I had a head like yours, I'd have it circumcised.

Dave Allen

The best heckle I ever heard was from a mime artist. He did his act for fifteen minutes then someone shouted out, 'For fuck's sake, tell us a joke, I'm blind!'

Malcolm Hardee

The house lights should immediately be trained on hecklers. Like owls they cannot hoot comfortably when illuminated.

Peter Ustinov

I don't even consider it heckling unless they stab me.

Roddy Piper

There have been nights when the audience reaction has left me wondering whether I'm a comedian at all, or a blind poet from the sixteenth century writing exclusively in Irish.   Kevin McAleer

Life: you get used to it, then you die. Comedy: you die and get used to it.
                                                              Simon Munnery

CRITICS

Those cut-throat bandits in the paths of fame.   Robert Burns

The critic's job is to walk on live bodies and make them bleed.
                                                              Eric Bentley

A sneer of critics.   Peter Nichols, suggested collective noun

A critic is a man whom God created to praise greater men than himself, but who, by a curious blindness, has never been able to find them.
                                                         Richard Le Gallienne

How much easier to be critical than to be correct.   Benjamin Disraeli

Believe a woman or an epitaph, or any other thing that's false, before you trust in Critics.   Lord Byron

A good review from the critics is just another stay of execution. Dustin Hoffman

The trouble with most of us is that we would rather be ruined by praise than saved by criticism.   Norman Vincent Peale

Actors only ever want one thing said to them after a performance: 'Hail to thee, oh God, rise and lead thy people.'   Michael Simkins

Occasionally, recipients of scathing reviews from A.A. Gill decide to take matters into their own hands. He…has received dog turds, indeterminate gunge, used loo-roll and tampons in the post over the years.   James Silver

Don't be taken in by the guff that critics are killing the theatre. Commonly they sit on the side of enthusiasm. Too often they give their blessing to trash.   Tallulah Bankhead

Summit of achievement for an artist: to reach that level of reputation at which audiences come to believe that failure on their part to appreciate your latest work points to a flaw in themselves (e.g. Pinter, Peter Hall and Stanley Kubrick).   Kenneth Tynan

The critic secretly wants to kill the writer. We all hate golden eggs. Bloody golden eggs again, you can hear the critics mutter as a good novelist produces yet another good novel; haven't we had enough omelettes this year?   Gustave Flaubert

Your function as a critic is to show that it is really you yourself who should have written the book, if you had had the time, and since you don't you are glad that someone else had, although obviously it might have been better done by you.   Stephen Potter

Remember that nobody will ever get ahead of you as long as he is kicking you in the seat of the pants.   Walter Winchell

Frankly, reviews are mostly for people who still read. Like most of the written word, it is going the way of the dinosaur.   Bruce Willis

GRUMPY
COMMUNICATION

NAMES

I can't remember your name. But don't tell me.   Alexander Woollcott

—You're Dirk fucking Benedict!
—I seldom use my middle name.
                    Donny Tourette and Dirk Benedict, *Celebrity Big Brother 5*

My name is Shazia Mirza – or at least that's what it says on my pilot's licence.   Shazia Mirza

'Sir Jasper Finch-Farrowmere?' said Wilfred. 'ffinch-ffarrowmere,' corrected the visitor, his sensitive ear detecting the capitals.
                                                            P.G. Wodehouse

They asked me to change my name. I suppose they were afraid that if my real name, Diana Fluck, was in lights, and one of the lights blew…
                                                            Diana Dors

Your name's Carina? That comes from the Celtic for 'parents with ideas above their fucking station'.   Al Murray, the Pub Landlord

Never allow your child to call you by your first name. He hasn't known you long enough.   Fran Lebowitz

—Have you ever met an American named Jeremy?
—No, it's too complicated. Three syllables.   Stephen Fry and Jeremy Clarkson

When I meet a man whose name I can't remember, I give myself two minutes, then if it is a hopeless case I always say, 'And how is the old complaint?'   Benjamin Disraeli

WORDS & GRAMMAR

The words and phrases I must overuse are: bollocks, bullshit, fucking idiot and I love you.

Dave Allen

Excuse me, but 'proactive' and 'paradigm' – aren't these just words dumb people use to sound important?

Cartoonist, *The Simpsons*

If the word *arse* appears in a sentence, even in a sublime sentence, the public will hear only that one word.

Jules Renard

A bishop and a young priest are seated next to each other on a plane. The bishop is passing the time doing the crossword. 'Do you know a four-letter word, referring to women only, ending in UNT?' he enquires. 'Aunt,' cries the priest. 'Damn,' said the Bishop, 'do you have an eraser?'

Anon

—She calls me up at my office, she says, 'We have to talk.'
— Ugh, the four worst words in the English language.
—That, or 'Whose bra is this?'

George Costanza and Jerry Seinfeld, *Seinfeld*

The saddest words are not, 'what might have been'. The saddest words are, 'Restrooms for customers only'.

Paul Kocak

—You split an infinitive on *The Nine O'Clock News*.
—I was under fire at the time.

His former Cambridge supervisor and John Simpson, journalist

An exclamation mark is a question mark with an erection.

Pierre Alechinsky

They put exclamation marks where there had been question marks.

**Dr Hans Blix, former UN Chief Weapons Inspector,
on the British Government's Iraq dossier**

I suggest that you should always flee from blind exaggeration as from a fiend... I have been told that when the late Sir Edward March, composing his memoir of Rupert Brooke, wrote 'Rupert left Rugby in a blaze of glory,' the poet's mother, a lady of firm character, changed 'a blaze of glory' to 'July'.

F.R. Lucas

LANGUAGE

—Maris is learning German.
—Just when you thought she couldn't get any cuddlier.

Niles and Martin Crane, *Frasier*

It isn't at all a becoming language. I feel quite plain after my German lesson.

Oscar Wilde

—Bonjour, Monsieur.
—Excuse me?
—It's French.
—So is eating frogs, cruelty to geese and urinating on the streets.

Edmund Blackadder and Mrs Miggins, *Blackadder the Third*

Weep not for little Léonie,
Abducted by a French Marquis!
Though loss of honour was a wrench
Just think how it's improved her French!

Harry Graham, 'Compensation'

The American arrives in Paris with a few French phrases he has culled from a conversational guide or picked up from a friend who owns a beret.

Fred Allen

Language primers and phrase books can be an odd introduction to a foreign country... The reader of *Teach Yourself Catalan* for instance, can only wonder what dire circumstances will require the use of the phrase, 'I am prepared to raffle the goat.'

Henry Alford

In 1945 an Italian-English phrase book was hastily compiled in Florence to promote a better understanding between the Florentines and British and American troops. It contained the following entry:

Italian: Posso presentare il conte. *English:* Meet the cunt.   **W.H. Auden**

Belladonna: in Italian a beautiful lady; in English a deadly poison. A striking example of the essential identity of the two tongues.
Ambrose Bierce

'Aloha' is an all-purpose Hawaiian phrase meaning 'hello', 'goodbye', 'I love you', and 'I wish to decline the collision damage waiver'.
Dave Barry

A knowledge of Sanskrit is of little use to a man trapped in a sewer.
C.H.W. Roll

I personally believe we developed language because of our deep inner need to complain.   **Jane Wagner**

My father, a Danish journalist, was faced with translators. His phrase 'The spirit is willing, but the flesh is weak', was translated as 'The vodka is good, but the meat is off.'   **Sandi Toksvig**

The interpreter was the harder to understand of the two.
Richard Brinsley Sheridan

What language are you talking in now? It appears to be bollocks.
Victor Meldrew, *One Foot in the Grave*

We need a president who's fluent in at least one language.   **Buck Henry**

COMMUNICATION

The problem in the world today is communication. Too much communication.
Homer Simpson

A quick way to start a conversation is to say something like 'What's your favourite colour?' A quick way to end a conversation is to say something like 'What's your favourite colour...person?'
Demetri Martin

No man would listen to you talk if he didn't know it was his turn next.
Ed Howe

Women speak until they have something to say.
Sacha Guitry

Conversing with Aunt Dahlia was like throwing chaff into the path of a lively tornado.
P.G. Wodehouse

I'm not saying she talks a lot but her mouth was open so often last winter, we had to lag her tonsils.
Les Dawson

The trouble with her is that she lacks the power of conversation, but not the power of speech.
George Bernard Shaw

I have noticed that nothing I never said ever did me any harm.
Calvin Coolidge

He just ignores me. It's as if I'd slept with him.
Carla Tortelli, *Cheers*

It was said of Helmuth Von Moltke that he could be silent in seven languages.
Alfred Pearce Dennis

Women like silent men. They think they're listening.
Marcel Archard

I love the fact that I've managed to generate myself an extraordinary amount of cash. I really am very proud of that – because it allows me to interrupt people.

Noel Gallagher

Most people have to talk so they won't hear.

May Sarton

One advantage of talking to yourself is that you know at least somebody's listening.

Franklin P. Jones

A young missionary went among cannibals. They listened with the greatest of interest to everything he had to say. And then they ate him.

Mark Twain

GOSSIP

My own business bores me to death; I prefer other people's.

Oscar Wilde

If you haven't got anything good to say about anyone, come sit by me.

Alice Roosevelt Longworth

She poured a little social sewage into his ears.

George Meredith

Satan's Tongue-Pie.

Anatole France

She always tells stories in the present vindictive.

Tom Peace

Men gossip less than women, but mean it.

Mignon McLaughlin

If all men knew what others say of them, there would not be four friends in the world.

Blaise Pascal

Run along home, now, the curtains won't twitch themselves, you know.

Eileen Grimshaw, *Coronation Street*

TELEPHONE

Alexander Graham Bell invented the telephone. Which was fine. Until he invented the second one.   Dave Allen

What fresh hell is this?   Dorothy Parker, answering the phone

Hi, this is Sylvia. I'm not at home right now, so when you hear the beep...hang up.   Nicole Hollander

I ordered a wake-up call the other day. The phone rang and a woman's voice said, 'What the hell are you doing with your life?'   Demetri Martin

Can you call me back? I'm right in the middle of someone.   Kinky Friedman

The worst thing about modern telecommunications is the Pavlovian pressure it places upon everyone to communicate whenever a bell rings.
                                                                Russell Baker

Any time, anywhere you can be interrupted at someone else's convenience.   Tom Briscoe

Mobile phones are everywhere. You see people walking up and down the streets, talking on their phones...and I'm dying, I'm waiting, I'm praying, oh, please God, I go to church, I light candles, I'm going, oh, please God, let one of those bastards walk into a lamp-post!   Dave Allen

If you don't own a cell phone you're either Amish or a certified freak.
                                                                Tom Briscoe

Mobile phones, like just about every other technological step forward, are both a blessing *and* a curse. With the airplane came the plane crash. With the car came pollution and road traffic accidents. With the television came *Deal Or No Deal*.   David Llewellyn

The itemised phone bill ranks up there with suspender belts, Sky Sports channels and *Loaded* magazine as inventions women could do without.

Maeve Haran

The technological advance I wish I could get added to my answering machine is a get-to-the-point button.

Alicia Brandt

What you say: Well, it was nice to hear from you. *What you mean*: Please hang up and call someone else.

Jeremy Hardy

I do wish we could chat longer, but I'm having an old friend for dinner.

Hannibal Lecter, *The Silence of the Lambs*

Oh, how often I wished that Thomas A. Watson had laid a restraining hand on Alexander Graham Bell's arm and said to him, 'Let's not and say we did.'

Jean Mercier

CUSTOMER SERVICE

Thank you for calling. To be placed on hold and listen to a tinny version of 'Greensleeves', press 1.To speak to a customer service representative who has no interest in your problem, press 2. To speak to someone who is very friendly and understanding, but no help whatsoever press 3. To be plunged into a telephonic abyss of silence, press 4. To be disconnected for no apparent reason, pre–

Anon

What they say: 'Your call is important to us.' *What they are thinking*: '...though not so important we'd pay someone minimum wage to answer it.'

Pam Sweeney

Hello, IT support, can I help you? ... Have you tried turning it off and on again?

Standard reply

A devious communication strategy I've noticed is becoming more common now, namely the attempt to make a problem disappear simply by acknowledging it... For example, how many times have you phoned up a monolithic corporation to complain about bad service, practically spewing tears as you relive the 15-month frustration you've just been through, only to be told: 'I hear what you're saying'? ... Of course they are hearing what you're saying, but it's no more effective a solution to your problem than declaring: 'I'm sitting on my buttocks.'

Armando Ianucci

Can I just give you my address and not do that thing where I give you the postcode and you work out the address like some kind of party trick?

Rick Spleen, phoning a call centre, *Lead Balloon*

A phone company rings me up and says, 'Are you interested in having a TV on your phone?' I go, 'No. I've got a TV.' I'm not interested in having a TV on my phone for the same reason I don't want a piss in my tumble drier.

Mark Watson

—Hi, would you be interested in switching over to TMI long-distance service?
—Oh, gee, I can't talk right now. Why don't you give me your home number and I'll call you later?
—Er, I'm sorry, we're not allowed to do that.
—Oh, I guess you don't want people calling you at home.
—Umm, no.
—Well, now you know how I feel. [*Hangs up phone*]

Telemarketer and Jerry Seinfeld, *Seinfeld*

This is the emergency service. Please listen carefully, as some of our menu items have changed: if you have a murder in progress to report, press 1; for assault with a deadly weapon, press 2; for a fire covering more than 1,000 square feet, press 3...

Andrew Cook

If you are deaf, press 1...

Maja Keech

For a list of all the ways technology has failed to improve the quality of life, please press 4.

Alice Kahn

This country used to have the mightiest army, the most powerful navy, and the mightiest air force the world has ever known to sustain the greatest empire that's ever existed in human history: The British Empire. Now everyone works in a call centre. If a new Hitler comes along, what are we going to do? Put him on hold?

Al Murray, the Pub Landlord

WRITER

Do you just do your writing now – or are you still working?

Waiter, *Charlie Bubbles*

Who would write, who had anything better to do? Lord Byron

I like to write when I feel spiteful: it's like having a good sneeze.

D.H. Lawrence

Getting even is one reason for writing. William Gass

If I didn't have writing, I'd be running down the street hurling grenades in people's faces. Paul Fussell

If you know somebody is going to be awfully annoyed by something you write, that's obviously very satisfying, and if they howl with rage or cry, that's honey.

A.N. Wilson

Writers are always selling somebody out. Joan Didion

It's no fun having dinner with other writers; they have crap social skills, poor personal hygiene and toxic jealousy.

Celia Brayfield

Last night I dined out in Chelsea, and mauled the dead and rotting carcasses of several works written by my friends.   Virginia Woolf

Writers are very, very good at hating one another. Perhaps not as good as ballet dancers, but certainly a lot better than politicians. And they hate because they hate what the other writer says and, even more, they hate the way they say it.   Toby Litt

No poet or novelist wishes he was the only one who had ever lived, but most of them wish they were the only one alive, and quite a number fondly believe their wish has been granted.   W.H. Auden

Teaching is a good profession for a writer, because it gives him a sharp sense of futility.   John Fowles

I had a friend who got onto the Tube at Piccadilly with the intention of getting off at the next station, Green Park, but found himself sitting next to a girl who was reading one of his novels. He knew that, about 50 pages further on, there was going to be a joke. So he sat on, until Cockfosters, in the hope of hearing a laugh that never came.
          Sir John Mortimer

Almost all American male writers are alcoholic, and as a result of the alcohol they become less capable sexually as they get older. They also become confused about which is their penis, which is their pen. Think of all those clones of Hemingway, drinking and worrying – fortunately they write very little.   Gore Vidal

Great Moments in Literature: in 1936, Ernest Hemingway, while trout fishing, caught a carp and decided not to write about it.   Roger Guindon

I'd rather have written *Cheers* than anything I've written.   Kurt Vonnegut

Marquis de Sade – a French nobleman keen on inflicting pain, primarily through several execrable novels.   Mike Barfield

Samuel Johnson's aesthetic judgements are almost invariably subtle, or solid, or bold; they have always some good quality to recommend them – except one: they are never right.   Lytton Strachey

One of my *fears* – I don't think I was quite alone in this – was that one day she would speak to me (but she never did).
                                               Hugo Dyson, on Virginia Woolf

Bernard Levin writes perfect English, he can be funny, albeit only as often as John the Baptist went shopping for balaclavas.   Jaci Stephen

BOOKS

[*Selling a book*] Enjoy. It's dreadful, but quite short.
                                               Bernard Black, *Black Books*

It often requires more courage to read some books than it does to fight a battle.   Sutton Elbert Griggs

Hey, I suffered for my art! Now it's your turn.   David Gerrold, publishing a book

—Oh, Mum, let me read this to you: 'He stood to attention, his sword erect, ready to take his punishment. He was a throbbing member of an exclusive club. The lord laughed as he thought of the noble lord's rogering.' It's the new Jeffrey Archer.
—Oh, that sounds great, Kim. What happens in the end?
—I don't know. I haven't started it yet. That was just the bio in the front.
                                        Kim Craig and Kath Day-Knight, *Kath & Kim*

The Jacket Fallacy: the deluded belief that the photograph on a book jacket resembles the writer of the book, or indeed that the blurb resembles the contents.   Miles Kington

I've got no right to say to anyone you should read Aeschylus and not Joan Collins… No right but a despotic, unarguable, Neronian conviction.
                                                                    George Steiner

My father thought Dickens would uncover the mysteries of English life. Instead I grew up thinking everyone had funny names.   Anita Brookner

Do you realise that all great literature – *Moby Dick, Huckleberry Finn, A Farewell to Arms, The Scarlet Letter, The Red Badge of Courage, The Iliad* and *The Odyssey, Crime and Punishment, The Bible*, and *The Charge of the Light Brigade* – are all about what a bummer it is to be a human being?   Kurt Vonnegut

Buying books would be a good thing if one could also buy the time to read them in: but as a rule the purchase of books is mistaken for the appropriation of their contents.   Arthur Schopenhauer

Where do I find all the time for not reading so many books?   Karl Kraus

How useful it would be to have an authoritative list of books that, despite the world's generally high opinion of them, one really need not read: books generally overrated or overwritten – books that somehow or other do not come near repaying the time required to read them.
                                                                    Joseph Epstein

Okay, have you ever finished *Ulysses*? Thought not.   Bulbosaur

Once I put it down, I just couldn't pick it up.
                                                                    Mark Twain

The most overrated book of the year was, and always is, the Booker Prize winner.   Jeffrey Bernard

Definition of a classic: a book everyone is assumed to have read and often thinks they have.   Alan Bennett

Chick Lit: just Mills & Boon with Wonderbras.　　　　　　Kathy Lette

Like dog food and coffins, children's books are usually picked out by someone other than the ultimate recipient.　　　　　　Tracy Mayor

Surely no one buys a book of quotations when sober... They always seem to be published around this time of year [Christmas] purely to trap the unwary luncher.　　　　　　Marcus Berkmann

The formula for a successful diet book is clear to me: one must inconvenience people, but not too much. Theodore Dalrymple

Plato's complaint against books was that when one tried to question them they remained silent and that if one sought to attack them they did not reply.　　　　　　Jean Gimpel

Someone once said there are only 2,400 people in the world worth writing for, anyway.　　　　　　Alexander Theroux

As repressed sadists are supposed to become policemen or butchers, so those with an irrational fear of life become publishers.　　　　　　Cyril Connolly

Taxi drivers in Frankfurt are said to dislike the annual Book Fair because literary folk, instead of being shuttled to prostitutes like respectable members of the other convening professions, prefer to stay in their hotels and fuck one another.　　　　　　Julian Barnes, *Cross Channel*

Today publishers are reluctant to publish first novels by anyone who has not been, at the very least, a movie star or serial killer.　　　　　　Gore Vidal

Geri Halliwell has now published two volumes of her autobiography. That means she's already published as many books as God. Or, if you're Jewish, twice as many.　　　　　　Mark Watson

Just as there is nothing between the admirable omelette and the intolerable, so with autobiography.
                                                              Hilaire Belloc

Hillary Clinton's 506-page memoir has come out. So much of her personality shines through, that in the end, you, too, will want to sleep with an intern.
                                                              Craig Kilborn

Simon Raven's second volume of memoirs…was published in 1990 and almost immediately withdrawn and pulped, as a result of Raven's libellous suggestion that a named friend had ejaculated into a stew before serving it up at a grand luncheon.
                                                              Daily Telegraph

I wasn't even in the index.   Edwina Currie, on John Major's autobiography

Please send a copy of your book to my office. I have a desk with one leg shorter than the other that needs propping up.
                                                    Sir Alan Sugar, letter to Piers Morgan

I hate libraries. I can never tell if the whispering is coming from inside my head or out.   Max Ryan, *The Geena Davis Show*

DIARY

Sunday, July 19th, slept, awoke, slept, awoke, miserable life.
                                                    Franz Kafka, diary entry

To write a diary every day is like returning to one's own vomit.
                                                    Enoch Powell

Manning's diaries are always written as though he were defending himself, on the Day of Judgement, before a hostile jury.   A.C. Benson

A diary is an assassin's cloak which we wear when we stab a comrade in the back with a pen.   William Soutar

Gaselee's diary, with the elaborate account book, etc. His only entry, on Jan.1. 'Got up at quarter to eight.'   A.C. Benson

I do not remember this day.
Dorothy Wordsworth, diary entry, 17 March 1798

POETRY

Novelist, Frank McCourt, recently described an encounter with a former student in New York. 'He said, "Hi, Mr McCourt." I said, "Hi, Moose." He said, "You know my name?" I said, "Yeah, Moose Kline." He said, "I was in your class 15 years ago!" I said, "I know, Moose. So, how are you doing?" He said, "I was in your writing class for a year and a half and now I'm a poet, and I'm starving. And fuck you!"'   Mark Sanderson

Receive Algernon Swinburne? I do not care to meet someone who is sitting in a sewer and adding to it.   Thomas Carlyle

Poets are revolting people, as a rule. They are dreadfully dressed, unpleasant people who don't pay for their drinks, and then all the girls fall for them.   Auberon Waugh

Poet T.S. Eliot had dinner with me on Monday – rather ill and rather American; altogether not quite gay enough for my taste.   Lytton Strachey

We had this rather lugubrious man in a suit and he read a poem… I think it was called 'The Desert'… At first the girls got the giggles, then I did, then even the King.
The Queen Mother, listening to T.S. Eliot reading from *The Waste Land*

My name is only an anagram of toilets.   T.S. Eliot

Haiku poems are limericks that don't make you laugh.   A.A. Gill

—Shall I do my war poem, sir?
—No. I'd rather French-kiss a skunk.
Baldrick and Edmund Blackadder, *Blackadder Goes Forth*

All I can recall of the actual poetry is the bit that goes Tum-tum, tum-tum, tum-tumpty-tum I slew him, tum-tum, tum.   P.G. Wodehouse

Very nice, though there are dull stretches.
Antoine de Rivarol, on a two-line poem

The Scots do make good whisky. In Robbie Burns, they had a great poet, but I've never drunk enough whisky to understand him.   Donald McCaig

I think writing about unhappiness is probably the source of my popularity, if I have any – after all, most people are unhappy, don't you think?   Philip Larkin

Preface to a Twenty Volume Suicide Note
Amiri Baraka, title of poetry collection

All bad poetry is sincere.   Oscar Wilde

…it annoys me when turds discuss 'the art of poetry' and so on. Poetry is nobody's business except the poet's, and everybody else can fuck off.
Philip Larkin

JOURNALISM

TITANIC GOES DOWN. EVERYONE SAFE.
Headline, *Daily Mirror*, April 1912

Why is there news? Why do they have it? It's so depressing.
Anna Nicole Smith

It's not the world that's got so much worse but the news coverage that's got so much better.   G.K. Chesterton

[*Sorting the sections of the newspaper*] Lifestyle – yours, Daphne. Sports – mine. The rest – recycling.   Martin Crane, *Frasier*

What is the difference between the *Pravda*, which didn't give any news, and the *New York Times* which gives too much?   Umberto Eco

The public have an insatiable curiosity to know everything. Except what is worth knowing. Journalism, conscious of this, and having tradesman-like habits, supplies their demands.   Oscar Wilde

Trying to determine what is going on in the world by reading newspapers is like trying to tell the time by watching the second hand of a clock.
                                                                    Ben Hecht

Journalism is full of lying, cheating, drunken, cocaine-sniffing, unethical people. It's a wonderful profession.   Piers Morgan

I listen to the snot in my hankie before I listen to you.

DCI Gene Hunt, to a journalist, *Life on Mars*

All journalists have one thing in common: a complete and utter inability to do anything else.   A.A. Gill

My experience with journalists authorises me to record that a very large number of them are ignorant, lazy, opinionated, intellectually dishonest, and inadequately supervised. The 'profession' is heavily cluttered with abrasive youngsters who substitute 'commitment' for insight, and, to a lesser extent, with aged hacks toiling through a miasma of mounting decrepitude. Alcoholism is endemic in both groups.   Conrad Black

A very nice bunch of bastards.   Graham Taylor

A newspaper is not the place to go to see people actually earning a living, though journalists like to pretend they never stop sweating over a hot typewriter. It is much more like a brothel – short, rushed bouts of really enjoyable activity interspersed with long lazy stretches of gossip, boasting, flirtation, drinking, telephoning, strolling about the corridors sitting on the corner of desks, planning to start everything tomorrow. Each of the inmates has a little speciality to please the customers. The highest paid ones perform only by appointment; the poorest take on anybody, the editors are like madams – soothing, flattering, disciplining their naughty, temperamental staff, but rarely obliged to satisfy the clients personally between the printed sheets.

Washington bureau manager, *United Press International*

I recall the comments of the owner of a tavern which was largely patronised by prostitutes. He gave drinks and meals to newspapermen at half rates. When asked the reason he replied, 'Commercial courtesy to an allied profession.'

Khushwant Singh

If you can't get a job as a pianist in a brothel you become a royal reporter.

Max Hastings

Piers Morgan is a relentless self-publicist whose every utterance is oral Rohypnol.

Anon, quoted by A.A. Gill

What a squalid and irresponsible little profession it is. Nothing prepares you for how bad Fleet Street is until it craps on you from a great height.

Ken Livingstone

Marianne Faithfull has been bleating about the trauma caused by a German journalist who asked her about the size of former boyfriend Mick Jagger's manhood. She said: 'I was absolutely gobsmacked.'

Daily Mail

Journalists belong in the gutter because that is where the ruling classes throw their guilty secrets.

Gerald Priestland

I believe in equality for everyone – except reporters and photographers.

Mahatma Gandhi

Serious, concerned, charitable, fashionable, crushingly humourless, tendentious, engaged, decent, the *Guardian* stands in an agnostic age for all the well-meaning Puritanism that still survives so strongly in the British character – liberal, egalitarian, feminist, middle class… I will not allow it in the house.
William Packer

How can one not be fond of something that the *Daily Mail* despises?
Stephen Fry

The key to the *Daily Telegraph*'s immense success…an excellent, fair, concise, informative newspaper; good sports coverage; a page three in which the kinkiest, gamiest, most salacious and most scatological stories in Britain were set out in the most apparently sober manner, but with sadistically explicit quotations from court transcripts; and extreme veneration of the Royal Family.
Conrad Black

Where I work, we have only one editorial rule. We can't write anything longer than the average person can read during the average crap.
Michael Gold, *The Big Chill*

People who read the tabloids deserve to be lied to.
Jerry Seinfeld

A really nasty nation can and should produce a really nasty press, but it is the nation we should detest – and, in my case, enjoy detesting – before the newspapers which mirror it.
Auberon Waugh

I wish I had gotten as much in bed as I got in the newspapers.
Linda Ronstadt

INTERVIEW

Do you know what a Pink Pussy is? Do you know what a Slippery Nipple is?
Jeremy Paxman, interviewing David Cameron

My interview technique rests on the question: Why is this lying bastard lying to me?
Jeremy Paxman

The difference between MPs and ordinary mortals is not that the average politician is more dishonest than the average voter but that our elected representatives are forced to submit themselves to interrogations on terms that no ordinary mortal would accept. Here are the seven responses a politician is not allowed to give to a question: 1) I don't know; 2) I don't care; 3) I won't say; 4) There's nothing I can do about it; 5) It's not my responsibility; 6) Mind your own business; 7) No comment.

Matthew Parris

Can I get this question in, Prime Minister, because we're having an interview, which must depend on me asking some questions occasionally.

Robin Day, to Margaret Thatcher

You'll interrupt yourself in a minute.

David Cameron, interviewed by John Humphrys

Taking on a Cabinet minister is as nothing to handling three tons of kicking cow.

John Humphrys, former farmer

—What makes you a good interviewer?
—I'm sincere. I'm really curious. I care what people think. I listen to answers and leave my ego at the door. I don't use the word 'I'.

Reporter and Larry King

Wait for those unguarded moments. Relax the mood and, like a child dropping off to sleep, the subject often reveals his truest self.

Barbara Walters

PUBLIC SPEAKING

Ladies and gentlemen, if I could say a few words...I'd be a better public speaker.

Homer Simpson

Shall we let the people enjoy themselves a little longer, or had we better make our speech now?

Joseph Chamberlain, at a civic dinner

I think it was Antonia Fraser who remarked that the thought of having to make a speech always ruined her mother's dinner, while the thought of not having to make one ruined her father's.
Godfrey Smith

Friends, relatives, and other people I can't stand...
Jack Sugden, wedding speech, *Emmerdale*

I feel like Zsa Zsa Gabor's fifth husband. I know what I'm supposed to do but I don't know if I can make it interesting.
Al Gore, as the 23rd speaker at a political dinner

At least you get paid for this.
Prince Philip, to toastmaster Ivor Spencer, during a tedious speech

When a man gets up to speak, people listen, then look. When a woman gets up, people look; then, if they like what they see, they listen.
Pauline Frederick

The most popular speaker is the one who sits down before he stands up.
John Pentland Mahaffy

GRUMPY
SOCIETY &
POLITICS

HISTORY

—How do you embarrass an archaeologist?
—Give him a used tampon and ask him which period it came from. **Anon**

History is just one fucking thing after another.   **Rudge, *The History Boys***

History tells me nothing that does not either vex or weary me; the men
are all so good for nothing, and hardly any women at all.   **Jane Austen**

History, or, to be more precise, the history we Germans have repeatedly
mucked up, is a clogged toilet. We flush and flush, but the shit keeps
rising.   **Günter Grass, *Crabwalk***

We have never closed the Dark Ages.   **Michel Butor**

History is what you hastily delete as you log off the Internet.   **Anon**

PROGRESS

How come we put a man on the moon before we figured out that wheels
on luggage might be a good idea?   **Anon**

In the olden days, when we had to use newspaper for toilet paper,
Mr Merton would become so engrossed in a news story he would
temporarily forget his mission. With the advent of soft toilet paper
Mr Merton is much quicker about his ablutions but now less informed
current affairs-wise. Progress really is swings and roundabouts.

Mrs Merton

Frozen food is not progress.   **Russell Baker**

Progress is what people who are planning to do something really terrible
always justify themselves on the grounds of.   **Russell Baker**

Humanity does not change much; in some ways it even improves. Our international football games are occasions for violence, but football began in England with a severed head for a ball.   **Anthony Burgess**

Progress was all right. Only it went on too long.   **James Thurber**

CIVILISATION

You can always tell the civilisation of a country by two things – its whores and its bread.   **Brendan Behan**

Civilisation is the distance man has placed between himself and his excreta.   **Brian Aldiss**

Civilised man arrived in the Pacific armed with alcohol, syphilis, trousers and the Bible.   **Havelock Ellis**

Barbarism is needed every four or five hundred years to bring the world back to life. Otherwise it would die of civilisation.   **Edmond de Goncourt**

Civilisation: Its Cause and Cure   **Edward Carpenter, essay title**

The end of civilisation is now marked by a lack of cell phone coverage.   **Tom Briscoe**

ROYALTY

You're going to the only place madder than Manchester United.
                    **Sir Alex Ferguson, to Patrick Harveson on quitting
                    the club to work for Prince Charles**

After you've met 150 Lord Mayors, they all begin to look the same.
                    King George V

The Duke of Edinburgh has perfected the art of saying hello and goodbye in the same handshake. Jennie Bond

—Do you know the Scilly Isles, off the coast of Cornwall?
—My son...er...owns them. Reporter and Prince Philip

One of the staples of the Queen's job is smiling relentlessly in the face of other people's folk-dancing. Robert Lacey

You *are* a woman, aren't you? Prince Philip, to a native Kenyan woman

Queen Mary's appearance was formidable, her manner – well, it was like talking to St Paul's Cathedral. Henry Channon

It's like opening a huge jar of sweets.
The Queen Mother, instructing Prince Charles on how to perform the royal wave

If it doesn't fart or eat hay, she's not interested.
Prince Philip, on Princess Anne

My boyfriend's chocolate-brown labrador has a pedigree that makes the Queen look positively arriviste. David Starkey

The Queen's accent has definitely changed from that Princess Elizabeth bray into something more middle class. I would like this process to speed up so that at the end of next year's Christmas address (in estuary English) she signs off with 'Luv you loads. Luv you like a bruvver.' Stephen Pile

There is only one certain way for the royal family to achieve huge popular support: produce a nude calendar. John Kilburn

POWER

If power is for sale, sell your mother to obtain it. Once you have the power, there are several ways of getting her back. Ashanti maxim

In government, the scum rises to the top.   Friedrich Hayek

I'm not a dictator. It's just that I have a grumpy face.

Augusto Pinochet

Say what you like about Genghis Khan but when he was around, old ladies could walk the streets of Mongolia safely at night.   Jo Brand

Mussolini never killed anyone. Mussolini used to send people on vacation in internal exile.   Silvio Berlusconi

There are two kinds of women: those who want power in the world, and those who want power in bed.   Jacqueline Kennedy Onassis

David Lloyd George did not care in which direction the car was travelling so long as he remained in the driver's seat.   Lord Beaverbrook

CNN is one of the participants in the war. I have a fantasy where Ted Turner is elected president but refuses because he doesn't want to give up power.   Arthur C. Clarke

Tyrants are always assassinated too late. That is their great excuse.

E.M. Cioran

DEMOCRACY

Democracy is the process by which people are free to choose the man who will get the blame.   Laurence J. Peter

A democracy is a means whereby we channel our contempt for our fellow man into a lively scorn for those elected to represent him. Kindly men and women accept invitations to appear on *Any Questions* to absorb the hatred that would otherwise spill onto the streets.

Stephen Fry, as Dr Trefusis

People who want to understand democracy should spend less time in the library with Aristotle and more time on the buses and in the subway.

Simeon Strunsky

The difference between a democracy and a dictatorship is that in a democracy you vote first and take orders later; in a dictatorship you don't have to waste your time voting.

Charles Bukowski

President Bush says the US has no plans to attack North Korea. He has something even more deadly in store for them: we're going to bring them democracy.

Bill Maher

My job is to teach these natives the meaning of democracy, and they're going to learn democracy if I have to shoot every one of them.

Colonel Purdy, *The Teahouse of the August Moon*

ELECTION

—Every thinking person will be voting for you.
—Madam, that is not enough. I need a majority.

Voter and Adlai Stevenson

In my lifetime we've gone from Eisenhower to George W. Bush. We've gone from John F. Kennedy to Al Gore. If this is evolution, I believe that in twelve years, we'll be voting for plants.

Lewis Black

The trouble with having the vote is that other people have it too.

J.R. Lucas

If pigs could vote, the man with the slop bucket would be elected every time, no matter how much slaughtering he did on the side.

Orson Scott Card

All politics are based on the indifference of the majority.

James Reston

I have voted only once in my life. On that occasion, I just had to. There was this one candidate who had been committed to an asylum and upon discharge was issued a Certificate of Sanity. Well, now, how could I resist? What other politician anywhere has an actual medical report that he is sane? I simply had to support him.   **Malcolm Muggeridge**

If Franklin D. Roosevelt became convinced tomorrow that coming out for cannibalism would get him the votes he sorely needs, he would begin fattening a missionary in the White House backyard come Wednesday.
                                                            H.L. Mencken

If a candidate wants it too much, the convention turns him down.   Malcolm Muggeridge

Never murder a man who is committing suicide.
                    Woodrow Wilson, on Charles Hughes' election campaign

I wouldn't vote for Ken Livingstone if he were running for Mayor of Toytown.   **Arthur Scargill**

If Jeremy Clarkson stood for mayor of London, he would win. But can you bloody imagine it? He'd be scary. He would roar around London in a Lamborghini with a huge mayoral flagpole, shooting cyclists.
                                                        Richard Hammond

That the refreshingly honest Christine Wheatley has been dropped from the Labour Party candidates' shortlist for admitting to having a youthful career in Paris as a '20-franc tart' seems very unfair. What better qualification for political office?   **Janice Turner**

If you're in politics, you're a whore anyhow. It doesn't make any difference who you sleep with.   **Robert S. Strauss**

If you agree with me on 9 out of 12 issues, vote for me. If you agree with me on 12 out of 12 issues, see a psychiatrist.
                    Ed Koch, campaigning to become Mayor of New York City

Vote for the man who promises least; he'll be the least disappointing.
Bernard M. Baruch

Be thankful only one of them can win.
Bumper sticker

I trust the intelligence of the Italian people too much to think that there are so many pricks around who would vote against their own best interests.
Silvio Berlusconi

The people have spoken, the bastards.
Dick Tuck

Contrary to reports that I took the loss badly, I slept like a baby: every two hours I work up and cried.
Bob Dole, on losing the presidential nomination, 1988

John Kerry can lose elections he's not even in.
David Letterman

It doesn't matter who you vote for, the government always gets in.   Anon

GOVERNMENT

[*Government official to staff member*] Leak this against my wishes.
David Sipress

Good news and government do not go hand in hand. When did you last see a council notice reading 'Park where you like'?   Keith Waterhouse

The government solution to a problem is usually as bad as the problem.
Milton Friedman

[*Government official to staff member*] I'm horny. Sex up this document.
David Sipress

Government is so tedious that sometimes you wonder if the government isn't being boring on purpose.   P.J. O'Rourke

The single most exciting thing you encounter in government is competence, because it's so rare.   Daniel Moynihan

If you put the federal government in charge of the Sahara Desert, in five years there'd be a shortage of sand.   Milton Friedman

Under consideration means we've lost the file. Under active consideration means we're trying to find it.   Bernard Woolley, *Yes, Minister*

Every government is a parliament of whores. The trouble is, in a democracy the whores are us.   P.J. O'Rourke

POLITICS – GENERAL

Politics is the gentle art of getting votes from the poor and campaign funds from the rich, by promising to protect each from the other.
                    Oscar Ameringer

Politics is made up of two words. 'Poli' which is Greek for 'many', and 'tics' which are bloodsucking insects.   Gore Vidal

One has to be a lowbrow, a bit of a murderer, to be a politician, ready and willing to see people sacrificed, slaughtered, for the sake of an idea, whether a good one or a bad one.   Henry Miller

A politician is a fellow who will lay down your life for his country.
                    Texas Guinan

There are two impossibilities in life: 'just one drink' and 'an honest politician'.   H.L. Mencken

In Mexico they call their air-conditioning machines 'politicians' because they make a lot of noise and don't work very well.   Len Deighton

It might appear that I'm being slightly hard on politicians, but in actual fact I've got a very soft spot for all of them. It's a bog in the west of Ireland.   Dave Allen

A politician is an arse upon which everyone has sat except a man.
E.E. Cummings

Political extremism involves two prime ingredients: an excessively simple diagnosis of the world's ills and a conviction that there are identifiable villains back of it all.   John W. Gardner

Never judge a country by its politics. After all, we English are quite honest by nature, aren't we?   Miss Froy, *The Lady Vanishes*

The problem is that many MPs never see the London that exists beyond the wine bars and brothels of Westminster.   Ken Livingstone

It is sometimes necessary to lie damnably in the interests of a nation.
Hilaire Belloc

I entered Parliament with what I thought to be the lowest possible opinion of the average member. I came out with one lower still.
John Stuart Mill

If you've got half a mind to go into politics, that's all you'll need. Will Rogers

My wife is smarter than me, which is one reason why she chose to go into the law and not politics.   Tony Blair

When I entered politics, I took the only downward turn you could take from journalism.   Jim Hightower

'But you're a politician,' I said. 'And you were a human being before you became a politician.'   Paul Theroux

The only people who say worse things about politicians than reporters do are other politicians.

Andy Rooney

Politicians are interested in people. Not that it's always a virtue. Fleas are interested in dogs.

P.J. O'Rourke

A politician divides mankind into two classes: tools and enemies.

Friedrich Nietzsche

There are too many politicians who believe, with a conviction based on experience, that you can fool all of the people all of the time.

Franklin P. Adams

Did you ever notice that when a politician does get an idea he usually gets it wrong.

Don Marquis

I have never found, in a long experience of politics, that criticism is ever inhibited by ignorance.

Harold Macmillan

A politician is a statesman who approaches every subject with an open mouth.

Adlai Stevenson

Politics is not the art of the possible. It consists in choosing between the disastrous and the unpalatable.

J.K. Galbraith

The choice in politics isn't usually between black and white. It's between two horrible shades of grey.

Peter Thorneycroft

There are no morals in politics; there is only expedience.

V.I. Lenin

—The right honourable gentleman will apologise for calling the honourable member a liar.
—Mr Speaker, I said the honourable member was a liar it is true and I am sorry for it. The honourable member may place the punctuation where he pleases.

Speaker of the House and Richard Brinsley Sheridan

Listen, I'm a politician, which means I'm a cheat and a liar, and when I'm not kissing babies I'm stealing their lollipops. But it also means I keep my options open.   Jeffrey Pelt, *The Hunt for Red October*

If there is one eternal truth about politics, it is that there are always a dozen good reasons for doing nothing.

John le Carré

I have always noticed in politics how often men are ruined by having too good a memory.   Alexis Comte de Tocqueville

When things don't go well for you, call in a secretary or a staff man and chew him out. You will sleep better and they will appreciate the attention.   Lyndon B. Johnson

If you don't like being shouted at, then politics is not the life for you.
George Osborne, Shadow Chancellor

I have one simple principle in foreign affairs. I look at what the Americans are doing and then do the opposite. That way I can be sure I'm right.   President Jacques Chirac

Any country which displays more than one statue of a living politician in a country is headed for trouble.   Paul Theroux

Politics, as a practice, whatever its professions, has always been the systematic organisation of hatreds.   Henry Brook Adams

I saw Heseltine in the post office of the Commons today, and said to him, 'I noticed when you were interviewed not long ago on television that one of my books was on the shelf behind you. I presume it was there to impress people.' 'I'll remove it at once,' he replied.
Tony Benn, on Michael Heseltine

If you're in politics and you can't tell when you walk into a room who's for you and who's against you, then you're in the wrong line of work.

Lyndon B. Johnson

Greater love hath no man than this, that he lay down his friends for his life.

Jeremy Thorpe

There are no true friends in politics. We are all sharks circling, and waiting, for traces of blood to appear in the water.

Alan Clark

There is no act of treachery or meanness of which a political party is not capable; for in politics there is no honour.

Benjamin Disraeli

There's nothing so improves the mood of the party as the imminent execution of a senior colleague.

Alan Clark

There is really nothing more delightful than carefully plotting a trap into which your enemy in the party is bound to fall, and then going to bed.

Josef Stalin

The dirty work at political conventions is almost always done in the grim hours between midnight and dawn. Hangmen and politicians work best when the human spirit is at its lowest ebb.

Russell Baker

I have climbed to the top of the greasy pole. Benjamin Disraeli, on becoming Prime Minister

I am the Jesus Christ of politics. I am a patient victim, I put up with everyone, I sacrifice myself for everyone.

Silvio Berlusconi

Silvio Berlusconi caught sight of me, clapped me on the shoulder and, in Italian, said, 'Ambassador! Have you found yourself a good lover yet?' I smiled wanly and Tony Blair said, 'What did he say?' I said, 'Oh, er, just a technical detail he wanted to follow up with me...'

Sir Ivor Roberts, HM Ambassador to Italy

The duty of an opposition is very simple – to oppose everything and propose nothing.
                                                                    Lord Derby

English experience indicates that when two great political parties agree about something, it is generally wrong.
                                                                    G.K. Chesterton

Welcome to Britain's New Political Order. No passion… No Right. No Left. Just multi-hued blancmange.
                                                                    Austin Mitchell

I am sure that the party system is right and necessary. There must be some scum.
                                                                    A.P. Herbert

So, God was creating Man, and his assistant came up to him and he said: 'Hey, we've got all these bodies left, but we're right out of brains, we're right out of hearts and we're right out of vocal chords.' And God said, 'Fuck it! Sew 'em up anyway, smack smiles on the faces and make them talk out of their arses.' And lo, God created the Tory Party.
                                                                    Phil, *Brassed Off*

The new logo of the Conservative Party is a tree, but if you look really closely you'll see an asylum seeker hanging from it.
                                                                    Frankie Boyle

I do not have a bleeper. I can't speak in soundbites. I refuse to repeat slogans… I hate focus groups. I absolutely hate image consultants.
                                                                    Kenneth Clarke

I'll be buggered if I'll join the Liberal Democratic Party.
                                                                    Ned Sherrin

The Sod 'Em All Party; Then Go to Blazes Party.
                                    The Official Monster Raving Loony Party, earlier incarnations

Nowadays my political militancy consists of sitting in front of the news saying, 'Bastards!' periodically.
                                                                    Jeremy Hardy

The mistake a lot of politicians make is forgetting that they've been appointed and thinking they've been anointed.   Claude D. Pepper

In politics, you can be a rooster one day, and a feather duster the next.

Frank McManus

Nothing is so abject and pathetic as a politician who has lost his job, save only a retired stud horse.   H.L. Mencken

No more than the whiff of scent on a lady's pocket handkerchief.
David Lloyd George, on Arthur Balfour's impact on history

Contradict me if you dare: no British Prime Minister in history has ever done anything seriously worthwhile or interesting after leaving Downing Street.   Matthew Parris

You might very well think that. I couldn't possibly comment.
Francis Urquhart, Chief Whip, *House of Cards*

THE HOUSE OF LORDS

We in the House of Lords are never in touch with public opinion. That makes us a civilised body.   Oscar Wilde

I am there as a pustule on the rump of the body politic.
The Earl of Onslow

I encountered Lord Longford once. He reminded me of a giant ant I met once, who had blundered blindly off the *Doctor Who* set and had to be led back by his antennae.   Nancy Banks-Smith

The House of Lords is like a club. And in the United Kingdom, if they ever brought back the death penalty, apart from cruelty to dogs and queue-jumping, it would be for bumptiousness in a club. I shall not commit that heinous offence.   Lord Conrad Black

MARGARET THATCHER

Jezebel.   Reverend Ian Paisley

Attila the Hen.   Clement Freud

The Immaculate Misconception.   Norman St John-Stevas

The Plutonium Blonde.   Arthur Scargill

The lips of Marilyn Monroe, the eyes of Caligula.
                                              President François Mitterand

To quote her own backbenchers, the Great She-elephant, She-Who-Must-Be-Obeyed, the Catherine the Great of Finchley...   Denis Healey

A half-mad old bag lady.   Tony Banks

When Lord Carrington and Margaret Thatcher were entertaining a VIP from overseas, he scribbled a note and slipped it in front of the Prime Minister: 'The poor chap's come 600 miles, do let him say something.'
                                                            Douglas Keay

Margaret Thatcher is democratic enough to talk down to everyone.
                                                            Austin Mitchell

The difference between Maggie Thatcher and Joan of Arc is that Thatcher only hears her own voice.   Peter Ustinov

She'll probably replace Guy Fawkes as an effigy.   **Ken Livingstone**

A big cat in a poodle parlour, sharpening her claws on the velvet.

Matthew Parris, on Lady Thatcher in the House of Lords

She is about as environmentally friendly as the bubonic plague. I would be happy to see her stuffed, mounted, put in a glass case, and left in a museum.   **Tony Banks**

A statue of Margaret Thatcher has been unveiled in the Houses of Parliament. It's been cast in solid bronze so it's a more cuddly version than the real thing. It's a good likeness, too, though you have to look quite closely under her heel to spot Arthur Scargill's testicles.

Clive Anderson

I might have preferred iron, but bronze will do. It won't rust.

Margaret Thatcher, on her statue

POLITICS – AMERICAN

The last thing I ever wanted was to be alive when the three most powerful people on the whole planet would be named Bush, Dick and Colon.   **Kurt Vonnegut**

Thomas Jefferson once said: 'Of course the people don't want war. But the people can be brought to the bidding of their leader. All you have to do is tell them they're being attacked and denounce the pacifists for somehow a lack of patriotism and exposing the country to danger. It works the same in any country.' I think that was Jefferson. Oh wait. That was Hermann Goering. Shoot.   **Jon Stewart**

Whatever it is that the government does, sensible Americans would prefer that the government do it to somebody else. This is the idea behind foreign policy.
P. J. O'Rourke

In American politics, nothing much happens until the status quo becomes more painful than change.
John Fischer

The Democrats are the party that says government will make you smarter, taller, richer, and remove the crabgrass on your lawn. The Republicans are the party that says government doesn't work and then they get elected and prove it.
P.J. O'Rourke

I didn't come to Washington to be loved and I haven't been disappointed.
Phil Gramm, Senator

After two years in Washington, I often long for the realism and sincerity of Hollywood.
Senator Fred Thompson, former actor

A group of politicians deciding to dump a President because his morals are bad is like the Mafia getting together to bump off the Godfather for not going to church on Sunday.
Russell Baker

Standing for governor is the most difficult decision I've made in my entire life, except the one I made in 1978 when I decided to get a bikini wax.
Arnold Schwarzenegger

Arnold Schwarzenegger is the Governor of California... And how did he get to be in that position? He got there by lifting things.
Dylan Moran

To link me to George Bush is like linking me to an Oscar – it's ridiculous.
Arnold Schwarzenegger

Politics is a dirty business. Hillary Clinton is running for President and the Republicans are already digging up dirt. They found out that once in her lifetime, she slept with Bill Clinton.
David Letterman

I said I didn't want to run for President. I didn't ask you to believe me.

Mario Cuomo

We have a presidential election coming up. And I think the big problem, of course, is someone will win.

Barry Crimmins

By the time a man gets to be presidential material, he's been bought ten times over.

Gore Vidal

People think I sit here and push buttons and get things accomplished. Well, I spent today kissing behinds.

Harry S. Truman

No easy problems ever come to the President of the United States. If they are easy to solve, somebody else has solved them.

Dwight D. Eisenhower

Being President is like being a jackass in a hailstorm. There's nothing to do but stand there and take it.

Lyndon B. Johnson

JFK's administration was called Camelot but it should have been called Comealot.

George Carlin

The country runs better with a good-looking man in the White House. Look what happened to Nixon...no one wanted to fuck him, so he fucked everyone.

Samantha Jones, *Sex and the City*

President Nixon's motto was, if two wrongs don't make a right, try three.

Norman Cousins

You know the difficulty with a President when he makes a statement is that everybody checks to see whether it's true.

Richard Nixon

When the President does it, it means it's not illegal.

Richard Nixon

Every President needs an S.O.B. – and I'm Nixon's.

H.R. Haldeman

I don't mind not being President. I just mind that someone else is.

Edward Kennedy

The President of today is just the postage stamp of tomorrow. Gracie Allen

The vice-presidency isn't worth a pitcher of warm piss. It doesn't amount to a hill of beans. John Nance Garner, Vice-President 1933–41

I spent several years in a North Vietnamese prison camp, in the dark, fed with scraps. Do you think I want to do that all over again as Vice-President of the United States? Senator John McCain

GEORGE W. BUSH

I would like to apologise for referring to George W. Bush as a 'deserter'. What I meant to say is that George W. Bush is a deserter, an election thief, a drunk driver, a WMD liar and a functional illiterate. And he poops his pants. Michael Moore

A shallow, arrogant, gun-loving, abortion-hating, Christian fundamentalist Texan buffoon. Unnamed European official

Unusually incurious, abnormally unintelligent, amazingly inarticulate, fantastically uncultured, extraordinarily uneducated, and apparently quite proud of these things. Christopher Hitchens

How come the Democrats couldn't find a candidate who could defeat Bush in 2004? It would be like finding a normal person who would lose in the Special Olympics. Lewis Black

—The President has fallen during a bike ride.
—Did the training wheels fall off? Reporter and Senator John Kerry

The White House is giving George W. Bush intelligence briefings. You know, some of these jokes just write themselves.   **David Letterman**

Do you do this with Christmas tree lights? You have a string of them and one bulb is dead, and you flick the bulb with your finger to get it to light up? Same thing they do with George Bush before a debate.   **Jay Leno**

The widespread suspicion he may be a dim bulb really lets Bush off too easily. It's not that he is incapable of thinking through the apparent contradictions in his own alleged core philosophy. It's that he can't be bothered.   **Michael Kinsley**

Nine o'clock and Mr Excitement is in bed and I am watching *Desperate Housewives*... I said to him, 'George, if you really want to end tyranny in this world you're going to have to stay up later.'
      Laura Bush, wife of George W. Bush

Personally, I think George W. Bush is further evidence that the Great Scriptwriter in the Sky has an overdeveloped sense of irony.   Molly Ivins

Ways George W. Bush Can Boost His Popularity...
Hang Saddam Hussein again.
Develop steamy 'will they or won't they' relationship with Nancy Pelosi.
Nail a heavyset intern.
Resign.   **David Letterman**

President Bush has been very clear that, through his leadership, he has made the world safer. My question to you is simply this: how much safer can the world afford to have him make us?   **Jon Stewart, *The Daily Show***

Stop Mad Cowboy Disease.   **Banner at peace rally**

POLITICAL ORATORY

I thought, when I first went to the English Parliament, that I'd hear wonderful oratory, learned debate, great discussions, passionate arguments, flashes of wit and verbal swordplay. You been in there? It's like the fourth form in a bad grammar school.   Dave Allen

Political language...is designed to make lies sound truthful and murder respectable, and to give an appearance of solidity to pure wind.

George Orwell

In politics, all abstract words conceal treachery.   C.L.R. James

I view Tony Blair as, kind of, the air-guitarist of political rhetoric.

Will Self

Oratory is just like prostitution: you must have little tricks.

Vittorio Emanuele Orlando

A candidate will always say the opposite of what he means and predict the opposite of what he thinks will occur.

David Broder, *The Legum Law of Inherent Opposites*

A politician will tip off his true belief by stating the opposite at the beginning of a sentence. For maximum comprehension, do not start listening until the first clause is concluded; begin at the word 'but' which begins the second – or active – clause.   Frank Mankiewicz

It is said that Mr Gladstone could persuade most people of most things, and himself of anything.   Dean W.R. Inge

Listening to a speech by Neville Chamberlain is like paying a visit to Woolworth's. Everything in its place and nothing above sixpence.

Aneurin Bevan

Neil Kinnock, who was one of the country's best orators in a hall, was often disastrous on TV. His delivery was once compared to a tortoise trying to reach orgasm.

Martha Kearney

His speeches leave the impression of an army of pompous phrases moving over the landscape in search of an idea.

Senator William McAdoo

He is one of those orators of whom it was well said, 'Before they get up, they do not know what they are going to say; when they are speaking, they do not know what they are saying; and when they have sat down, they do not know what they have said.'

Winston Churchill, on Lord Charles Beresford

One of the most fascinating aspects of politician-watching is trying to determine to what extent any politician believes what he says.

Gore Vidal

Since a politician never believes what he says, he is quite surprised to be taken at his word.

Charles de Gaulle

What about the unfortunate politician who stood up on the first day of the new Northern Irish Assembly, and said: 'I'd like to congratulate Northern Ireland at the Commonwealth Games. We've just won a gold medal in the shooting.'

Jimeoin

If all politicians fished instead of spoke publicly, we would be at peace with the world. Things in our country run in spite of government, not by aid of it.

Will Rogers

POLITICAL INSULTS

Gordon Brown has the charisma of a coffin lid.

Michael Portillo

The only time I've seen a smile like that is in crowd scenes of *The Wicker Man*.

Andy Hamilton, on Gordon Brown

Cameron versus Brown: 'Style without Substance' versus 'Substance
without Style'?   Gavin Esler

I was at an event recently where I was introduced to a huge hog who was
called Boris. But he was nothing like our Boris – at least the pig had its
hair brushed.   David Cameron, on Boris Johnson

My chances of being elected leader of the Conservative Party are about as
likely as being locked in a disused fridge.   Boris Johnson

I had absolutely no expectations of Tony Blair, and even I have been
disappointed.   Linda Smith

Tony Blair appears to have no clear political view except that the world
should be a nicer place and that he should be loved and trusted by
everyone and questioned by no one.   Norman Tebbit

Tony Blair is so vain, he'd take his own hand in marriage.
Greg Knight

Tony Blair is sanctimonious and cloaks himself in righteousness.
John Major

Some people were calling Tony Blair Bambi...so I tried it for a bit but it
didn't really work. Bambi doesn't have teeth, whereas Blair has far too
many. I even tried drawing him as Andy Pandy, but much preferred
Harriet Harman as Looby Loo. Draw a rounded square, put an eyeball in
each top corner and bingo! It's Harriet.   Steve Bell, political cartoonist

Tony Blair's expanding forehead bears the vivid imprint of the ravages of
power. Sometime in 2004, after the invasion of Iraq...I noticed it had
taken on a kind of Klingon quality. Yet by the time of the general election
campaign in spring 2005, his forehead had become like a cross between a
baby's bum and a snare drum. I'd be prepared to bet that he'd had Botox.
Steve Bell, political cartoonist

Is he really 83? My goodness, who would have thought it?
Nelson Mandela, to Hilary Benn, confusing Tony Blair and Tony Benn

John Prescott has been a gargoyle on the guttering of government. Quentin Letts

John Prescott's job? To shaft the working classes in their own accent.
Jeremy Hardy

—Who's a Cheeky boy! Who's a Cheeky boy!
— I think honourable members should leave any cheeky business to me.
I should point out that the other sister is still single.
MPs barracking Lembit Opik in the Commons over
his relationship with Cheeky Girl twin, Gabriela Irimia

Our relationship is not based on lust; it's primarily a relationship of intellect, a meeting of minds.
Liberal Democrat MP Lembit Opik, on what
attracted him to Cheeky Girl Gabriela Irimia

Lembit Opik is not the first middle-aged man to have his head turned by a fetching young woman in want of a visa. Sarah Sands

Simon Hughes give me the creeps. He's so sanctimonious – like a bicycling curate. Matthew Parris

You know it's bad when more people turn up to your gang bangs than your polling booths. Alan Carr, on Mark Oaten

The good fairy gave David Owen thick dark locks, matinee idol features and a frightening intellect. Unfortunately, the bad fairy also made him a shit. Denis Healey

When Edwina Currie goes to the dentist, *he's* the one who needs the anaesthetic. Frank Dobson

Does the honourable lady remember that she was an egg herself once: and very many members of all sides of this House regert that it was ever fertilised.

Nicholas Fairbairn, to Edwina Currie, during the Salmonella in Eggs crisis

I am a little surprised, not at Mrs Currie's indiscretion, but at a temporary lapse in John Major's taste.

Mary Archer, on John Major's affair with Edwina Currie

The thing about Mrs Thatcher was there was a character to assassinate. The problem with Mr Major is that you look and look – and where is it?

Gerald Kaufman

Being attacked by Denis Healey is like being savaged by a dead sheep.

Geoffrey Howe

Michael Heseltine couldn't see a parapet without ducking underneath it.

Julian Critchley

A boil on a verruca.   *Neil Kinnock, on Norman Tebbit*

A semi house-trained polecat.   *Michael Foot, on Norman Tebbit*

If Harold has a fault it is that he will smother everything with HP sauce.

Mrs Harold Wilson

Michael Foot is a good man fallen among politicians.   *Daily Mirror*

Norman Lamont's mouth is like the neck of a party balloon.

Alec Guinness

George Canning's time as Prime Minister is a fly in amber: nobody cares about the fly; the only question is, 'How the devil did it get there?'

Rev Sydney Smith

The right honourable gentleman is indebted to his memory for his jests and to this imagination for his facts.

Richard Brinsley Sheridan, on the Earl of Dumas

I don't object to the Old Man's always having the ace of trumps up his sleeve, but merely to his belief that God Almighty put it there.

Henry Labouchere, on William Gladstone

William Gladstone has not a single redeeming defect.   Benjamin Disraeli

He made his conscience not his guide but his accomplice.

Benjamin Disraeli, on William Gladstone

A sophisticated rhetorician, inebriated with the exuberance of his own verbosity, and gifted with an egotistical imagination that can at all times command an interminable and inconsistent series of arguments to malign an opponent and to glorify himself.

Benjamin Disraeli, on William Gladstone

The right honourable gentleman is reminiscent of a poker. The only difference is that a poker gives off occasional signs of warmth.

Benjamin Disraeli, on Sir Robert Peel

The right honourable gentleman's smile is like the silver fittings of a coffin.   Benjamin Disraeli, on Sir Robert Peel

Your Lordship is like a favourite footman on easy terms with his mistress. Your dexterity seems a happy compound of the smartness of an attorney's clerk and the intrigue of a Greek of the lower empire.

Benjamin Disraeli, on Lord Palmerston

If a traveller were informed that such a man was the leader of the House of Commons, he might begin to comprehend how the Egyptians worshipped an insect.   Benjamin Disraeli, on Lord John Russell

He insults the House of Lords and plagues the most eminent of his colleagues with the crabbed malice of a maundering witch.

Benjamin Disraeli, on the Earl of Aberdeen

William Gladstone is honest in the most odious sense of the word.
Benjamin Disraeli, *attrib.*

The difference between a misfortune and a calamity is this: if Gladstone fell into the Thames, it would be a misfortune, and if someone hauled him out again, that would be a calamity.
Benjamin Disraeli

I am told that this is a face which has sunk a thousand scholarships.
Aneurin Bevan, to Florence Horsbrugh, Minister for Education, on cuts in education

Henry Campbell-Bannerman is remembered chiefly as the Prime Minister about whom all is forgotten.
Nicolas Bentley

Anthony Eden is forever poised between a cliché and an indiscretion.
Harold Macmillan

Clement Attlee brings to the fierce struggle of politics the tepid enthusiasm of a lazy summer afternoon at a cricket match.
Aneurin Bevan

Andrew Bonar Law is honest to the point of simplicity.
David Lloyd George

The right honourable and learned gentleman has twice crossed the floor of this House, each time leaving behind a trail of slime.
David Lloyd George, on Sir John Simon

John Simon has sat on the fence so long that the iron has entered his soul.
David Lloyd George

When they circumcised Herbert Samuel, they threw away the wrong bit.
David Lloyd George

David Lloyd George has sufficient conscience to bother him, but not sufficient to keep him straight.
Ramsay MacDonald

One could not even dignify him with the name of stuffed shirt. He was simply a hole in the air.
George Orwell, on Stanley Baldwin

Occasionally he stumbled over the truth, but hastily picked himself up and hurried on as if nothing had happened.

Winston Churchill, on Stanley Baldwin

The candle in that great turnip has gone out.

Winston Churchill, on hearing of Stanley Baldwin's death

Fifty per cent of Winston is genius, fifty per cent bloody fool.

Clement Attlee, on Winston Churchill

Anthony Eden is not a gentleman. Dresses too well. Bertrand Russell

—Do you support Anthony Eden?
—Well, he is the best Prime Minister we have.

Reporter and Richard Austen Butler

Harold Wilson did not have political principle... He had short-term opportunism allied with a capacity for self-delusion, which made Walter Mitty appear unimaginative. Denis Healey

A shiver looking for a spine to run up.

Harold Wilson, on Edward Heath

The Incredible Sulk. Greg Knight, on Edward Heath

James Callaghan was skilful in debate, persuasive in speech – and disastrous at his job. Lord Wyatt

William McKinley walked among men a bronze statue, for thirty years determinedly looking for his pedestal. William Allen White

How can I talk to Woodrow Wilson, a fellow who thinks himself the first man in two thousand years to know anything about peace on earth?

Georges Clemenceau

Oh, if I could piss the way he speaks!

Georges Clemenceau, on David Lloyd George

Grover Cleveland sailed through American history like a steel ship loaded with monoliths of granite.
                                                                    H.L. Mencken

What a disgusting, dishonest fakir Bryan is! When I see so many Americans running after him, I feel very much as I do when a really lovely woman falls in love with a cad.
                                                                    Elihu Root

One could drive a schooner through any part of his argument and never scrape against a fact.
                                            David Houston, on William Jennings Bryan

Calvin Coolidge didn't say much, and when he did, he didn't say much.
                                                                    Will Rogers

Calvin Coolidge's perpetual expression was of smelling something burning on the stove.
                                                                    Sherwin L. Cook

Calvin Coolidge was distinguishable from the furniture only when he moved.
                                                                    George Creel

Herbert Hoover, if elected, will do one thing that is almost incomprehensible to the human mind: he will make a great man out of Calvin Coolidge.
                                                                    Clarence Darrow

I don't know how many times I pulled that bumbling, brainlack bubblehead's chestnuts out of the fire and he never thanked me once.
                                            Lyndon Johnson, on Dwight D. Eisenhower

John Tyler has been called a mediocre man, but this is unwarranted flattery.
                                                                    Theodore Roosevelt

If ignorance ever goes to $40 a barrel, I want drillin' rights on that man's head.
                                                        Molly Ivins, on Dick Armey

The air currents of the world never ventilated his mind.

Walter H. Page, on Woodrow Wilson

The Wizard of Ooze.   *John F. Kennedy, on Everett Dirksen*

Adlai Stevenson was a man who could never make up his mind whether to go to the bathroom or not.   *Harry S. Truman*

Richard Nixon could shake your hand and stab you in the back at the same time.   *Hunter S. Thompson*

Jimmy Carter is a great ex-president. It's a shame he couldn't have gone directly to the ex-presidency.   *Thomas Edward Mann*

Ronald Reagan can't remember whether he was born in a log cabin or a manger.   *Barry Goldwater*

Ronald Reagan…wasn't without leadership ability, but he lacked most of the management skills that a President needs. But let me give him his due: he would have made a hell of a king.   *Thomas 'Tip' O'Neill*

Walter Mondale has all the charisma of a speed bump.   *Will Durst*

What do you do if you're in a room with Muammar Qaddafi, Saddam Hussein and John Sununu, and you have a gun that has only two bullets? Shoot Sununu twice.
          Michael Dukakis, on the White House Chief of Staff under George Bush

Being attacked by Rush Limbaugh is somewhat akin to being gummed by a newt. It doesn't actually hurt, but it leaves you with slimy stuff on your ankle.   *Molly Ivins*

When Bob Dole does smile, he looks as if he's just evicted a widow.   *Mike Royko*

Real Texans do not use the word 'summer' as a verb.
                          Molly Ivins, on George Bush

Choosing between Bush, Clinton and Perot is like needing a pair of underpants but being forced to decide between three dirty pairs.

Michael Dalton Johnson

—Congressman Dan Burton called Bill Clinton a 'scumbag'.
—The use of a two-syllable vulgarity by the chairman was rather ambitious.   **Reporter and Mike McCurry**

Dan Quayle says he intends to be a pit bull during the presidential campaign. My, that's got every fire hydrant in America worried.

Bill Clinton

Bill Clinton's foreign policy experience is pretty much confined to having had breakfast once at the International House of Pancakes.   **Pat Buchanan**

I'm just sick and tired of presidents who jog. Remember, if Bill Clinton wins, we're going to have another four years of his white thighs flapping in the wind.   **Arianna Huffington**

—Bill Clinton is said to be giving away his pet cat, Socks.
—It is the first time Clinton has ever rejected pussy in his life.

Reporter and G. Gordon Liddy

If I were in the President's place I would not have gotten a chance to resign. I would be laying in a pool of my own blood, hearing Mrs Armey standing over me saying, 'How do I reload this damn thing?'

Dick Armey, US Congressman

Condoleezza Rice is the whitest woman ever. She makes Oprah Winfrey look like a crack whore.   **Robin Williams**

Give him enough rope and he'll hang you.   **Anon, on Charles Haughey**

Robert Muldoon is a bull who carries his own china shop with him. **Anon**

Malcolm Fraser was born with a silver spoon in his mouth, speaks with a forked tongue, and knifes his colleagues in the back.   **Bob Hawke**

Like being flogged with a warm lettuce.
John Hewson, after being attacked by Paul Keating, Australian prime minister

John Howard is the greatest job and investment destroyer since the bubonic plague.   **Paul Keating**

TERRORISM

I went to the airport to check in and they asked what I did because I looked like a terrorist. I said I was a comedian. They said, 'Say something funny then.' I told them I had just graduated from flying school.
Ahmed Ahmed

Irish people love Muslims. They have taken a lot of heat off us. Before, we were 'the terrorists' but now, we're 'the Riverdance people'.
Andrew Maxwell

My dad is Irish and my mum is Iranian, which meant that we spent most of our family holidays in customs.   **Patrick Monahan**

The Pakistani president claimed Osama bin Laden is hiding in Afghanistan; the Afghan president said he's in Pakistan; and President Bush said, 'I like sprinkles on my ice cream.'   **Conan O'Brien**

A rattlesnake loose in the living room tends to end all discussion of animal rights.   **Lance Morrow, after 9/11**

Rules for conversing with a potential suicide bomber: 1. Be polite, but firm. 2. Resist the temptation to discuss your own problems.
Simon Munnery

After 7/7 for the first time in my life I was able to say, 'What?! You're going to England?! I wouldn't go there! It's full of terrorists.'
Dara O'Briain

If a terrorist organisation wanted to knock out the moral compass of Britain, all they'd have to do is kill a hundred celebrities at random. The country would have an instant nervous breakdown.   **Chris Morris**

WAR

All men are brothers. Hence, war.   **Simon Munnery**

If a woman ran the United States, we would never declare war. We would just attack, and when the country asked us why, we'd say, 'Oh, I think you know why.'   **Seth Brown**

I was in a library in Toronto in 1915, studying a Latin poet, and all of a sudden I thought, war can't be this bad. So I walked out and enlisted.   **Lester Pearson**

A general and a bit of shooting makes you forget your troubles… It takes your mind off the cost of living.   **Brendan Behan**

You obviously require a battle plan. My second husband, the general, always advocated attacking from the rear, which, although it did nothing to enhance our marriage, did bring him some success on the field.   **Lady Conway, *Mrs Henderson Presents***

This the whole secret of successful fighting. Get your enemy at a disadvantage; and never, on any account, fight him on equal terms.   **George Bernard Shaw**

—I fought in the war, you know.
I killed four men.
—He was in the catering corps.
He poisoned them.   **Basil and Sybil Fawlty, *Fawlty Towers***

We spend so much money on the military, yet we're slashing education budgets throughout the country. No wonder we've got smart bombs and stupid fucking children.   Jon Stewart

You have to just marvel at the stun-gun absurdity of fighting to the death over what happens when you die.   Dennis Miller

All wars are fought for money.   Socrates

The Vietnam War only made billionaires out of millionaires. Today's war is making trillionaires out of billionaires. Now I call that progress.

Kurt Vonnegut

If you're bothered about getting shot don't join the army.   Noel Gallagher

I would rather die in Wolverhampton that in Aix.   John Betjeman

The closest I've ever been to combat is wrestling with a tough-to-open ketchup sachet in a motorway service station.   Charlie Brooker

Clearly I've never been there, but it feels like we are in the centre of hell.
Bernard Shaw, CNN reporter in Baghdad, 1991

I believe in compulsory cannibalism. If people were forced to eat what they killed, there would be no more wars.   Abbie Hoffman

We have women in the military, but not in the front lines. Don't know if we can kill. I think we can. All the general has to do is walk over to the women and say, 'You see the enemy over there? They say you look fat in those uniforms.'   Elayne Boosler

If you look from far enough away, all wars are civil wars.   Jason Love

As for Iraq, I'll believe it's calmed down when Margaret Beckett goes on a caravanning holiday to Basra.   Andy Hamilton

VIOLENCE

We live in perilous times. You gotta keep alert. You don't want your life to wind up as black-and-white newsreel footage scored by a cello in a minor key.
                                            David Dobel, *Anything Else*

The world is a dangerous place; only yesterday I went into Boots and punched someone in the face.
                                            Jeremy Limb

I woke up with a bloody nose this morning, and I wondered how it got into bed with me.
                                            Emo Philips

In the pub, I saw six men hitting my mother-in-law with bar stools. My friend said, 'Are you going to help?' I said, 'No. Six of them should be enough.'
                                            Les Dawson

Look at this lot. I've not seen them so excited since they printed that paedophile's address in the paper.
                                            Jerry St Clair, *Phoenix Nights*

They do say that verbal insults hurt more than physical pain. They are, of course, wrong, as you will soon discover when I stick this toasting fork in your head.
                                            Edmund Blackadder, *Blackadder the Third*

—What happened to your face?
—I won second prize in a fight.

                                            Harry Moseby and Quentin, *Night Moves*

—Ten minutes ago, you beat a man senseless.
—He was senseless before I beat him.
                                            Dilbert and Alice, *Dilbert*

Don't stare at me like that. I'm a humane man, but right now I could kick a kitten through an electric fan.
                                            Frasier Crane, *Frasier*

I'm non-violent, but if a hawk comes when I'm feeding birds, I lose my temper and get my air rifle.
                                            Dalai Lama

—Sorry, the law requires a five-day waiting period before you can purchase a gun. We've got to run a background check.
—*Five days*? But I'm mad now!

Gun shop owner and Homer Simpson, *The Simpsons*

Hold it! Or I'll pump you so full of lead you'll be using your dick for a pencil.   **Lucky Day, *Three Amigos!***

Must be his golf jacket – got eighteen holes.   **Policeman, *Clockers***

I live in a neighbourhood so bad you can get shot while getting shot. Chris Rock

South Florida residents own as many guns as the North Korean army, although ours are generally of a higher calibre.   **Dave Barry**

—It makes me glad we don't have so many guns in England.
—You don't need guns, you have kidney pie.

Frasier Crane and Daphne Moon, *Frasier*

Satan Kidney Pie   **Album title, Ten Benson**

We have always said that in our war with the Arabs we had a secret weapon – no alternative.   **Golda Meir**

You can put up a sign on the door, 'Beware of the Dog', without having a dog.   **Dr Hans Blix, former UN Chief Weapons Inspector**

The papers are full of the atomic bomb which is going to revolutionise everything and blow us all to buggery. Not a bad idea.

Noël Coward, 1945

I'm sorry. I had to give in. She threatened to tickle me.

Sophia Petrillo, *The Golden Girls*

CRIME – GENERAL

I wouldn't live in London now. You can't walk down the street without getting mugged.
Reggie Kray

More and more people are having phones snatched. The safest place to use one is actually inside a telephone kiosk.
Chris Webb

In Chicago, it is unwise to take your eyes off any asset smaller than a locomotive.
Keith Wheeler

What contemptible scoundrel stole the cork from my lunch?
W.C. Fields

He's got more fingers in more pies than a leper on a cookery course.
DCI Gene Hunt, *Life on Mars*

A burglar dropped a testicle when he broke into the home of pensioners Joyce and Leslie Edwards. The clumsy thief slipped as he tried to climb through their window and sliced off one of his testicles on the shards of glass. When 80-year-old Mrs Edward went to investigate, she found the man dangling half in and half out of the window, his private parts firmly impaled on a vicious spike of glass and blood pouring from his wounds. 'He cried out to me, "I'm dying, please help me," but I was so cross I shouted back, "Good!" and ran out of the house,' said sprightly Mrs Edwards.
Metro News

A priest in New York City was arrested on gun possession. These days, you better be happy that the bulge in his pocket is a .38.   **David Letterman**

It's rumoured that Gary Glitter will be out of Ho Chi Minh City jail by next spring, and may return to the UK to relaunch his career. In fact, there's even talk that he might be in panto next year, doing *Babes in the Wood*.
Victor Lewis-Smith

—Hey, kid, if I give you a sweetie, will you come in my car?
—Gimme the bag and I'll come in your mouth.
Anon

Serial pederast, Jonathan King…is clearly a threat to society. Who can forget his vile crimes? 'Everyone's Gone To The Moon', 'Una Paloma Blanca', 'Johnny Reggae' and 'Sugar Sugar', to name but four.

Jonathan Gornall

Almost every desire a man has is a punishable offence.

Louis-Ferdinand Celine

I think pot should be legal, I do. I also think if your cousin is really hot, you should be able to fuck one time. **Dave Attell**

I was raped by a doctor. Which is so bittersweet for a Jewish girl.

Sarah Silverman

I got arrested for flashing. They took me to a small claims court.

Rodney Dangerfield

When you walk past the bank and there's a security man in blue, carrying a sack full of money, you always think, 'God, I bet if I just grabbed it and ran, he'd be so surprised, he wouldn't even follow me.' **Jeremy Hardy**

Arson, after all, is an artificial crime… A large number of houses deserve to be burnt. **H.G. Wells**

MURDER

Every normal man must be tempted at times to spit upon his hands, hoist the black flag, and begin slitting throats. **H.L. Mencken**

Lately, the only thing keeping me from being a serial killer is my distaste for manual labour. **Scott Adams**

Not everybody knows that looking at people in 'a funny way' is the commonest cause of sudden murder. I happen to know that because I read a Home Office brochure once.

Tom Baker, *Who on Earth is Tom Baker?*

If Looks Could Kill He Wouldn't Need a Chainsaw.
Tagline, *Texas Chainsaw Massacre: The Next Generation*

Late last night I slew my wife,
Stretched her on the parquet flooring;
I was loath to take her life,
But I *had* to stop her snoring.

Harry Graham, 'Necessity'

Killing your wife is a natural thing that could happen to the best of us.
Brendan Behan

Each year, 18,000 Americans are shot to death, and 2,000 more are stabbed. Americans...have no imagination.
Tagline, *Hostel 2*

She didn't quite chop his head off. She made a Pez dispenser out of him.
Dwight, *Sin City*

—She murdered herself in her sleep, sir.
—You mean suicide?
—Oh, no, it was murder, all right. Mrs Twain *hated* herself.
Jamesir Bensonmum and Dick Charleston, *Murder by Death*

Fortunately, not everyone who could kill you does.
Mignon McLaughlin

I defended about 140 people for murder in America and I think in all of the cases I received just one Christmas card from all of these defendants.
Samuel Leibowitz

I found criminal clients easy and matrimonial clients hard. Matrimonial clients hate each other so much and use their children to hurt each other in beastly ways. Murderers have usually killed the one person in the world that was bugging them and they're usually quite peaceful and agreeable.
Sir John Mortimer

Sex and murder are the same. Well, you say the same after both, don't you? Damn, I got to get the hell out of here! What was I thinking!

Dave Attell

—Don't you want to hear my last words?
—I just did.

Mickey Bergman and Joe Moore, Heist

POLICE

Don't move! You're surrounded by armed bastards.

DCI Gene Hunt, Life on Mars

—You're a killer.
—Partly. I'm a cop.

Sgt Pete Menzie and Capt Hank Quinlan, Touch of Evil

The police attack people and people forgive them. 'Well, it is a difficult job,' they say, 'after all, the police are just normal people.' Police are *not* normal people. Who do you know who rides a horse round a shopping centre?

Jeremy Hardy

The police only exist insofar as they can demonstrate their authority. They say they're here to preserve law and order but in fact they'd go absolutely mad if all the criminals of the world went on strike for a month. They'd be on their knees begging for a crime. That's the only existence they have.

William S. Burroughs

Think of all the people you know who've been burgled, car-robbed and all that, when do the police ever find anyone? They're useless! Imagine if the fire service, for example, was like that: they never ever put a fire out, but there were just a few houses that they hosed down by mistake.

Mark Steel

I've come at this from more angles than Linda Lovelace.

DCI Gene Hunt, Life on Mars

There was a howl of fury which caused the local policeman, who had just been about to turn into the street, to stop and tie his bootlace.

P.G. Wodehouse

Is this 'stop and search' policy really a good thing? Even I don't want to know what's in some of my pockets.   Jeremy Hardy

Don't go causing any trouble now; we haven't got any room left in the prisons.   John Reid, Home Secretary, passing drinkers outside a Westminster pub

PUNISHMENT

Nelson Mandela, incarcerated for 25 years, out 14 years and he hasn't reoffended, which goes to show that prison works.   Ricky Gervais

It's not the people in prison who worry me. It's the people who aren't.

Earl of Arran

You don't need to electronically tag teenagers. Just shove 'em in front of a PlayStation with a bucket of sugar. They're not gonna move.

Linda Smith

—I got 40 hours of community service. I have to pick up trash for the next two weeks.
—Yeah, at least this trash won't call you the next morning.

Jack McFarland and Will Truman, *Will and Grace*

Cyril Osborne is the only man in Britain who would ring the speaking clock just to hear the voice saying, 'At the third stroke.'

Bernard Levin, about the pro-hanging MP

Prison is like mime or juggling – a tragic waste of time.   Malcolm Hardee

You know what I'm gonna tell God when I see him? I'm gonna tell him I was framed.   Longbaugh, *The Way of the Gun*

LAW & LAWYERS

—Do you think we should send for a lawyer?
—Certainly not. We're in enough trouble.

Bert Winstanley and Bob Maltravers, *Cockeyed Cavaliers*

—All lawyers are assholes.
—I resent that!
—Why, are you a lawyer?
—No, I'm an asshole.

Anon

Some men are heterosexual, and some are bisexual, and some men don't think about sex at all...they become lawyers.

Woody Allen

Lawyers fall more into the category of politicians, civil servants and jockeys – some of them are probably honest, but how can you be sure?

Lloyd Cutler

—Her husband is a lawyer, and an honest man.
—Bigamist!

Cartoon, *Punch*

...as a lawyer, and I am one, if in remission...

Jeff Park

My father was a criminal lawyer. There are some people who will tell you that's redundant.

Lynn Lavner

Lawyers do tricks even I can't figure out.

Harry Houdini

—What's black and brown and looks great on a lawyer?
—A Dobermann.

Anon

It is lawyers who run our civilisation for us – our governments, our businesses, our private lives... We cannot buy a home or rent an apartment, we cannot get married or try to get divorced, we cannot leave our property to our children without calling on the lawyers to guide us. To guide us, incidentally, through a maze of confusing gestures and formalities that lawyers have created... The legal trade, in short, is nothing but a high-class racket.

Fred Rodell

A lawyer with a briefcase can steal more than a thousand men with guns.

Mario Puzo

There are more lawyers in just Washington, DC than in all of Japan. They've got about as many lawyers as America has sumo-wrestlers.

Lee Iacocca

Someone once told me that New York has more lawyers than people.

Warren Buffet

You have an excellent case, Mr Peabody, how much justice can you afford?

Punch

Timothy McVeigh's lawyer got him the death penalty, which, quite frankly, I could have done.

Jon Stewart

I get paid for seeing that my clients have every break the law allows. I have knowingly defended a number of guilty men. But the guilty never escape unscathed. My fees are sufficient punishment for anyone.

F. Lee Bailey

—What's the difference between a prostitute and a lawyer?
—Very little, but a prostitute will stop screwing you once you're dead.

Anon

I'm not an ambulance chaser. I'm usually there before the ambulance.

Melvin Belli

A lawyer is never entirely comfortable with a friendly divorce, any more than a good mortician wants to finish his job and then have the patient sit up on the table.

Jean Kerr

Judicial wigs are uncomfortable, scratchy and of questionable hygiene, even if they no longer provide a home for a variety of tiny animals.

High Court judge

—What do you call a barrister with an IQ of 50?
—Your Honour.

Anon

I remember once sitting next to a judge who was in the middle of trying a sensational murder case. I asked him how he felt during the opening speeches. 'They went on for so long. They don't understand that, by half past three, my whole body is crying out for a chocolate biscuit.' It's important to remember that in all the great and significant moments of life, someone is probably crying out for a chocolate biscuit.

Sir John Mortimer

I decided law was the exact opposite of sex; even when it was good, it was lousy.

Mortimer Zuckerman

Any profession that suffers from so foul a reputation must, in some way, provoke it.

Alan Dershowitz

Bar associations are notoriously reluctant to disbar or even suspend a member unless he has murdered a judge downtown at high noon, in the presence of the entire committee on Ethical Practices.

Sydney J. Harris

If war is too important to be left to the generals, surely justice is too important to be left to lawyers.

Robert McKay

May your life be filled with lawyers.

Mexican curse

GRUMPY SCIENCE & TECHNOLOGY

SCIENCE
– GENERAL

There is no gravity. The earth sucks.   **Brett Easton Ellis**

Welcome to *Brainiac*, the show that does for science what five pints of
lager does for ugly women.   **Richard Hammond**

The great tragedy of science – the slaying of a beautiful hypothesis by an
ugly fact.   **Thomas. H. Huxley**

I can't help thinking that science would be more appealing if it had no
practical use.   **Claude Lévi-Strauss**

It is, of course, a bit of a drawback that science was invented after I left
school.   **Lord Carrington**

A great poet is always timely. A great philosopher is an urgent need.
There's no rush for Isaac Newton. We were quite happy with Aristotle's
cosmos. Personally, I preferred it. Fifty-five crystal spheres geared to
God's crankshaft is my idea of a satisfying universe. I can't think of
anything more trivial than the speeed of light. Quarks, quasars – big
bangs, black holes – who gives a shit?   **Bernard, *Arcadia* by Tom Stoppard**

Marx, Darwin and Freud are the three most crashing bores of the
Western world. Simplistic popularisation of their ideas has thrust our
world into a mental straitjacket from which we can only escape by the
most anarchic violence.   **William Golding**

There are two kinds of statistics, the kind you look up and the kind you
make up.   **Rex Stout**

If there's a 50–50 chance that something can go wrong, then 9 times out
of 10 it will.   **Paul Harvey**

Statistics moron: two apples a day keep two doctors away.   **Rey Barry**

Nobody, not even in the provinces, should ever be allowed to ask an intelligent question about pure mathematics across a dinner table.

Oscar Wilde

In my day, we didn't have hand-held calculators. We had to do addition on our fingers. To subtract, we had to have some fingers amputated.

Jon Patrick Smith

Have you noticed that there are some numbers that never change? Six, for instance. This is the number of times, while sitting in an airport lounge, you take out your passport and ticket, to make sure they're still there, before you decide the whole thing is ridiculous and you put them in a special safe place.

Miles Kington

In my opinion, we don't devote nearly enough scientific research to finding a cure for jerks.

Bill Watterson

If only politicians and scientists were lazier how much happier we would be.

Evelyn Waugh

Scientists have odious manners, except when you prop up their theory; then you can borrow money off them.

Mark Twain

I'd push the lot of you [scientists] over a cliff myself. Except the one in the wheelchair, I think I'd lose the sympathy vote before people had time to think it through.

Bernard, *Arcadia* by Tom Stoppard

I wanted to talk to him about the universe but he just wanted to watch the girls.

Peter Stringfellow, on Professor Stephen Hawking's visit to his nightclub

Is the universe expanding? Is it contracting? Is it standing on one leg and singing 'When Father Painted the Parlour'? Leave me out. I can expand my universe without you. 'She walks in beauty, like the night of cloudless climes and starry skies, and all that's best of dark and bright meet in her aspect and her eyes.' There you are, he wrote it after coming home from a party.

Bernard, *Arcadia* by Tom Stoppard

ASTRONOMY

Humans: advanced enough to land on the moon, petty enough to leave a flag.
                                                                    Jason Love

Astronauts are really just engine drivers who have been shot into space.
                                                                    Craig Brown

For years I've been campaigning for a British space programme for pop stars. It basically involves sticking a rocket up Elton John's arse. I like to think of it as one small step for man...and a good laugh.
                                        Mark Lamarr, *Never Mind the Buzzcocks*

There is no such planet as Uranus. It was invented by a researcher working on *The Sky at Night* in order to humiliate Patrick Moore.   Mrs Merton

I'd like to assume that any species intelligent enough to get from one planet to another will have a highly developed moral system, but that's an assumption. H.G. Wells pointed out in *The War of the Worlds* that maybe they're just hungry.   David Gerrold

I think that if advanced beings were visiting Earth, we'd know it by their laughter.
                                                                    Bill Amend

I believe there is something out there watching over us. Unfortunately, it's the government.
                                                                    Woody Allen

TECHNOLOGY

I have always hated machinery, and the only machine I ever understood was a wheelbarrow, and that but imperfectly.   E.T. Bell

The pencil sharpener is about as far as I have ever got in operating a complicated piece of machinery with any success.   Robert Benchley

I have a sun lamp that rains on me.   **Woody Allen**

Smoke detectors come with simple installation instructions. Insert
batteries and place smoke detector as directed. Now light a cigar.
Bzzzzzzzzzzzzzz. Build a fire in the fireplace. *Bzzzzzzzzzz.* Try to cook
dinner. *Bzzzzzzzzzzzz.* Remove batteries and give the smoke detector to
the dog to play with.   **P.J. O'Rourke**

Fire alarms are a damn nuisance. I've got one in my bathroom and every
time I run my bath the steam sets it off and I've got the fire brigade at the
door.   **Prince Philip, to Sue Parkin, campaigner for**
smoke alarms, whose two sons died in a fire

Bill Gates is not necessarily so different from the rest of us. I went into
his den and his VCR is still flashing 12:00.   **Jay Leno**

My VCR flashes 01.35, 01.35, 01.35...   **Steven Wright**

The trouble with machinery is that charm doesn't work.

Franklin 'Hawkeye' Pierce, *M*A*S*H*

Air-conditioning is an efficient and widely used method for spreading
disease.   **John Ralson Saul**

Technology is the knack of so arranging the world that we don't have to
experience it.   **Max Frisch**

Technology throws daily another loop of fine wire around our souls...
We need increasingly to take the reading of a needle on a dial to discover
whether we think something is good or bad, or right or wrong.
Adlai Stevenson

Technology interrupts our ability to have a thought or a daydream, to
imagine something wonderful because we're too busy bridging the walk
from the cafeteria back to the office on the cell phone.   **Steven Spielberg**

What next? The Paintings of Leonardo Da Vinci – All Digitally
Remastered.   **Sidney Harris**

I would trade all of my technology for an afternoon with Socrates.
                              Steve Jobs, co-founder of Apple Computers

COMPUTER

The only thing God didn't do to Job was give him a computer.   **I.F. Stone**

I think I bought a bad computer. The mouse bit me.   **David Letterman**

Buying the right computer and getting it to work properly is no more
complicated than building a nuclear reactor from wristwatch parts in a
darkened room using only your teeth.   **Dave Barry**

Part of the inhumanity of the computer is that, once it is competently
programmed and working smoothly, it is completely honest.   **Isaac Asimov**

If you put tomfoolery into a computer, nothing comes out of it but
tomfoolery. But this tomfoolery, having passed through a very expensive
machine, is somehow ennobled and no one dares criticise it.   **Pierre Gallois**

All sorts of computer errors are now turning up. You'd be surprised to
know the number of doctors who claim they are treating pregnant men.
                                                        Isaac Asimov

Ours is the age that is proud of machines that think and suspicious of
men who try to.   **H. Mumford Jones**

Computers operate on simple principles that can easily be understood by
anybody with some common sense, a little imagination and an IQ of 750.
                                                        Dave Barry

A printer consists of three parts: the case, the jammed paper tray and the blinking red light.   **Dave Barry**

Imagine if every Thursday your shoes exploded if you tied them the usual way. This happens to us all the time with our computers, and nobody thinks of complaining.   **Jeff Raskin**

In life: You spill your cereal at breakfast, you get fired from your job, your dog dies, and your house burns down.
Computer equivalent: Virus Detected.

In life: You've finished a 900-page novel. Your life's work. You will be a famous author worldwide; but then, it falls into the lit fireplace.
Computer equivalent: Quitting without saving.

In life: A solution to all problems is found. World peace is achieved, all conflicts end, and everyone is happy.
Computer equivalent: Ctrl+Alt+Del.   **Anon**

How does Bill Gates change a light bulb? He doesn't. He just declares darkness the new industry standard.

Anon

The most overlooked advantage of owning a computer is that if they foul up there's no law against whacking them around a little.   **Eric Porterfield**

In all large corporations, there is a pervasive fear that someone, somewhere is having fun with a computer on company time. Networks help alleviate that fear.   **John C. Dvorak**

Programming today is a race between software engineers striving to build bigger and better idiot-proof programs, and the Universe trying to produce bigger and better idiots. So far, the Universe is winning.

Rich Cook

INTERNET

A million monkeys were given a million typewriters. It's called the Internet.   Simon Munnery

The Internet is just the world's biggest bog wall.   Phill Jupitus

Blogger, *n*: someone with nothing to say writing for someone with nothing to do.   Guy Kawasaki

Personal web pages are the equivalent of home video, except that you don't have to visit somebody else's house to fall asleep – you can do so in the comfort of your own home.   Ray Valdes

People tell me that blogs are the future. Oh, well, maybe I won't be a part of it. I've redefined the website of *Private Eye* so that when you go on there's a big message flashes up which says: GO AND BUY THE MAGAZINE.   Ian Hislop, editor, *Private Eye*

Modern cyberspace is a deadly festering swamp, teeming with dangerous programs such as 'viruses', 'worms', 'Trojan horses', and 'Licensed Microsoft software' that can take over your computer and render it useless.   Dave Barry

The World Wide Web is like being in a library where someone has scattered all the books on the floor, attached them together with threads and you are in the dark.   CBC Radio

On the downside, MySpace is loaded with sexual predators. On the plus side, it's also loaded with sexual prey.   Demetri Martin

They're bringing out a new Barbie doll called 'Internet Barbie', which is really a fat guy claiming to be a hot blonde.   Bill Maher

On the Internet, nobody knows you're a dog.   Peter Steiner

I think it would be cool, if you were writing a ransom note in Microsoft Word, the paperclip popped up and said, 'It looks like you're writing a ransom note...need some help? You should curse more.'   Demetri Martin

If you receive an email with a subject of 'Badtimes', delete it immediately *without* reading it! This is the most dangerous email virus yet. It will re-write your hard drive. Not only that, but it will recalibrate your refrigerator's coolness setting so all your ice-cream goes melty, drink all your beer, make you fall in love with a penguin, give you nightmares about circus midgets, leave the toilet seat up and kill your dog.

Badtimes Virus Alert

UNIVERSAL LAWS

Left to themselves, things will always go from bad to worse.

Steen's Law

The more crap you put up with, the more crap you are going to get.

Scott Adams

Every time you come up with a great idea, you will find someone else has thought of it first.   Arney's Law

If you think big enough, you'll never have to do it.

Reisner's Law of Conceptual Inertia

In crises, most people will choose the worst possible course of action.

Rudin's Law

There are more horses' asses than there are horses.   Soderquist's Paradox

If it requires a uniform, it's a worthless endeavour.   George Carlin

If an experiment works, something has gone wrong.   Finagle's First Law

Whenever an astronomical event takes place, a natural phenomenon obscures the event.

Spode's Law

Auditors always reject any expense account with a bottom line divisible by five or ten.

O'Brien's Principle

When stupidity is a sufficient explanation, there is no need to have recourse to any other.

Mitchell Ulmann

If an article is attractive, or useful, or inexpensive, they'll stop making it tomorrow; if it's all three, they stopped making it yesterday.

Mignon McLaughlin

Is there a law which dictates that those who hold tickets for the centre seats in the row of a theatre always arrive last?

Anon

Kington's Syndrome: the tendency to put a passport, visa and tickets in a safe place and then mislay the safe place.

Miles Kington

A flying particle will always seek the nearest eye.

Ken's Law

That which does not kill us is often made of foam.

Tony Law

Everything has an except in it.

Lynne's Law

GENERAL APPEARANCE

Oh my God, look at you. Anyone else hurt in the accident?
Don Rickles, to Ernest Borgnine

He has a strange growth on his neck – his head.   **Arthur Godfrey**

Look at that face! I bet his cornflakes try to climb out of the bowl.
Bernard Black, *Black Books*

It's a face that only a fist could love. **Mark Lamarr, *Never Mind the Buzzcocks***

—Do you think these glasses make me look smarter?
—No, you can still see your face.
Marty Maraschino and Betty Rizzo, *Grease*

—You look like hell.
—Yeah? I just got back.
Heather Duke and Veronica Sawyer, *Heathers*

I will never be the woman with perfect hair, who can wear white and not
spill on it.   **Carrie Bradshaw, *Sex and the City***

My God! She looks like I do in a spoon.   **Mrs Patrick Campbell**

Her neck was reminiscent of drought-resistant cattle from India.
Peter Carey

I can't take a well-tanned person seriously.   **Cleveland Amory**

Dale Winton is so orange, if you lick him he cures scurvy.   **Ross Noble**

Carla, do you realise you're the same height kneeling down as you are
standing up?   **Cliff Clavin, *Cheers***

The first time I realised I was small was at a school sports day. I was in a race and ran right under the finishing line.

Lynsey de Paul

People can be very heightist. I am 42 years old and I cannot tell you the number of people who have just met me who pat me on the head. Grown men in meetings will get up and put their arm round me in a very chummy sort of way and I absolutely hate it. I feel as though I'm being leant upon like a doorstop. And my response is just to wither them if I can, and they usually only do it once. Many of them haven't had an erection since.

Sandi Toksvig

Never trust men with short legs. Brains too near their bottoms.

Noël Coward

All I say is, nobody has any business to go around looking like a horse and behaving as if it were all right. You don't catch horses going around looking like people, do you?

Dorothy Parker

Nudity is a deep worry, if you have a body like a bin bag full of yoghurt, which I have.

Stephen Fry

FASHION & DRESS

Marlo Thomas – look at you! Vintage sixties with a plunging neckline – oh, and I love your dress, honey!

Karen Walker, *Will and Grace*

Here comes Ashley Judd in her no-yeast-infection-here Oscar gown...

Libby Gelman-Waxner

It's not bloody Pret A Manger in here, you know.

Unnamed Tory MP, shocked at Lib Dem MP Julia Goldsworthy entering the House of Commons wearing blue pedal-pushers and white slip-on shoes

Bumpy bra, smooth T-shirt – not a good look, darling.

Anne Robinson, to a TV producer on her first day at work

Sporting a look only Wayne Rooney could find attractive, Botox-addled Anne Robinson was in the question master's role, wearing leather trousers, bomber jacket and a push-up bra.

Ally Ross

Why does everything you wear look as if it's bearing a grudge?

Edina Monsoon, *Absolutely Fabulous*

Grace, we talked about the beret. Patty Hearst couldn't even pull one off and she had money and a gun.

Karen Walker, *Will and Grace*

If you have a pear-shaped body, you should not wear pear-coloured clothes, or act juicy.

Demetri Martin

—This tweed suit is vintage.
—I'll think you'll find it's just old.

Edina Monsoon and Patsy Stone, *Absolutely Fabulous*

And, honey? That colour doesn't even look good on an orange, okay?

Karen Walker, *Will and Grace*

Your dresses should be tight enough to show you're a woman, and loose enough to show you're a lady.

Edith Head

She wore far too much rouge last night, and not quite enough clothes. That is always a sign of despair in a woman.

Oscar Wilde

She's all fur coat and no knickers! Anon

—Fifty animals died because of that coat you're wearing!
—Wanna make it fifty-one?

Anti-Fur Protestor and Suzanne Sugarbaker, *Designing Women*

If I wear high heels, I need a handicapped parking space.   **Margaret Smith**

A woman can tell you exactly what she was wearing during every crisis in her life.

Mignon McLaughlin

Pubic topiary is the new pashmina!   Caroline Todd, *Green Wing*

There is no fashion so absurd, even grotesque, that it cannot be adopted, given two things: the authority of the fashion-setter (Dior, Jackie Onassis) and the vacuity or noughtness of the consumer e.g. bustles in the West, bound feet in the East.   **Walker Percy**

As far as the outrageous outfits go, whatever Dame Edna Everage has worn as a joke, Jordan has worn for real, to her own wedding, with pride.   **Caitlin Moran**

Larry Blackman used to wear a codpiece which, if you don't know, is a garish piece of cheap plastic that nestles your genitals. If you're listening, Peter Andre, you don't marry it!   **Mark Lamarr**, *Never Mind the Buzzcocks*

Women should never wear anything that panics a cat.   P.J. O'Rourke

—You're not wearing that tonight, are you?
—No, this is what I'm wearing to your funeral. I was just practising.   **Judith Cottrill**

...the woman who sneers at you from the pages of the glossy magazines, the model ideal of superb meanness, a long slink of classical contempt...begs for defilement, like an American tourist travelling second-class in Europe.   **John Osborne**

I figured out Victoria's Secret. Starvation and liposuction.   **Mel Fine**

Men want the same thing from their underwear that they want from their women: a little bit of support, and a little bit of freedom.   **Jerry Seinfeld**

My husband is constantly revolted by men in flip-flops. I have heard him exclaim, 'Oh, the mandals!'   **R.F.S. Greene**

I was once startled on the subway by a flying toenail hitting me in the forehead – a guy sitting diagonally from me was actually clipping them on a crowded car, one of the most despicable displays I've ever encountered, and one enabled by the 'easy access' afforded by flip-flops (he was wearing them, of course). Flip-flops are the fannypacks of footwear.
Boris Vian

I'm getting sick of the urban flip-flop phenomenon... If we let this go on, pretty soon we're going to see guys walking the streets of Chelsea wearing towels.
Glenn O'Brien

The fashion world leaves me cold. I have never finished an article on anyone called Armani. Nor, in fact, do I think I have ever started one.
Miles Kington

I frankly admit to not knowing who I am. This is why I refuse to buy brand-name clothes that will tell people who I want them to think I am.
Russell Baker

I may not know styles, but I'm an excellent judge of price tags. Bill Hoest

The older you get, the higher your underwear gets. Like rings on a tree. When you're 80 years old, your breasts are inside 'em. When you die, they just pull 'em up over your head.
Margaret Smith

My dream is to see the Pope in a T-shirt, a huge gold Medusa head on the front and 'Versace is the Best' on the back.
Donatella Versace

The fluorescent jacket is the true costume of Official Britain, where the standard keywords are 'health and safety'.
Jonas Andersson

HAIR

—Close the window, dear, it messes up my hair.
—Ma, your hair hasn't moved since I was 12.
Virginia and Cybill Sheridan, *Cybill*

Your hair's already such a disaster that the Red Cross wouldn't give it coffee.
Karen Walker, *Will and Grace*

It's a hair-don't!
Geometry teacher, *Hairspray*

I just found something in my hair. That's never a good thing. That's never gonna be, like, a treat.
Demetri Martin

These days he doesn't need shampoo and conditioner – just a duster and a squirt of Pledge.
Frances Edmonds

Charlton Heston wears a hairpiece. His character in *A Man for All Seasons* was bald. Instead of doing without a hairpiece, he put a bald pate *over* it.
Dustin Hoffman

Oh, keep your hairpiece on!
Christopher Hitchens, to Charlton Heston during an altercation on CNN news

I wonder why all the men in Iraq have black moustaches? They can't *all* think it suits them.
Paul Merton

It is impossible to dry a beard. Mine was damp all day long. At night they are at their worst. They tickle one's chest, you know, and keep one awake. I used to wake up under the impression that I had fallen asleep in some undergrowth in the forest.
Maurice Baring

I once dated a girl with pigtails. Under her arms.
Rodney Dangerfield

You have a lot of nerve telling me to get a wax. If you were in Aruba the natives could bead your back.
Samantha Jones, *Sex and the City*

PERSONAL HYGIENE

Abandon Soap all ye who enter here! **Harry Graham**

What separates two people most profoundly is a different sense and degree of cleanliness. **Friedrich Nietzsche**

My wife kisses the dog on the lips, yet she won't drink from my glass. **Rodney Dangerfield**

A man at the next table spent five minutes hawking into a handkerchief before sitting back, candidly examining the contents and announcing, 'That's got rid of *that* one!' **Charles Jennings, *Up North***

Like orgasm, ninety per cent of a sneeze is sheer anticipation. **Bia Lowe**

I'm not a bath man myself. More of a cologne man. **Homer Simpson**

You're sweating like Peter Andre on *Mastermind*. **Rick Spleen, *Lead Balloon***

Do you mind if I sit back a little? Because your breath is very bad. **Donald Trump, to Larry King, interviewer**

Since I've been married I don't have to worry about bad breath. I never get a chance to open my mouth. **Rodney Dangerfield**

Britain is not a country that has a reputation for changing its underwear very often. **Elle Macpherson**

Supped at the Club D'Elysée with Marlene Dietrich and Ginette, and it was gay and sweet and terribly exciting, and we were joined by Burt Bacharach and got into a discussion about crabs. Marlene sorrowfully announced that she had once had them for Christmas. **Noël Coward**

She's got crabs, dear, and I don't mean Dungeness.

Daniel Hillard, *Mrs Doubtfire*

I was acting opposite Marlon Brando in the play *Rampant Eagle*. I asked if we could change the title because the only thing rampant about the goddamn thing was Brando's crabs. **Tallulah Bankhead**

The door handle of a public lavatory is statistically more dangerous than standing in downtown Baghdad wrapped in the Stars and Stripes, shouting, 'Come on, if you're man enough, towelhead.' **A.A. Gill**

Do they still make that really hard toilet paper which you could use as tracing paper at school if you were stuck? **Jonathan Ross**

Once I went to a ghastly orgy in a tower block in Paddington... What stuck in my mind the most were the refreshments...saucers of nibbles here and there. I won't eat peanuts at a bar because they're supposed to have twenty types of wee on them, so who's going to eat Smarties at an orgy? **Russell Brand**

Wash your hands and say your prayers, 'cause germs and Jesus are everywhere. **Kinky Friedman**

BEAUTY & UGLINESS

Hey, you want to feel really handsome? Go shopping at Asda.

Brendon Burns

Good looks are a curse, Deirdre. You and Ken should count yourselves lucky. **Blanche Hunt, *Coronation Street***

I know you hate being ugly, but someone has to make everyone else look good. **Chicken, *Cow and Chicken***

—My teacher tells me beauty is on the inside.
—That's just something ugly people say.

Max and Fletcher Reede, Liar, Liar

One of the *big* weaknesses of the male sex is just being completely unable to see through beauty.

Candace Bushnell

Women are judged by their looks... Men are judged by what they do. An ugly woman could be a genius; she could cure cancer and somebody would still say, 'Hey, did you hear about that ugly woman who cured cancer?' There would be jokes on late-night television shows: 'Did you hear about the ugly scientist who cured cancer? Yeah, that's great. You know how she found the cure? Apparently, she just looked at the cancer and scared it away.'

Wanda Sykes

Beauty is all very well at first sight; but who ever looks at it when it has been in the house three days?

George Bernard Shaw

—I can still turn a few heads.
—...and a few stomachs!

Cynthia and Roxanne Purley, Secrets and Lies

I was so ugly as a kid, my parents had to tie a pork chop around my neck so the dog would play with me.

Rodney Dangerfield

From thirty feet away she looked like a lot of class. From ten feet away she looked like something to be seen from thirty feet away.

Raymond Chandler

I'm not saying she looks like the back of a bus, but I've noticed that no one ever overtakes her on the inside.

Les Dawson

They did a makeover on Ann Widdecombe, but it's pointless, isn't it? It's like sprinkling glitter on dog shit.

Dave Spikey

She went to see the film *The Elephant Man* and the audience thought he was making a personal appearance.

Les Dawson

What I love about goths is when they pretend to be ugly on purpose. It's genius.

Dr McCartney, Green Wing

It was not until I had attended a few post-mortems that I realised that even the ugliest human exteriors contain the most beautiful viscera, and was able to console myself for the facial drabness of my neighbours in omnibuses by dissecting them in my imagination.   J.B.S. Haldane

The Ambassador has had a change of heart. A lot of good that'll do him. He's still got the same face.   Groucho Marx

COSMETIC SURGERY

Karen Walker, in the flesh! Whose flesh is unclear.
                                        Beverly Leslie, *Will and Grace*

She's much prettier since her surgery. You look at her face and you can't even tell where it used to be.   Daphne Moon, *Frasier*

I had to do something about my looks. A peeping Tom once threw up on my windowsill.   Phyllis Diller

If I see something sagging, dragging or bagging, I get it sucked, tucked or plucked.   Dolly Parton

Her breasts scare me. They're like Mickey Mouse's ears. Whichever way she turns, they're still facing you.   Susan Walker, *Coupling*

—[*Pointing*] Implants?
—[*Pointing*] Lobotomy?   Chuck Smith

I haven't had a boob job. Short of letting everyone have a feel, I don't know what else to do.   Jennifer Aniston

—You're looking at my girlfriend's breasts!
—First of all, Richard, they're not breasts. They're just big chemical balls, okay?   Richard Jeni and Larry David, *Curb Your Enthusiasm*

Everyone knows Denise Kilcannon had a backstreet boob job for a hundred quid and now her boobs look like the Mitchell brothers in *EastEnders*.
                                    Vicky Pollard, *Little Britain*

—How do you like my perky new bosoms?
—My rear tyres have less pressure in them.
                    Blanche Devereaux and Dorothy Zbornak,*The Golden Girls*

If your breasts are too big, you'll fall over – unless you wear a rucksack.

Ivor Cutler

Sharon Osbourne has had liposuction. She had fat sucked out of her, then pumped into her daughter. I think that's cruel.
                            Mark Lamarr, *Never Mind the Buzzcocks*

My husband, Ozzie, says I've been lifted so many times that I fart through the back of my neck.
                                    Sharon Osbourne

You may be looking at a brand new face, but you'll still be hearing the same old mouth.
                                    Florida Evans, *Maude*

This cosmetic surgery is getting out of hand. Now the only way to tell if people are naturally ugly is to see how their baby turns out.   Wanda Sykes

In California, plastic surgery is now so common that when the cops pull someone over they have to ask for identification with two pictures – Before and After.
                                    Arnold Schwarzenegger

I went to have Botox. The surgeon said to me, 'That's $8,000.' I couldn't even look shocked.
                                    Shazia Mirza

Death is not going to be any easier just because your face can't move.
                                    Cate Blanchett

Not to accept growing old is the sign of a misspent life.   Clive James

It's sad. Melanie Griffith was a beautiful woman and now she has a face like a catfish.
Lorraine Kelly

She told a reporter that she hasn't had plastic surgery. Come on! She's had more tucks than a motel bed sheet.
Joan Rivers

Sophia Loren has had so much surgery she now shits through her ears.
Joan Rivers

Hey, if you go to that plastic surgeon, don't you let him put you all the way under. I knew a guy in Stateville one time, went to get his face fixed. Woke up and the sucker had given him a pair of tits. He landed back in jail but he never had to want for cigarettes.
Bobby Blane, *Heist*

My doctor told me to smile more. It's an instant face lift. I just wish my ass had a sense of humour.
Joy Behar

HEALTH & MEDICINE

Two kids were trying to figure out what game to play. One suggests, 'Let's play doctors.' 'Good idea,' says the other. 'You operate, and I'll sue.' **Anon**

[*Receptionist to a patient in a doctor's waiting room*] Your appointment with the doctor is at 11.15 but his appointment with you is at 12.15.
David Sipress

[*Receptionist to patients in a doctor's waiting room*] We're running a little behind, so I'd like each of you to ask yourself, 'Am I really that sick, or would I just be wasting the doctor's valuable time?' **David Sipress**

Receptionists in doctors now are there to protect the doctor: 'I'd like to see the doctor, please.' '*Why?*' 'Well, I was hoping he'd help me change the tyres of the bloody car.'
Dave Allen

In the future we'll have 15 minutes of fame and 15 minutes of health care.
                                                                    Nicole Hollander

I suppose one has a greater sense of intellectual degradation after an interview with a doctor than from any human experience.   Alice James

My new doctor asked me for a list of the medications I take. He took one look at the list and said, 'Well, you look healthier in person than you do on paper.'
                                                                    Ed Green

What do doctors know? They practise medicine for 15 years and they still don't know to warm their hands before a breast examination.
                                                    Sophia Petrillo, *The Golden Girls*

I said, 'Doctor, every morning when I get up and look in the mirror I feel like throwing up. What's wrong with me?' He said, 'I don't know, but your eyesight's perfect.'
                                                                    Rodney Dangerfield

My doctor grabbed me by the wallet and said, 'Cough!'   Henny Youngman

I see your medical insurance covers little green pills, little yellow pills, little white pills, little red pills and little purple pills. What I'm going to give you are some little *orange* pills.   Sidney Harris

—How do you know which pills to take?
—Doesn't make any difference. Whatever they fix, I got.
                                        Oscar Madison and Felix Unger, *The Odd Couple*

A miracle drug is any drug that will do what the label says it will do.
                                                                    Eric Hodgins

A man's health can be judged by which he takes two at a time – pills or stairs.

Joan Welsh

On the plane was a *Time* magazine. There was a 30-page article about diabetes and I read every page. By the time that plane landed, I had diabetes.
Lewis Black

Victor's one of the few men that suffers from hot flushes. He's had them ever since he stumbled across the details one day in his medical encyclopaedia. Most people have a medical dictionary so that when they get something wrong with them they can find out what it is. With Victor it's the other way round. He looks up a disease and then develops the symptoms to fit it. Treats it more in the way of a Freeman's catalogue, really. Browsing through to see what he can die of next.
Margaret Meldrew, *One Foot in the Grave*

[*Reading a medical dictionary*] Colon tumour: offers no symptoms in the early stages – oh God, that's exactly what *I've* got!
Victor Meldrew, *One Foot in the Grave*

The trouble with being a hypochondriac these days is that antibiotics have cured all the good diseases.
Caskie Stinnett

Everyone has a body, and many, revelling in its disorders, really enjoy bad health. There are those who divide their lives into two parts – 'before my operation' and 'since my operation'.
Lord Hill

It's exactly 15 years today since my hysterectomy, but I don't like to dwell.
Mrs Merton

For each illness that doctors cure with medicine, they provoke ten in healthy people by inoculating them with the virus that is a thousand times more powerful than any microbe: the idea that one is ill.
Marcel Proust

Imaginary pains are by far the most real we suffer, since we feel a constant need for them and invent them because there is no way of doing without them.
E.M. Cioran

I don't want a flu jab. I like getting flu. It gives me something else to complain about.
David Letterman

—How are you feeling?
—Not too bad, apart from the agonising pain.
Doctor and Mrs Jones, *Victoria Wood – As Seen on TV*

The radiographer seems to think it is a spastic colon. All meals are followed by pain... One LONGS to be able to fart. I told Gordon Jackson and he said, 'Oh! My trouble is the desperate desire to BURP...'
Kenneth Williams

Nasty thing, prostates. My first husband had one. He said it was like trying to empty a hot water bottle with someone standing on the nozzle.
Meg, *One Foot in the Grave*

—What's grey, sits at the end of the bed and takes the piss?
—A kidney dialysis machine.
Anon

Mrs Berkeley has contributed nothing to the world except her constipation.
Dr Frederick C. Irving

Bowel troubles flaring up again. I've spent so much time in the bathroom, I'm thinking of sending out change of address cards.
Owen Newitt, *The Vicar of Dibley*

Stool softener is not a foam cushion.
Carl Maietta

Chronic constipation has gained for me an unrivalled knowledge of all laxatives, aperients, purgatives and cathartic compounds. At present I arrange two gunpowder plots a week. It's abominable. Best literature for the latrine: picture puzzles.
W.N.P. Barbellion

The enemas take some getting used to, but, in time, you'll learn to look forward to them, like an old friend with a cold nose.
Endymion Hart-Jones, *The Road to Wellville*

Piles are a Jewish man's affliction. Piles and mothers. What causes them?
Stephen Fry

My bowels are as regular as a Kennedy funeral.
Brian Potter, *Phoenix Nights*

There is no human activity, eating, sleeping, drinking or sex, which some doctor somewhere won't discover leads directly to cardiac arrest.

Sir John Mortimer

I think the worst time to have a heart attack is during a game of charades. Especially if your team-mates are bad guessers. The only time worse would be during a game of 'Fake Heart Attack' followed by naps.

Demetri Martin

What do you mean, heart attack? You've got to have a heart before you can have an attack. Billy Wilder, on Peter Sellers

A person seldom falls sick, but the bystanders are animated with a faint hope that he will die.

Ralph Waldo Emerson

Father always said laughter was the best medicine. I guess that's why so many of us died of tuberculosis.

Jack Handey

A Short History of Medicine...
2000 BC   Eat this root.
AD 1000   That root is heathen, don't eat it. Say this prayer.
AD 1850   That prayer is superstition, don't say it. Drink this potion.
AD 1940   That potion is snake oil, don't drink it. Take this pill.
AD 1985   That pill is ineffective, don't take it. Take this antibiotic.
AD 2000   That antibiotic is artificial, don't take it. Eat this root.   **Anon**

An osteopath is one who argues that all human ills are caused by the pressure of hard bone upon soft tissue. The proof of his theory is to be found in the heads of those who believe it.

H.L. Mencken

Holistic medicine: not taking any notice of one's doctor.   **Malcolm Burgess**

When it comes to homeopathy all I know is that if I'm in an accident, I want to hear sirens not wind chimes.

Sean Lock

When the pain is great enough, we will let anyone be a doctor.

Mignon McLaughlin

Isn't it a bit unnerving that doctors call what they do 'practice'? Steven Wright

My brother is the youngest member of the College of Physicians and Surgeons. And I wouldn't let him cut my nails. **Alan King**

I often say a great doctor kills more people than a great general.

Gottfried Wilhelm von Leibniz

What they say: 'Now, this mammogram won't hurt at all.' *What they are thinking*: 'Just pretend that your breast is caught in the freezer door.'

Marty McCullen

The specialist did these tests, pulled the leg every way imaginable, and then did some X-rays. After lengthy analysis he told me, 'Your knee is fucked.' **Julian Dicks**

I saw a specialist who asked me: 'Are you familiar with the phrase faecal impaction?' I said I think I saw that one with Glenn Close and Michael Douglas. **Bob Monkhouse**

A colonoscopy? Count your blessings. In the old days, they had to send a sketch-artist up there. **Charlie Harper, *Two and a Half Men***

The doctor says I have pre-cancer. Pre-cancer? Isn't that...like life?

Lorrie Moore, *Like Life*

When the doctor broke the news that I had cancer, I said, 'Tell me straight, doc, how long do I have?' He said, 'Ten...' I said, 'Ten what? Years, months, weeks?' He said, 'Nine, eight, seven...' **Bob Monkhouse**

You have cancer, I have asthma. We all have to die some time.

Mohannad Al-Fallouji, a doctor now struck off, to a patient

Professor Ellwell, you are the only man I know who can say 'malignant' the way other people say 'Bingo!'   **Doctor Praetorius**, *People Will Talk*

—Isn't treating patients why we become doctors?
—No, treating illnesses is why we become doctors. Treating patients is what makes most doctors miserable.
                                        Dr Foreman and Dr House, *House*

I'm thankful that no one on my kid's soccer team knows that I'm a doctor, because when the coach's kid broke his leg and people were shouting for a doctor, I was making a run for high score in Tetris on my cell phone.   **Jeff Brechlin**

My doctor once said to me, 'Do you think I'm here for the good of your health?'   **Bob Monkhouse**

He was one of those doctors who run their practice on the firm theory that 99 per cent of their patients are quacks.   **Peter de Vries**

Cancer can do many things to the human spirit but it can't make boring people interesting. A pensioner in a baseball cap showed us pictures of his diseased organs, speaking of them with a curious twinkle like they were his grown-up children in Canada.
                                        Rab C. Nesbitt, *A Stranger Here Myself*

My doctor told me, 'No more wine and women but sing all the songs you want.'
                                        Bob Monkhouse

If a lot of cures are suggested for a disease, it means that the disease is incurable.   **Anton Chekhov**

She had broken down the process of dying into five stages: anger, denial, bargaining, depression and acceptance. Sounds like a Jewish law firm.
                                        Davis Newman, *All That Jazz*

Never go to a dentist who's had his office soundproofed.   Milton Berle

The dentist is the estate agent of the medical world.   Simon Nye

Dentistry: once you sat in a chair, now you lie down on a sort of couch. Nastier for you, producing feelings of helplessness among the old and nervous, but nicer for him because he can sit down. A good textbook example of sod the patient.   Kingsley Amis

—What's the difference between a gynaecologist and a dentist?
—Teeth.   Jackie Martling

My sister-in-law, who is pregnant, told me the other day that she was afraid to bother her gynaecologist with questions for fear of 'getting on his wrong side'.   Nora Ephron

Randolph Churchill went into hospital...to have a lung removed. It was announced that the trouble was not 'malignant'... It was a typical triumph of modern science to find the only part of Randolph that was not malignant and remove it.   Evelyn Waugh

A trip to hospital is always a descent into the macabre. I have never trusted a place with shiny floors.   Terry Tempest Williams

WET FLOOR – This is Not an Instruction.
          Notice in the men's toilets, Leicester General Hospital

Hospitals are spending too much on art pieces and not enough on patient care. I suspect there are already enough unmade beds in hospitals to constitute an 'arty' presence.   Carol Thatcher

The NHS – much praised around the world...but never copied.
          Graeme Garden

In the good old days, you got ill, you were poor, you died. Today, everyone seems to think they have the right to be cured. Result of this sloppy socialist thinking? More poor people.
          Alan B'Stard, *New Statesman*

Anyone contemplating euthanasia would do better to be admitted to an NHS hospital: it saves having to travel abroad.   **Derek Annis**

I have investigated slaughter houses cleaner than some hospitals.
                                                    Professor Hugh Pennington, microbiologist

[*To a nurse*] Don't touch me! I don't know where you've been.
                                                    Basil Fawlty, *Fawlty Towers*

In every hospital, sooner or later, you're gonna get an enema. Some nurse will say, 'It's time for your enema, what are you here for?' 'I came to visit my sister-in-law.'   **Jackie Mason**

T.F. Bundy: Totally Fucked But Unfortunately Not Dead Yet.
                                                    Medical acronym

The NHS don't think of it as having lost a patient, more as having gained a bed.   **Doctor Flynn,** *Tlc*

Doctors think a lot of patients are cured who have simply quit in disgust.
                                                    Don Herold

I stopped taking the medicine because I prefer the original disease to the side effects.   **Sidney Harris**

An apple a day, if aimed straight, keeps the doctor away.   **P.G. Wodehouse**

DISABILITY

Is it fair to say there'd be a lot less litter in Britain if blind people were given pointed sticks?   **Adam Bloom**

—Did you hear about the blind circumciser?
—He got the sack.   **Anon**

I bought my grandmother a Seeing Eye dog. But he's a little sadistic. He does impressions of cars screeching to a halt.   **Larry Amoros**

I hear blind people are complaining that Seeing Eye dogs are expensive, difficult to train, and hard to get. I say, let 'em use midgets. They can use the work.   **Chris Rock**

—That guy over there – is he a midget?
—Yes, Ma.
—Thank God, I thought I was having another stroke.
                Sophia Petrillo and Dorothy Zbornak, *The Golden Girls*

My worst moment on radio came when I was interviewing two women – one who'd had a stroke and one who looked after the stroke victim – but unable to decide which was which.   **Gerry Anderson**

Blonde bombshell, Diana Dors, was approached, in a bar, by a vertically challenged lech who'd had one too many beers. 'I'd really like to fuck you!' he exclaimed. Without missing a beat, Diana replied, 'Well, if you do, and I ever find out about it...'   **Mark Morris**

I realised I was dyslexic when I went to a toga party dressed as a goat.
                                                        Marcus Brigstocke

I'm working with a clothing company for disabled adults. We do a T-shirt that says, 'If You Stare At Me Long Enough I'll Do A Trick'.
                                            Dame Tanni Grey-Thompson

She has 112 unpaid parking tickets – what do you expect from a woman who thinks a chocolate allergy entitles her to use a handicapped space?
                                                    Frasier Crane, *Frasier*

In California, handicapped parking is for women who are frigid.
                                                            Joan Rivers

DRUGS

Having a wonderful time. Wish I were here.

Tagline, *Postcards from the Edge*

The majority of humankind only enjoy life by forgetting that they
are alive.   **Count Maurice Maeterlinck**

It's great to be back. It's great to be anywhere.

Keith Richards, on tour with the Rolling Stones, 2003

I can remember my first wife's mother's telephone number, but I can't
remember what I said to you ten minutes ago.   **Ozzy Osbourne**

I hate people who think it's clever to take drugs – like customs officers.
Aren't they a bunch of bastards, all that finger up the arsehole, all day
long. They put a uniform on, for a job like that, can you imagine doing
that? 'Just off to work now, dear.' 'Have a nice day at the orifice.'

Jack Dee

—Spread!
—What d'you think you're gonna find up there, eh? A new striker for
Newcastle United?

Customs official and 'Oz' Osbourne, *Auf Wiedersehen, Pet*

There are drugs tests everywhere in sports now. Even the old guys who
play crown green bowls have been giving samples. They don't mean to…

Jasper Carrott

They kept Lance Armstrong's urine for a year. It was like a Chardonnay
by then.   **Robin Williams, on the champion cyclist**

Marijuana? It's harmless, really, unless you fashion it into a club and beat
somebody over the head with it.   **Bill Bailey**

Marijuana is self-punishing. It makes you acutely sensitive, and in this
world, what worse punishment could there be?   **P.J. O'Rourke**

The others had their drugs and booze. I had my women. I thought that was safer: you can't overdose on women.   **Bill Wyman**

All drugs of any interest to any moderately intelligent person in America are now illegal.   **Thomas Szasz**

Human drug mules smuggle cocaine into the country by swallowing it in the form of 'pellets'– condoms stuffed with drugs, which they then pass by taking laxatives. Why would I want to shove something up my nose that's already been through someone else's digestive system? **Mark Collins**

Drugs, eh? What's the point? They make you forget, make you talk funny, make you see things that aren't there. My old grandma got all of that for free when she had a stroke.   **DCI Gene Hunt, *Life on Mars***

I was high on life, but eventually I built up a tolerance.   **Arj Barker**

ADDICTION

Hi, my name is Barry and I check my email two to three hundred times a day.   **David Sipress**

Sudokuku: addicted to filling in numbers in little grids.   **Pam Sweeney**

If addiction is judged by how long a dumb animal will sit pressing a lever to get a 'fix' of something, to its own detriment, then I would conclude that Netnews is far more addictive than cocaine.   **Rob Stampfli**

It's not inevitable that you'll turn from a hobby to a habit. No more than boiling an egg and swearing turns you into a celebrity chef.   **Mike Gunn**

Every form of addiction is bad, no matter whether the narcotic be alcohol or morphine or idealism.   **Carl Jung**

America is addicted to oil.   **George W. Bush**

I used to be a food addict, but I switched to alcohol. It's a much better addiction because you can drink enough to forget you're a drunk. You can't eat enough to forget you're fat. **Basil White**

Drink and sex killed my father. He couldn't get either so he shot himself.
Dusty Young

ALCOHOL

Well, well, Candy Pruitt, as I live and drink!   **Karen Walker, *Will and Grace***

—Get me a vodka rocks.
—Mom, it's breakfast.
—…and a piece of toast.   **Lucille and Michael, *Switch Hitter***

You can either watch me drink or you can join me. One of them is more fun.   **Alan Swann, *My Favorite Year***

'Booze make you sad. It makes you depressed. It makes you cry. It gives you headaches. Makes you bad-tempered. Makes you want to shoot your wife. Makes you miss. Gives you double vision. Shakes. Destroys your stomach lining. Kills your liver. Causes hardening of the arteries. And total destruction of the brain cells.' 'Then why do you drink it?' 'For pleasure – what else?'   **Dave Allen**

Alcohol is the anaesthesia by which we endure the operation of life.
George Bernard Shaw

—What would you say to a cold one, Norm?
—See you later, Vera, I'm going to Cheers.   **Woody Boyd and Norm Peterson, *Cheers***

I don't use this pub, it's too piss cute, with its baseball artefacts on the walls and its designer bar staff forever running their hands through their hair like any minute now those smug cunts from *Friends* will run in and they'll all have a big bonding hug. It still goes against the grain for us to call a pub a 'bar' and I'd sooner cut my paw off than high-five anybody.

Rab C. Nesbitt, *A Stranger Here Myself*

Homer, lighten up. You're making 'Happy Hour' bitterly ironic.

Marge Simpson, *The Simpsons*

Is Anybody Ever Really Happy Hour 6–7

Sign in window of bar, David Sipress

Most people hate the taste of beer to begin with. It is however a prejudice many have been able to overcome.   Winston Churchill

Real ale fans are just like trainspotters, only drunk.   Christopher Howse

—What's the difference between London beer and making love in a punt?
—They're both fucking close to water.   Victor Lewis-Smith

Gin makes you say things like, 'Nobody likes my shoes! I made...I made 50 fucking vol-au-vents, and not one of you...not *one* of you... said thank you.' And my favourite: 'Everybody, shut up. Shut up! This song is all about me.'   Dylan Moran

Brandy: a cordial composed of one part thunder-and-lightning, one part remorse, two parts bloody murder, one part death-hell-and-the-grave and four parts clarified Satan.   Ambrose Bierce

A clear white local fluid in which toasts are drunk, *mao-tai* has the same effect as inserting your head into a cupboard and asking a large male friend to slam the door.   Clive James

—Refill?
—Does the Pope shit in the woods?

Jackie Treehorn and The Dude, *The Big Lebowski*

I distrust a man that says 'when'. If he's got to be careful not to drink too much, it's because he's not to be trusted when he does.

Kasper Gutman, *The Maltese Falcon*

I saw a wino. He was eating grapes. I was like, 'Dude, you have to wait.'

Mitch Hedberg

When ordering wine, it is wrong to do what everyone else does – namely, to hold the wine list just out of sight, look for the second cheapest claret on the list, and say, 'Number 22, please.'

Stephen Potter

What wine goes with mood stabilisers?

Will Truman, *Will and Grace*

—This wine tastes like the back of a fucking LA school bus. Now they probably didn't de-stem, hoping for some semblance of concentration, crushed it up with leaves and mice, and then wound up with this rancid tar and turpentine bullshit.
—Tastes pretty good to me.

Miles Raymond and Jack, *Sideways*

Alan Clark could detect a bogus Bellini at 50 paces and a bottle blonde at 100 yards.

Boris Johnson

Last week I had to offer my publisher a bottle that was far too good for him, simply because there was nothing between the insulting and the superlative.

A.J. Liebling

Appreciating old wine is like making love to a very old lady. It is possible. It can even be enjoyable. But it requires a bit of imagination.

André Tchelistcheff

I recently discovered the appropriate word for the modern brand of telly wine bores. You know, the ones who insist on telling us that 'I can smell wet nappies in there and burned toast and newly mown grass and creosote and Sunday newspapers'. What better name for such a pretentious group of plonk experts than 'plonkers'?

Victor Lewis-Smith

DRUNK & HANGOVER

Richard Burton once said that the first thing he asked each morning was, 'Who do I send flowers to?' – on the basis that he was bound to have behaved abominably the previous evening.   Emer O'Kelly

I was at one of those student parties – the ones where you wake up still drunk with a strange pair of feet wrapped round your head. It wasn't till I got up to leave that I realised they were mine.   Sean Hughes

I can't think of anything worse after a night of drinking than waking up next to someone and not being able to remember their name, or how you met, or why they're dead.   Laura Kightlinger

I had one too many of those nights where you drink so much you wake up the next morning and you can't get the toothpaste to foam.

Margaret Smith

Kingsley Amis once recommended sex as a cure for a hangover, which must be the case, because if I thought Kingsley Amis was going to make love to me, I'd certainly avoid getting drunk in the first place.

Joseph O'Connor

Pink elephants take aspirin to get rid of W.C. Fields.   Charlie McCarthy

I never got hangovers because I never sobered up.   Clarissa Dickson-Wright

Every time my friend Pat Green leaves a bar, he always asks himself the same question: 'Can I puke in a straight line?'   Kinky Friedman

I am as drunk as a lord, but then, I am one, so what does it matter?

Bertrand Russell

You know that kind of drunk when you're a drink away from yelling 'Faggot' or being one.   Dave Attell

Esplanade: to attempt an explanation while drunk.   Kevin Mellema

Alcopops really sums up my drinking problem – not the drink, it's the
nickname my kids had for me.   Jack Dee

—What's up, Mr Peterson?
—The warranty on my liver.   Woody Boyd and Norm Peterson, *Cheers*

But a man shouldn't fool with booze until he's 50; then he's a damn fool
if he doesn't.   William Faulkner

You guys made a lot of bad decisions because you were drunk. I *wish* I
could blame alcohol. I'm just a fucking asshole.   Louie, *Lucky Louie*

TEETOTAL

My ol' man was tough. He allowed no drinking in the house. I had two
brothers who died of thirst.   Rodney Dangerfield

Some years ago a couple of friends of mine stopped drinking suddenly
and died in agony. I swore then that such a thing should never happen
to me.   John Barrymore

—You've given up drinking before.
—Worst eight hours of my life!
                          Edina Monsoon and Patsy Stone, *Absolutely Fabulous*

I distrust camels and anyone else who can go a week without a drink. Joe E. Lewis

I am now starting to realise how the world's non-drinkers such as
President Bush are such dangerous men. The truth is that sobriety can go
to your head just as certainly as alcohol.
                          Peter Oborne, on giving up alcohol for a month

The fact that you don't drink at all is the greatest advertisement for
drunkenness I know.   **Harry Dawes,** *The Barefoot Contessa*

SMOKING

Pull out a Monte Cristo at a dinner party and the political liberal turns
into the nicotine fascist.   **Martyn Harris**

It should not be an act of social disobedience to light a cigarette – unless
you're actually a doctor working at an incubator.   **Dylan Moran**

Kids don't smoke because a camel in sunglasses tells them to. They smoke
for the same reasons adults do, because it's an enjoyable activity that
relieves anxiety and depression.   **George Carlin**

I smoke for my mental health. Tobacco gives you little pauses, a rest
from life. I don't suppose anyone smoking a pipe would have road rage,
would they?   **David Hockney**

—Don't you know that smoking kills?
—Yes, and I've been meaning to ask: when the smokers are all dead, who
will you annoy then?   **Interviewer and Tom Kreitzberg**

The worst kind of non-smokers are the ones that come up to you and
cough. That's pretty fucking cruel, isn't it? Do you go up to cripples and
dance too?   **Bill Hicks**

—First, no smoking in bars. What's next, no fucking in bars?
—Well, first, there would have to be a no-fucking section.
          Samantha Jones and Miranda Hobbes, *Sex and the City*

They say if you smoke you knock off ten years. But it's the last ten.
What do you miss? The drooling years?   **John Mendoza**

Give up smoking by sticking one cigarette from each new pack up a fat friend's arse, filter first, then replacing it in the box. The possibility of putting that one in your mouth will put you off smoking any of them.

Viz magazine

I quit smoking recently because I wanna live. And now I've quit smoking, I don't wanna live any more. I don't feel healthier. My clothes don't smell like cigarette smoke, that's a big plus. They smell a lot like Scotch and marijuana.

Gregg Rogell

He had quit once in Rome, for seven hours after breakfast, during the last two of which his wife was begging him to take it up again.

John Berryman

I have no objection to people smoking on my premises. It's good for business.

Alan Puxley, undertaker

I've stopped smoking. Why should I pay someone else to kill me?

Dave Allen

FOOD & DRINK
– GENERAL

—You are what you eat.
—Robbie, give your father his order of miserable bastard.

Frank and Marie Barone, *Everybody Loves Raymond*

At dinner, the tension was so thick you could cut it with a knife – which is more than I can say for the liver.

Eugene Jerome, *Brighton Beach Memories*

I didn't squawk about the steak, dear. I merely said I didn't see that old horse that used to be tethered outside.

W.C. Fields

Eww... this is what Evil must taste like.

Phoebe Buffay, *Friends*

—I may pop by later with some of my mother's drop scones.
—Good, we can build a rockery.

> Nick Swainey and Victor Meldrew, *One Foot in the Grave*

I once cut my mouth on my wife's soup.

Milton Berle

I would like to find a stew that will give me heartburn immediately, instead of at 3 o'clock in the morning.

John Barrymore

I'm so full of acid that I could etch a plate with my water.

Sir Lionel Lindsay

Next time you feel desperate for an egg, lad, pause, and remember where it came from. The world's full of nasty places, Granville.

Albert Arkwright, *Open All Hours*

In my experience, the dominant smell at most barbecues is sizzling human flesh, after a drunken guest decides to pour a can of petrol over the coals 'to get it going', and ends up wondering why they now look like Simon Weston.

Victor Lewis-Smith

I'm a man. Men cook outside. Women make the three-bean salad. That's the way it's always been.

William Geist

Is this the steak or the charcoal?

Bill Hoest

Pick up your pants, Grandpa. That's not how you put out a barbecue.

David Letterman

You can't barbecue in New York. You'd have to keep vacuuming the meat.

Rhoda Morgenstern, *Rhoda*

If ever the sun rises upon Barbecue, its flavour vanishes like Cinderella's silks, and it becomes cold baked beef – staler in the chill dawn than illicit love.

William Allen White

Think of the man who first tried German sausage.   Jerome K. Jerome

The proper way to cook cockatoo is to put the bird and an axe head into a billy. Boil them until the axe head is soft. The cockatoo is then ready to eat.   **Old Australian cookbook**

—Try some of this 'Scheese' – it's animal-free, dairy-free, lactose-free, gluten-free vegan cheese.
—I'll smell it, but I don't want to eat it.
—No wonder you don't pull much any more.
     Jonathan Ross and Graham Norton

—I liked it, Mom. Tasted kind of like chicken.
—It was chicken.   **Tommy and Mary Woodry**, *The Window*

You know an odd feeling? Sitting on the toilet eating a chocolate candy bar.   **George Carlin**

Some people pretend to like capers, but the truth is that any dish that tastes good with capers in it, tastes even better with capers not in it.**Nora Ephron**

I have a nut allergy. At school, the other kids used to push me up against the wall and make me play Russian roulette by force-feeding me a bag of Revels.   **Milton Jones**

Allergies? Well, I'm not good on strawberries. Come out in a bit of a rash. The worst one though is Marmite. Only got to smell the stuff and I start voting Conservative.   **Stephen Fry**, *A Bit of Fry and Laurie*

I do not like broccoli. And I haven't liked it since I was a little kid and my mother made me eat it. I'm President of the United States, and I'm not going to eat any more broccoli.   **George Bush**

Broccoli is one of the deadliest plants on earth. It tries to warn you itself with its terrible taste.   **Dr Hibbert**, *The Simpsons*

The first courgette I ever saw I killed it with a hoe.   **John Gould**

I am very fond of mushrooms. Often I go out into the country and gather a whole basketful. I carry them part of the way home; then I throw them away.   Stephen Leacock

Cabbage she serves me. In ten minutes I could be sky-writing.
Sophia Petrillo, *The Golden Girls*

Cauliflower is nothing but cabbage with a college education.   Mark Twain

Gave up spinach for Lent.   F. Scott Fitzgerald

Parsley is gharsley.   Ogden Nash

The durian is a melon-like fruit with a yellow, pudding-textured flesh, its odour is best described as pig shit, turpentine, and onions garnished with a dirty gym sock... It is forbidden to eat durian on the subway in Singapore.   Richard Sterling

Eating of the flesh of the durian was not much different from having to consume used surgical swabs.   Alan Davidson

Clams: I simply cannot imagine why anyone would eat something slimy served in an ashtray.   Miss Piggy

Dr Buckland used to say that he had eaten his way straight through the whole animal creation, and that there was one thing worse than a mole, and that was a blue-bottle fly.   Augustus Hare

It doesn't matter who you are, or what you've done, or think you can do. There's a confrontation with destiny awaiting you. Somewhere there is a chilli you cannot eat.   Daniel Pinkwater

Chilli represents your three stages of matter: solid, liquid, and eventually gas.   Dan Conner, *Roseanne*

What's the difference between a Brussel sprout and a bogey? You can't get kids to eat a Brussel sprout.

Anon

Who says he's not gettin' his five fruit and veg a day? Ketchup's made of tomatoes.

Les Battersby, *Coronation Street*

When I was a kid, my dad used to say to me, 'Eat your peas. It'll put hair on your chest.' I'm five. I'm Italian. I already have hair on my chest.

Maria Menozzi

Flo went over to her sister's yesterday. I hate having to get my own meals. All that looking through Yellow Pages, dialling and opening doors for delivery boys.

Andy Capp

I like my marshmallows like my men – crispy on the outside and stuck to the end of a fork.

Roseanne

The only thing I ever got from a fondu is a third-degree burn in the gob.

Terry Wogan

—Water?
—It's a mixer, Patsy. We have it with whisky.

Patsy Stone and Edina Monsoon, *Absolutely Fabulous*

Tea is not a Cossack drink.

Alexander Pushkin

Garlic is the ketchup of intellectuals.

Anon

Oregano makes everything taste like pizza. Saffron makes everything taste bright yellow. Parsley, sage, rosemary and thyme make lamb taste like Simon and Garfunkel records.

P.J. O'Rourke

A dessert without cheese is like a beautiful woman with only one eye.

Anthelme Brillat-Savarin

An apple is a spherical object created by 32 chemical products, then dipped in wax, then gassed. In the long run an apple is as likely to bring on a doctor as to keep one away.   John Ralston Saul

Organic food is a rip-off. I reckon what supermarkets do is get all the old unsold, non-organic veg, wait till it goes mouldy and rotten, then put it in the organic section and charge us double.   Carol McGiffin

I have often wondered what goes into a hot dog. Now I know and I wish I didn't.   William Zinsser

The better a pie tastes, the worse it is for you.   Edgar Howe

The food at Ian Fleming's was so abominable that I used to cross myself before I took a mouthful. I used to say, 'Ian, it tastes like armpits.'
                                                              Noël Coward

My mother is famous in our family for favouring a kill-by rather a sell-by date.
                                                              Ruth Watson

Cockroaches and socialites are the only things that can stay up all night and eat anything.   Herb Caen

A.A. Gill says that dogs cannot tell the difference between foie gras and Chappie...but I have discovered something much more interesting: most people cannot tell the difference between foie gras and Chappie.
    Consequently, the Millses' traditional Boxing Day party was the cheapest one in years.   Mrs Mills

The French'll eat anything. Over here, My Little Pony is a toy. Over there, it's a starter.   Paul Merton

The food in Yugoslavia is either very good or very bad. One day they served us fried chains.   Mel Brooks

German food is so bad, even Hitler was a vegetarian. 'Would you like some more shtrudleghraf on your shamlw?' How appetising does that sound?   **Dylan Moran**

Rumanian-Yiddish cooking has killed more Jews than Hitler.   **Zero Mostel**

If you can't recognise what you're eating, wait until you finish it before asking what it is. You'll enjoy it more.   **Richard Sterling**

Beware the term 'local delicacy'. It's usually code for something revolting.
Lillian Marsano

Malta is the only place in the world where the local delicacy is the bread.
Alan Coren

Greek food is always better outside Greece than inside it.   David Dale

A taco is not a living thing – until a few hours after you've eaten it.
Nathan Lane

There's only one secret to bachelor cooking – not caring how it tastes.
P.J. O'Rourke

A recipe is a series of step-by-step instructions for preparing ingredients you forgot to buy in utensils you don't own to make a dish the dog won't eat the rest of.   **Henry Beard**

Skid Road Stroganoff: add the flour, salt, paprika and mushrooms, stir, and let cook for five minutes while you light a cigarette and stare sullenly at the sink.   **Peg Bracken**

Emergency tomato soup: made with hot water and ketchup.   **P.J. O'Rourke**

Don't take any recipe on faith. There are some hostile recipes in this world.   **Peg Bracken**

A recipe my dear old mother gave me for those frequent evenings when you can't think what to give your returning-home-from-work husband for his supper: 'Give the bugger an egg,' she used to say.   Lady Cudlipp

Luckily for him, the average Englishman has no culinary sense at all. His palate is burned by tobacco, cocktails and whisky, and cannot appreciate fine savoury sauces.   *L'Epoque* magazine

Toast-making is like nose-picking: it's best if you do it yourself.   Anon

VEGETARIAN

Hitler was a vegetarian. It's a cautionary tale: in large doses, it can cause genocide.   Bill Bailey

Meat is murder but fish is justifiable homicide.   Jeremy Hardy

Most vegetarians I ever saw looked enough like their food to be classed as cannibals.   Finley Peter Dunne

If you're slower than me, stupider than me and you taste good... tough shit.   Anthony Bourdain

I'm a post-modern vegetarian. I eat meat ironically.   Bill Bailey

Recognise meat for what it really is: the antibiotic-and-pesticide-laden corpse of a tortured animal.   Ingrid Newkirk

Why do so many vegans, some of whom eschew the very idea of meat with a jihad-like fervour, try to create all these bastardised products that are supposed to be like meat?   Chuck Taggart

Tasting some of the faux-meat products, I tend to think they're manufactured by people in the meat industry to try and make vegetarians recant.

Casey

If slaughterhouses had glass walls, everyone would be a vegetarian.

Sir Paul McCartney

RESTAURANT

I never eat in a restaurant that's over a hundred feet off the ground and won't stand still.

Calvin Trillin

The disparity between a restaurant's price and food quality rises in direct proportion to the size of the pepper mill.

Bryan Miller

Bring the one you love. It's too good for the husband.

Slogan of Memsahib Indian restaurant, London

The key to a successful restaurant is dressing girls in degrading clothes.

Michael O'Donoghue

Sadly Maris won't be joining us at Orsini's. She had a bad experience there one Christmas Eve. The Italian soccer team was at the next table. Maris announced she was in the mood for a goose, and, perhaps inevitably, tragedy occurred.

Niles Crane, Frasier

What would you recommend to a family that's not sure they should be here?

Marge Simpson, to the waiter in a sushi bar, The Simpsons

Japanese food is very pretty and undoubtedly a suitable cuisine for Japan, which is largely populated by people of below average size. Hostesses hell-bent on serving such food to Occidentals would be well advised to supplement it with something more substantial and to keep in mind that almost everyone likes French fries.

Fran Lebowitz

Why doesn't someone go to the bathroom? It always makes the food come.   Carol Bennett, *Divine Secrets of the Ya-Ya Sisterhood*

Avoid any restaurant where a waiter arrives with a handful of knives and forks just as you reach the punchline of your best story and says, 'Which of you is having the fish?'   **Sir John Mortimer**

Hey, I asked for ketchup! I'm eating salad here!   **Homer Simpson**

—How was your roast woodcock?
—Too much wood, too little cock!   **Waiter and Noël Coward**

[*Waiter to diners*] Can I bring you something else to complain about?
                   David Sipress

—I found this in my food. It's a cockroach.
—Listen. With paella, ingredients vary from place to place.
                   Malcolm Gluck and waiter, in a New York restaurant

G.K. Chesterton once said that all dining out begins with fear of the waiter... In London, dining out begins with fear of the waiter and ends with the same feeling.   **Tom Baker, *Who On Earth is Tom Baker?***

In Jewish restaurants the waiter is always right.   Maureen Lipman

The Fashion Café in London is the worst restaurant that I have ever reviewed... I didn't put a single thing in my mouth twice. It all went back.   **A.A. Gill**

The best way to launch an Italian restaurant is to have it raided because the Mafia eats there. Everybody knows they eat well.   **Mario Puzo**

—Do you know where there's a good Korean restaurant?
—Korea?   **Jean Pargeter and Lionel Hardcastle, *As Time Goes By***

Eating food with a knife and fork is like making love through an interpreter.

Anon

I had calves' liver with sauté mushrooms. I've always wondered what it would be like to eat a baby. I think it would taste like this.

Gail Greene

Slow-baked cheese-and-onion tart – snot in a box. Grilled kipper – smoked postman's Odor Eater. Battered saveloy – a thing that only specialist medical staff handle, with rubber gloves.

A.A. Gill, on the Langley, London

Once a man next to me found the handle of a radiator in his mashed potato; he said nothing, merely moving it to the side of his plate after sucking the mashed potato off it first. Nobody else said anything either. If the truth was known several of us were probably jealous.

Tom Baker, on army food, *Who on Earth is Tom Baker?*

The baklava tasted like balaclava.

Victor Lewis-Smith

—The chef sent it over with his compliments.
—I wonder what his insults are like.

Martin and Frasier Crane, *Frasier*

My cooking is Modern Scottish – if you complain you get headbutted.

Chris Bradley, chef of Michelin-starred Mr Underhill's restaurant

I've got Gordon Ramsay's new book, *Take Two Eggs and Fuck Off*.

Jack Dee

M. Bourgignon, our *chef saucier*, told me that by the time a cook is 40 he is either dead or crazy.

David Ogilvy

Anthony Worrall Thompson once banned Michael Winner from all his restaurants, and placed a picture of Winner's face on his toilet seat.

David Rowan

Somebody said to me the other day, 'Shall we eat or have a McDonald's?'

Dave Allen

A Big Mac: the communion wafer of consumerism.   John Ralston Saul

Do you want lies with that?

Tagline, *Fast Food Nation*,
a film examining the health risks of the fast-food industry

McDonald's breakfast for under a dollar is actually more expensive than that. You have to factor in the cost of bypass surgery.   George Carlin

A woman went into a McDonald's in California, ordered a salad, and found a rat in it. It was the healthiest thing in the salad.   David Letterman

Fitness magazine has come out with a list of the healthiest foods to eat at McDonald's. Number one on the list is a stack of napkins.   Conan O'Brien

Eating salad at McDonald's is like going to a porn club and reading the Bible.   Dave Hughes

Having KFC is like porn. It feels good while you do it, but you feel dirty afterwards, and your hands are all sticky.   Dave Hughes

New York City has banned trans fats from fast foods. Don't worry, you can still get E-coli.   David Letterman

I met my future husband at Starbucks. Not at the same Starbucks; we saw each other at different Starbucks across the street from each other.

Meg Swan, *Best in Show*

—I'll have the French roast coffee, with three shots of espresso.
—The Defibrillator?

Niles Crane and Daphne Moon, *Frasier*

Motorway service-station snacks are very expensive. You get a cup of tea and a banana, go up to the counter and say to the woman, 'Sorry, I've only got a ten-pound note.' And she says, 'Well, you'll have to put that banana back then.'   Linda Smith

I ate the most expensive meal of my life today: breakfast at the airport.

Elayne Boosler

Restaurants have this in common with ladies: the best are often not the most enjoyable, nor the grandest the most friendly, and the pleasures of the evening are frequently spoiled by the final writing of an exorbitant cheque.   **Sir John Mortimer**

WEIGHT

—So, what brought you to Miami?
—My guess is, a small barge.
                              Dorothy Zbornak and Sophia Petrillo, *The Golden Girls*

My, she's a big woman. She has a job with British Airways. Kick-starting Boeings.   **Les Dawson**

And what a bra! She hung it on the line to dry and a camel made love to it.   **Les Dawson**

She was so fat, when she bent down in Liverpool they had an eclipse in Bournemouth.   **Les Dawson**

Her calves are so fat, they moo.   **Joan Rivers**

She could model car covers.   **Sophia Petrillo**, *The Golden Girls*

Two guys could fuck her at the same time and still never meet.
                                          Gigi Cestone, *The Sopranos*

Some men climb mountains; others date 'em.
                                                  Louie De Palma, *Taxi*

Bottoms are our natural enemy. They follow us around our entire lives, right behind us, and constantly growing. How do they do that? I'm sure mine's back there now, secretly snacking.   **Sally Harper**, *Coupling*

It's easy to distract fat people. It's a piece of cake.　　　Chris Addison

I don't have a waist. I've just got a sort of place a bit like an unmarked level-crossing.　　　Victoria Wood

Her bathtub has stretchmarks.　　　Rodney Dangerfield

Flabbergasted: appalled over how much weight you have gained.　　　Michelle Feeley

If you really want to be depressed, weigh yourself in grams.　　　Jason Love

Chin up, darling…both of them.　　　Lola Brewster, *The Mirror Crack'd*

He's gigantic! You could show a movie on his back.　　Daphne Moon, *Frasier*

I don't want to suggest that he's large, but when he was a kid, he could only play 'seek'.
Spencer Christian

When you have a fat friend there are no see-saws. Only catapults.　　　Demetri Martin

I can practically *hear* you getting fatter.　　　Richard Hayden, *Tommy Boy*

One day I was out jogging, listening to my iPod. Photo of me in the *Sun* the next day. Headline: 'iPodge'.　　　Ricky Gervais

Did you see his butt? You could park a car in the shadow of his ass.　　　Thelma Dickinson, *Thelma and Louise*

I'm not fat. I'm festively plump.　　　Eric Cartman, *South Park*

I hear they're going to tear you down and put up an office building where you're standing.　　　Groucho Marx, *Duck Soup*

Dawn French and I are both fat, but we're not in the same category. There are many other things in between. Some of them have to go back into the sea. Some of them have to be shot from helicopters with tranquilliser darts. **Ricky Gervais**

A cannibal king, beholding them, would have whooped with joy and reached for his knife and fork with the feeling that for once, the catering department had not failed him. **P.G. Wodehouse**

Fat grown-ups may be jolly, but fat children stare at you malevolently in every public place. **Mignon McLaughlin**

DIET

If you can't control your peanut butter, you can't expect to control your life. **Bill Watterson**

What would Kirstie Alley do? **David Letterman**

She went on one of those exercise shows on television. She started jumping up and down, and my TV fell off the stand. **Rodney Dangerfield**

TV cameras seem to add 10 pounds to me. So I make it a policy never to eat TV cameras. **Kitty Carlisle**

I'm one stomach-flu away from reaching my goal weight.

Emily Blunt, *The Devil Wears Prada*

Quiet, I'm ordering me dinner...one lettuce leaf, a grated carrot, three lightly boiled peas and a nut... Better cut that nut in half. We mustn't go mad. **Tony Hancock**, *Hancock's Half Hour*

Dieting can be hazardous! Take Oprah Winfrey, you never quite know where you are with her. I was fiddling with the horizontal hold for ages one week till I realised she'd put on three stones since the week before.

Mrs Merton

I'm glad you're going to be photographing me on the new movie, Jack. Don't worry about this fat round my middle. I'll fuck it off in three days.

Errol Flynn, to Jack Cardiff, cinematographer

According to a new report, you can lose 200 calories having sex. Hell, I burn up 200 calories just trying to get the safety cap off the Viagra.

David Letterman

How did I lose all this weight? I did it the old-fashioned way: laxatives and smokes.

Kim Craig, *Kath & Kim*

I know I'll never have a weight problem. You know why? First morning I wake up and can't see my dick? I STOP EATING.

Denis Leary

Doughnut manufacturers announced this week they are starting to develop healthy doughnuts. Doughnuts with more natural ingredients and no trans fats. This is like gun-makers coming out with bullets that contain eight essential vitamins.

Conan O'Brien

American consumers have no problem with carcinogens, but they will not purchase any product, including floor wax, that has fat in it.

Dave Barry

I hate mineral water freaks. Drink from the tap and take what's coming to you.

Ralph Steadman

I've just lost 250 pounds of unsightly fat. I got divorced.

Alison Long

EXERCISE

I'm bad at exercising. I once joined a gym but the smell was so appalling I had to be taken outside.

Bill Nighy

You can't go to a public pool and splash around any more. Everyone is swimming laps now. Some guy jumped in behind me and said, 'How long you gonna be using this lane?' And I said, 'Until my bladder's empty.'

Tommy Sledge

This morning, I rode the exercise bike for an hour and a half. If it was a real bicycle I would have been in Belgium by now.

C.J. Cregg, *The West Wing*

I think anyone who comes upon a Nautilus machine suddenly will agree with me that its prototype was clearly invented at some time in history when torture was considered a reasonable alternative to diplomacy.

Anna Quindlen

The word 'aerobics' comes from two Greek words: 'aero', meaning 'ability to', and 'bics', meaning 'withstand tremendous boredom'.

Dave Barry

In my day, we didn't do all this keep fit. We got our exercise lowering coffins out of upstairs windows.

Old bag, *Victoria Wood – As Seen on TV*

My friend called on his sister and found her standing on her head. 'The trouble with doing yoga exercises at home,' she said, 'is you're forever seeing a lot of places you forgot to dust.'

H. Peplow

Jogging is an urban sport whose principal long-term effect is to cripple middle- and upper middle-class professionals. Enthusiasts include orthopaedic surgeons and running-shoe manufacturers.   John Ralston Saul

Joggers are people who really believe that they can recapture their youth by taking exercise. The brutal facts suggest that unless you have never lost your youth, and have been taking exercise all the time, then trying to get fit will kill you as surely as a horse-kick to the heart.   Clive James

The beneficent effects of the regular quarter-hour's exercise before breakfast is more than offset by the mental wear and tear in getting out of bed fifteen minutes earlier than one otherwise would.   Simeon Strunsky

Exercise is bunk. If you are healthy you don't need it, if you are sick you shouldn't take it.   Henry Ford

People seem to think there is something inherently noble and virtuous in the desire to go for a walk.   Max Beerbohm

I like long walks, especially when they are taken by people who annoy me.   Fred Allen

Health nuts are going to feel stupid someday, lying in hospital dying of nothing.   Redd Foxx

—Your body is the only home you'll ever have.
—Yes, my home is pretty messy. But I have a woman who comes in once a week.   Mr Universe and Johnny Carson, *The Johnny Carson Show*

YOUTH

I hate the young, and particularly the fact that they have so much time on their hands. Still, the consolation is that they'll never be able to afford a house.   James Delingpole

The only thing I envy about young people is their livers.   Brendan Behan

—I have underpants older than her.
—Thanks for that image.   DC Terry Perkins and DC Jo Masters, *The Bill*

—What is it with kids these days? If they're not cracking your skull open for pleasure and profit they're vandalising your back wall, and shoving bottles of urine through your letter box.
—Shoving *what* through the letter box? That was a free sample of Lucozade.   Margaret and Victor Meldrew, *One Foot in the Grave*

There's nothing wrong with the younger generation that becoming taxpayers won't cure.   Dan Bennett

AGE & AGEING

We're adults. When did this happen? And how do we make it stop?
     Meredith Grey, *Grey's Anatomy*

You know you're not a kid any more when you can live without sex but not without your glasses.   Jeff Foxworthy

I found my first grey hair the other day. It was in a kebab, but there you go.   Jeff Green

It's a downhill slope to gum disease, wheelchair rides and death.
     Sue Townsend

Yeah, you never forget that trip to the doctor, do you? The day he says, 'There's nothing I can do for you, you're just getting old, sport.'
     Martin Crane, *Frasier*

[*Doctor to elderly patient*] Is your body actually two write-offs welded together?   'Matt', cartoon, Matt Pritchett

When he turned 50, Bob Geldof went off to have his prostate checked because he kept reading he should. ('Fucking finger up the arse, I can do without that again.') Apart from that, he isn't finding ageing difficult and actually welcomes the idea of death as a form of oblivion.   Barbara Ellen

I'm 52 but I prefer to think of myself as 11 centigrade.   Jeremy Bernstein

I've got four daughters – one who's older than me.
Des O'Connor

He was pushing 50 – back from the wrong side; the sort of age when evenings are passed in contemplation of one's pension and spending it on coach tours of the bulbs fields in Holland, a lifetime subscription to *The Oldie* and a bulk purchase of tartan slippers.

Nick Shannon, *The Money Race*

Surrounded by men in tartan trousers and bifocals and women whose last orgasm coincided with the Suez crisis, it was like being in the waiting room for heaven.   Gareth McLean

It is said that at the age of 55 each man becomes what he most despised at the age of 25. I live in constant fear lest I become a badly organised trip to Bournemouth.   Simon Munnery

—Does it ever occur to you that age brings wisdom and greater confidence?
—Age just brings you more to shave.

Susan Walker and Jane Christie, *Coupling*

I am only about eight hours a week away from looking like a bag lady, with the frizzled flyaway grey hair I would probably have if I stopped dyeing mine; with a pot belly I would definitely develop if I ate just half of what I think about eating every day; with the dirty nails and chapped lips and moustache and bushy eyebrows that would be my destiny if I ever spent two weeks on a desert island.   Nora Ephron

I've started to use my left breast as a bath plug.   **Joan Rivers**

On a recent train journey, I asked the ticket inspector if he would like to see my senior rail card, to which he replied: 'No, thank you, sir, that won't be necessary.'   **George Pratt**

You know you're getting older when you're more attractive hanging upside down.   **Cathy Ladman**

101 Ways to Stay Looking Young. No. 102: Iron your face.   **Tom Witte**

Anti-wrinkle cream there may be, but anti-fat-bastard cream there is not.
                    Dave, *The Full Monty*

I'm disgusted by the way old people are depicted on television. We are not all vibrant, fun-loving sex maniacs. Many of us are bitter, resentful individuals, who remember the good old days, when entertainment was bland and inoffensive.   **Grampa Simpson, *The Simpsons***

Joan Bakewell is still dubbed the thinking man's crumpet even if she has been in the bread bin a while.   **Patrick Kidd**

Nobody hears old people complain because people think that's all old people do. And that's because old people are gnarled and sagged and twisted into the shape of a complaint.   **Edward Albee**

I based the 'Old Woman' character in my sketch show on someone in an old people's home. I went there as a drama student to entertain the old folks. As I was singing 'Don't Sit Under The Apple Tree', this old woman shouted, ''Ere, is she gonna stand in front of the telly all day?'
                    Catherine Tate

The British loathe the middle-aged and I await rediscovery at 65, when one is too old to be in anyone's way.   **Sir Roy Strong, 1988**

Chatting with some children at the primary school where I am a volunteer, I was asked my age. When I told them I was 72, one child asked, 'Are you still alive?'   **Mary Blumeneau**

You're old when most people would rather have you dead.

William Wharton

I'm pretty good at spotting the warning signs of death... 1) your children start visiting during the week; 2) your doctor won't let you post-date a cheque; 3) you can't eat cream of wheat because it's too spicy.

Sophia Petrillo, *The Golden Girls*

I am having to learn to accept a new me; one who dials a telephone number and, while the phone is ringing, forgets whom he is calling.

Bill Cosby

But just imagine what life would be like if you could recite every word of Britney Spears' latest hit.

Sir John Mortimer

Did you ever think you'd live so long that your prostate would be bigger than your ego?

Susie Essman

No candles on my cake, please. This is a birthday party not a torchlight procession.

Ethel Barrymore

The woman is 100 years old. If you're 100 years old, that means that when you were a kid and the phone would ring, that shit would scare you.

Richard Blackwood

They say the first thing to go when you're old is your legs or your eyesight. It isn't true. The first thing to go is parallel parking.

Kurt Vonnegut

I'm an old man and I can't pee, and I asked the doctor about it, and the doctor asked me how old I am, and I said 90, and he said, 'You've pissed enough.'

Billy Wilder

I visited a new dentist for my six-monthly check-up. Having given me the all clear, he glanced at my notes, then remarked, 'Those should see you out.'
Angela Walder, 72

I've lived through two world wars, fifteen vendettas, four operations and two Darrins in *Bewitched*.
Sophia Petrillo, *The Golden Girls*

When you get to our age, they miss out every other day.
Anon

I don't have a pension. People say, 'Oh, you've got to make provision for your old age,' but I've done that by resolving that I'm going to be a burden on people.
Jeremy Hardy

—Did you know that there's a one in four chance you'll end up having to be looked after by a carer?
—Well, as long as it's not Bill Oddie, I don't mind.
Gary Strang and Tony Smart, *Men Behaving Badly*

Ah, the brochure for Dad's retirement home: 'Golden Acres: We care, so you don't have to.'
Niles Crane, *Frasier*

All I have to live on now is macaroni and memorial services.
Margot Asquith

Senior Citizen: Give me my Damn Discount. **Slogan on senior citizen's T-shirt**

RETIREMENT

I can just see my retirement – twenty years of own-brand baked beans, scratchy toilet paper and economy mints.
Colin, *Going For Broke*

I'm retired. I'm now officially a lower form of life than a Duracell battery. I've been replaced by a box. It's standard procedure apparently for a man of my age. The next stage is to stick you inside one.
Victor Meldrew, *One Foot in the Grave*

Seven months ago I could give a single command and 541,000 people would immediately obey it. Today I can't get a plumber to come to my house.   General Norman Schwarzkopf

Retirement is...a shortcut to death. Golf courses are too much like cemeteries.   Saul Bellow

After 48 years of fairly continuous employment, I have just retired. My working colleagues ask incredulously: 'What are you doing to do?' This preoccupation with activity seems a singularly British trait. In Italy, I feel sure, a similar announcement would be greeted with cries of, 'Bravo! Is your hammock comfortable? Is your cellar sufficient?'   Patrick Middleton

Sir Terence Conran has reached an age when many men's thoughts turn to retirement or to their granddaughters' schoolfriends. But this driven knight is no more likely to tend a bungalow garden in Peacehaven than he is to do a five-year stretch after being grassed up to Childline.
                                                      Jonathan Meades

Retirement? Twice as much husband, half as much pay.   Annie Wilks

DEATH

What do I dislike about death? Must be the hours.   Woody Allen

Death, or middle age as it is known in Govan...
                                    Rab C. Nesbitt, *A Stranger Here Myself*

I'm petrified of dying; there's no future in it.   Peter O'Toole

Don't worry, people die all the time. In fact, you could wake up dead tomorrow.   Homer Simpson

I think drowning would be a horrible experience, but I bet a little less horrible if, right before, you're really thirsty.   Demetri Martin

I'd like to die like my father died. He died fucking. He was 57. The woman was 18. My father came and went at the same time. **Richard Pryor**

The difference between sex and death is that with death you can do it alone and no one is going to make fun of you. **Woody Allen**

The first sign of his approaching end was when my old aunts, while undressing him, removed a toe with one of his socks. **Graham Greene**

In her last days, she resembled a spoiled pear.
Gore Vidal, on Gertrude Stein

I'd hate to die twice. It's so boring. **Richard Feynman**

Only think of Mrs Holder's being dead! Poor woman, she had done the only thing in the world she could possibly do to make one cease to abuse her. **Jane Austen**

—I hate Joan Crawford. She couldn't act, she was a whore!
—Miss Davis, excuse me. Miss Crawford was a great star and a great lady, besides which she is dead. You should not speak ill of the dead.
—Just because someone's dead doesn't mean they've changed.
Bette Davis and interviewer

He may be dead; or, he may be teaching English. **Cormac McCarthy**

—How can you tell if your wife is dead?
—The sex is the same but the dishes pile up. **Anon**

Most people's deaths are a sham. There's nothing left to die.
Charles Bukowski

What a disgusting verdict: he choked on his own vomit. You never hear of anyone choking on someone else's vomit. **Jeffrey Bernard**

What I look forward to is not a violent death, but dying in the normal way, with my head in the gas oven.   Leo Pavia

Everybody has got to die, but I have always believed an exception would be made in my case. Now what?   **William Saroyan, last words**

The farce is finished. I go to seek a vast perhaps.   François Rabelais

FUNERAL & EPITAPH

—So you're not coming to my aunt's funeral?
—No, sorry. I wouldn't enjoy it.

Jane Christie and Steve Harper, *Coupling*

I was on the golf course the other day with a friend when a funeral went by. My friend, in the middle of his swing, stopped and removed his hat until the cortège had passed. 'That was a very decent gesture,' I said. 'Least I could do, old boy,' he replied. 'She was a damn good wife to me.'

Les Dawson

I don't like funerals. In fact, I may not even go to my own.   **Brian Behan**

I'd rather just be shuffled off. No flowers. No candles. No long faces standing around in the rain, staring down into a hole in the ground while someone drones on about how wonderful I was. Just drop me into one of those black plastic bags and leave me by the trash can.   **Quentin Crisp**

Do-It-Yourself Coffins for Pets and People by Dale Power: Colour photographs illustrate every step in the construction of three pet-size and three human-size coffins… One box-design even doubles as a beautiful blanket chest or coffee table… With full colour illustrations and detailed instructions, this book is a challenge to the novice and a joy for the experienced craftsman.   **Editorial blurb, Amazon.com**

I have built one of the coffins following the directions in the book, *Do-It-Yourself Coffins for Pets and People*. Some measurements are missing, and some are not correct. This cost me in materials and time. Beware!
Eric Garwood, Amazon.com, customer review

The coffin reminds me of that IKEA couch your mother bought us.
Eileen Piper, *Six Feet Under*

—Tie's a bit bright, isn't it, Major, for a memorial service?
—Oh, I didn't like the chap.
Basil Fawlty and Major Gowen, *Fawlty Towers*

Damn, what am I going to wear? I don't have one thing in black that isn't see-through.
Blanche Devereaux, *The Golden Girls*

The modern funeral seems to have become a 'live obituary'... These days you have to supply the priest or the rabbi or the humanist with a supporting statement. We can't pass to the other side without an up-to-date CV. Which is rather hard on people who were a bit rubbish or never really got it together: 'And so we mourn the loss of Kevin who was well meaning... Ashes to ashes, dust to dust, Amen.'
Jeremy Hardy

Please forgive me if I appear down in the mouth this evening but I've had some bad news. Tomorrow it's the mother-in-law's funeral. And she's cancelled it.
Les Dawson

I want my tombstone to say, 'Too late, he's already dead,' just in case more people show up wanting to screw my life over.
Darien Fawkes, *The Invisible Man*

My Uncle Sammy was an angry man. He had printed on his tombstone: 'What are you looking at?'
Margaret Smith

If the whole human race lay in one grave, the epitaph on its headstone might well be: 'It seemed a good idea at the time.'
Rebecca West

GRUMPY
MIND
& SOUL

EDUCATION

The main purpose of education is to keep them off the streets. The teachers, I mean.
Katharine Whitehorn

Every schoolmaster after the age of 49 is inclined to flatulence, is apt to swallow frequently, and to puff.
Harold Nicolson

I am inclined to think that one's education has been in vain if one fails to learn that most schoolmasters are idiots.
Hesketh Pearson

Men are born ignorant, not stupid; they are made stupid by education.
Bertrand Russell

Education is what remains when you have forgotten everything you were taught.
A.C. Benson

If there were no schools to take the children away from home part of the time, the insane asylum would be filled with mothers.
Edgar Watson Howe

—Getting our son into this school may be the most important thing we ever do to ensure his happiness.
—Not counting our divorce.
Frasier Crane and Lilith Sternin, *Frasier*

—I was at Eton for six years and my people spent a lot of money on it, and I haven't any idea what I got out of it.
—Why, that's the beauty of it.
Hornby and O.E., quoted by A.C. Benson

I am inclined to agree with the headmaster of Eton that pederastic passions among schoolboys 'do no harm'; further, I think them the only redeeming feature of sexual life at public schools.
Aleister Crowley, 1909

I went to a convent in New York and was fired finally for my insistence that the Immaculate Conception was spontaneous combustion.
Dorothy Parker

When I went to school all I had was a pencil and the kid sitting next to me. If he had really applied himself I could have been somebody.

Joey Adams

[*Answering an exam question*] I am not currently able to divulge this information, as it may compromise our agents in the field.   Bill Watterson

Examinations are pure humbug from beginning to end. If a man is a gentleman, he knows quite enough, and if he is not a gentleman, whatever he knows is bad for him.

Oscar Wilde

You can get all As and still flunk life.

Walker Percy

COLLEGE

—Look at me, I'm a grad student, I'm 30 years old, and I made $600 last year.
—Don't make fun of grad students. They've just made a terrible life choice.   Bart and Marge Simpson, *The Simpsons*

Every man should have a college education in order to show him how little the thing is really worth.   Elbert Hubbard

What drove you to Bradford University? Your grades?   Phill Jupitus

Cambridge – the romantic dream of those who never went there.

Malcolm Muggeridge

I find Cambridge an asylum, in every sense of the word.   A.E. Housman

A great many Cambridge buildings remind one of the Tower of London.

C.S. Lewis

It's no use trying to be *clever* – we are all clever here; just try to be *kind* – a little kind.

Professor Foakes Jackson, to a young don at Jesus College, Cambridge

The image of the Oxford interview is that of an arcane rite in which dons toss bizarre questions around the room like cricket balls. There are, it seems, almost as many urban myths as spires. There's the don who allegedly asked a candidate to throw a brick through the window and then demanded to know why, on obeying instructions, he hadn't opened it first.

Liz Lightfoot

Like so many ageing college people, he had long ceased to notice the existence of students on the campus.

Vladimir Nabokov

The lecture theatre – the place where information passes from the notebook of the lecturer to the notebook of the student without necessarily passing through the mind of either.

Jim White

We never clean the toilet, Neil. That's what being a student is all about. No way, Harpic.

Rick, *The Young Ones*

Everyone has a right to a university degree in America, even if it's in hamburger technology.

Clive James

You're in for a lifetime of 'And you went to Harvard?' Accidentally give the wrong amount of change in a transaction and it's 'And you went to Harvard?' Forget just once that your underwear goes inside your pants and it's 'And you went to Harvard?' Get your head stuck in your niece's doll's house because you wanted to see what it was like to be a giant and it's 'Uncle Conan, you went to Harvard?'

Conan O'Brien

—I went to the University of Life.
—Really? I hear that's where everyone goes when they can't get accepted anywhere else.

Bridget Nylund and Michael Zbornak, *The Golden Girls*

I wanted to go to the University of Life but they wouldn't have me, so I had to go to Southampton.

Jeremy Hardy

INTELLIGENCE

Ah, Jack. Cute as a button but not quite as smart.

Will Truman, *Will and Grace*

What's on your mind, if you'll forgive the overstatement?   **Fred Allen**

John is a lunkhead. He would think it was raining if you pissed in his eyes.   **Scott Turow**

If his IQ gets any lower, we'll have to water him twice a week. **Molly Ivins**

I'm thick. I'm as thick as the big-print version of the *Complete Works of Charles Dickens*.   **Lt George Colthurst St Barleigh, *Blackadder the Third***

If you were any thicker, you'd set.   **Ken, *Early Doors***

If brains were lard, you couldn't grease a pan.

Jed Clampett, *The Beverly Hillbillies*

I've heard that Michael Winner was bragging recently about having 'slept with over 130 women'. Christ, and women still believe that they're the more intelligent sex.   **Victor Lewis-Smith**

I'm not saying my wife's thick but she was late for work the other day because she got stranded on an escalator during a power failure.

Les Dawson

Scientists have discovered that most women will, at some time in their life, contain intelligent DNA. Unfortunately, over 95 per cent of them spit it out.   **Anon**

Brains are never a handicap to a girl if she hides them under a see-through blouse.   **Bobby Vinton**

—Does your dick do all the thinking, Patrick?
—Er, I don't know. I'll ask it.

Susan Walker and Patrick Maitland, *Coupling*

TRUTH & LIES

I was working in Burger King when Andrew Lloyd Webber walked in.
He said, 'Give me two whoppers.' I said, 'You're good-looking and your
musicals are great.'   **Tim Vine**

The road to truth is long and lined the entire way with annoying
bastards.   **Alexander Jablokov**

I usually say, 'Fuck the truth,' but mostly, the truth fucks you.
                                    Prior Walter, *Angels in America*

I think she's as fake as a tranny's fanny.   **DCI Gene Hunt**, *Life on Mars*

What they say: 'Sure, I'll be happy to feed your cat for a few days.' *What
they mean*: 'Sure, I'll enjoy looking through all your drawers.'
                                                        Drew Bennett

'I just need to pay the mortgage.' The Yuppie Nuremberg defence.
                           Nick Naylor, *Thank You for Smoking*

You know, if you were Pinocchio, you'd have just poked my eye out.

                                      DCI Gene Hunt, *Life on Mars*

No Shame. No Mercy. No Sequel.   **Tagline**, *Scary Movie*

We Lied.   **Tagline**, *Scary Movie 2*

A commentary on the times is that the word 'honesty' is now preceded by
'old-fashioned'.   **Larry Wolters**

When someone says, 'Tell me honestly,' they mean, 'Lie to me with
conviction.'   **Jeremy Hardy**

Truth has been replaced by 'believability' as the test of the statements which dominate our lives. Almost anything can be made to seem true – especially if we wish to believe it.   Daniel J. Boorstin

When there are two conflicting versions of a story, the wise course is to believe the one in which people appear at their worst.   H. Allen Smith

Richard Nixon's a no-good lying bastard. He can lie out of both sides of his mouth at the same time, and if he ever caught himself telling the truth, he'd lie just to keep his hand in.   Harry Truman

I've been trying to think of a President in my life who didn't lie to the American people.   E.L. Doctorow, defending Bill Clinton

Without lies humanity would perish of despair and boredom.
                                                              Anatole France

The best measure of a man's honesty isn't his income tax return. It's the zero adjust on his bathroom scale.   Arthur C. Clarke

Speak the truth, but leave immediately after.   Slovenian proverb

RIGHT & WRONG

It is dangerous to be right when the government is wrong.   Voltaire

There is a demand today for men who can make wrong appear right.
                                                      Terence, *circa* 160 BC

The mark of a basic shit is he has to be *right*.   William S. Burroughs

Every woman is wrong until she cries, and then she is right – instantly.
                                                 Thomas Chandler Haliburton

GOOD & BAD

Bless me, Father, for I have sinned, it's been a minute since my last
confession.
Frank, *Angela's Ashes*

Christ died for our sins. Dare we make his martyrdom meaningless by
not committing them?
Jules Feiffer

There is more real pleasure to be gotten out of a malicious act, when
your heart is in it, than out of thirty acts of a nobler sort.
Mark Twain

K is for 'Kenghis Khan'; he was a very nice person. History has no record
of him. There is a moral in that, somewhere.
Harlan Ellison

Expecting the world to treat you fairly because you are good is like
expecting a bull not to attack you because you are a vegetarian.
Dennis Wholey

—Of all the terrible things you've ever done in your life, this is the worst,
the most despicable!
—But, Marge, I swear to you – I never thought you'd find out!
Marge and Homer Simpson, *The Simpsons*

The essence of a man's character is what he would do if he knew he
would never be found out.
Thomas Macaulay

Everything I did in my life that was worthwhile I caught hell for. Earl Warren

To act boastfully about something we should be ashamed of. That's a
trick that never seems to fail.
Joseph Heller

He has all the virtues I dislike and none of the vices I admire.
Winston Churchill, on Stafford Cripps

The death of Simon Raven, at the age of 73 after suffering a stroke, is proof that the devil looks after his own. He ought, by rights, to have died of shame at 30, or of drink at 50.   **Michael Barber**

You never see an old estate agent, do you? That's because it *is* possible to die of shame.   **Al Murray, the Pub Landlord**

To say that he has no shame is to drastically exaggerate the amount of shame he has.   **Journalist, on Malcolm Hardee**

Yes, Jamie, he was a bad man, but he might have been worse; he was an Irishman, but he might have been a Scotchman; he was a priest, but he might have been a lawyer.   **Samuel Parr**

MORALS & ETHICS

Being called 'immoral' by Jodie Marsh is like being told to sit up straight by the Hunchback of Notre Dame.   **George Galloway**

Moral indignation is in most cases 2 per cent moral, 48 per cent indignation and 50 per cent envy.   **Vittorio De Sica**

She had no use for morals and always omitted 'Lead us not into temptation' from the Lord's Prayer. 'It's no business of His,' she proclaimed.   **Philip Ziegler, on Lady Diana Cooper**

Never let your sense of morals get in the way of doing what's right.   **Isaac Asimov**

[*Bank manager to customer*] So, you're interested in ethical investing. *How* ethical?   **Sidney Harris**

There's just so far you can go with ethics, and then the real world kicks in.   **Sidney Harris**

—You have no values. With you it's all nihilism, cynicism, sarcasm and orgasm.
—Hey, in France I could run for office with that slogan, and win!
Doris and Harry Block, Deconstructing Harry

PHILOSOPHY

When the seagulls follow the trawler it is because they think sardines will be thrown into the sea.
Eric Cantona

If a Frenchman goes on about seagulls, trawlers and sardines, he's called a philosopher. I'd just be called a short Scottish bum talking crap.
Gordon Strachan

When he who hears doesn't understand him who speaks, and when he who speaks doesn't know what he himself means – that is philosophy.
Voltaire

—Why is there something rather than nothing?
—Even if there were nothing you'd still be complaining!
Student and Professor Sidney Morgenbesser

There was never yet philosopher that could endure the toothache patiently.
William Shakespeare, Much Ado About Nothing

Organic Life, we are told, has developed gradually from the protozoon to the philosopher and this development, we are assured, is indubitably an advance. Unfortunately it is the philosopher, not the protozoon, who gives us this assurance.
Bertrand Russell

I have studied many philosophers and many cats. The wisdom of cats is infinitely superior.
Hippolyte Taine

All men are mortal. Socrates was mortal. Therefore, all men are Socrates.
Woody Allen

One horse-laugh is worth ten thousand syllogisms.   **H.L. Mencken**

—I now have three philosophies... 'Life goes on,' 'Who cares?' and
'How should I know?' Pretty profound, huh?
—Maybe a little too profound...
—Who cares? How should I know? Life goes on!
                                                    Sally and Charlie Brown

This is my philosophy of life: if I can make just one person laugh, I'm
already doing better than Tony Danza.   **Emo Philips**

BELIEFS

If you believe the doctors, nothing is wholesome; if you believe the
theologians, nothing is innocent; if you believe the military, nothing
is safe.   **Lord Salisbury**

There are two things that will be believed of any man whatsoever, and
one of them is that he has taken to drink.   **Booth Tarkington**

Every man, wherever he goes, is encompassed by a cloud of comforting
convictions, which move with him like flies on a summer's day.
                                                         Bertrand Russell

—If you believe in angels then why not unicorns or leprechauns?
—Oh, Lisa, everyone knows leprechauns are extinct.
                        Lisa Simpson and Kent Brockman, *The Simpsons*

I knew there was no tooth fairy even before my teeth fell out.
                                  Larry David, *Curb Your Enthusiasm*

If a man doesn't believe as we do, we say he is a crank, and that settles it.
I mean, it does nowadays, because now we can't burn him.   **Mark Twain**

I don't believe any survey because they didn't ask *me*.   **Frank Muir**

If I ever find myself sharing a belief with Jane Fonda, I re-examine it immediately.

Clive James

No human beings are more dangerous than those who have suffered for a belief: the great persecutors are recruited from the martyrs not quite beheaded. Far from diminishing the appetite for power, suffering exasperates it.

E.M. Cioran

The curse of man, and the cause of nearly all our woes, is his stupendous capacity for believing the incredible.

H.L. Mencken

Delusions are both contagious and incremental: when you succumb to one, you are far more susceptible to others. Acquire a horoscope habit, say, and soon you'll be buying into feng shui, homeopathy and the Da Vinci Code. Eventually, you might hire Carole Caplin as your lifestyle guru.

Francis Wheen

Feng shui is the ancient Chinese art of sticking the telly on the other side of the room. It's defined as 'feng' – a Chinese word meaning 'sense', and 'shui' meaning 'more money than'.

Francis Wheen, *The News Quiz*

ASTROLOGY

You know, I'm a little psychic. Remember when I predicted that driver was going to lose his job, and then two days later I fired him?

Karen Walker, *Will and Grace*

My wife's an earth sign. I'm a water sign. Together we make mud.

Rodney Dangerfield

How can you believe in a science predicated on Hitler and Shirley Temple being born in the same month?

Helen Gurley Brown

Virgo (23 Aug – 22 Sep): Certain shortcomings in your education and upbringing cause you to read meaning into the relationships among various celestial bodies.   *The Onion* online newspaper

If you had been born two days later you would have been kind, generous and witty.   **Bill Hoest**

A touchstone to determine the actual worth of an 'intellectual': find out how he feels about astrology.   **Robert A. Heinlein**

Why, actually, are not professional astrologers jailed for fraud?
                                                              Richard Dawkins

Soothsayers make a better living in the world than truthsayers.
                                                        Georg Christoph Lichtenberg

If you keep saying things are going to be bad, you have a chance of being a prophet.   **Isaac Bashevis Singer**

Every Halloween the buddies of Houdini hold a séance to try to contact him. Now don't get me wrong but isn't one of the great things about being dead that you don't have to take calls?   **David Letterman**

GOD & THE DEVIL

Is man one of God's blunders or is God one of man's blunders?
                                                              Friedrich Nietzsche

If God is up there, he's obviously a shit.   **Brian Aldiss**

Why is God making me suffer so much? Just because I don't believe in him?   **Professor Sidney Morgenbesser**

I hate you, God. I hate you as though you existed.
                                        Maurice Bendrix, *The End of the Affair*

I wanted to play football for England and score three goals in the World Cup final like Geoff Hurst did in 1966. I used to pray for that every night. That is why I no longer believe in God. He let me down.

Hugh Grant

God is a DJ. He doesn't do requests.

Simon Munnery

The notion that God was everywhere put paid to any possible peace of mind by the time I was six... I was quite an imaginative child so going to the lavatory was torture. It still is. I still cannot do a big job if my wife is in the house, or if the light is on. I can't even evacuate if the telly is on.

Tom Baker, *Who on Earth is Tom Baker?*

—You think I was made in God's image? Take a look at me. You think He wears glasses?
—Not with those frames.

Boris Grushenko and Sonja, *Love and Death*

Why attack God? He may be as miserable as we are.

Erik Satie

If God were suddenly condemned to live the life which he has inflicted upon men, he would kill himself.

Alexandre Dumas

Ask people about God nowadays and they usually reply, 'I'm not religious, but deep down, I'm a very spiritual person.' What this phrase really means is, 'I'm afraid of dying, but I can't be arsed going to church.'

Colin Ramone

When I found out I thought God was white, and a man, I lost interest.

Alice Walker, *The Color Purple*

There is no God, because I think if there was a God, they would make sure that the clitoris was *in* the vagina.

Joy Behar

I cannot believe in a God that wants to be praised all the time.

Friedrich Nietzsche

I have more faith in my plumber than I do the eternal being. Plumbers do a good job. They keep the shit flowing.

Charles Bukowski

I distrust those people who know so well what God wants them to do because I notice it always coincides with their desires.   Susan B. Anthony

I'm sorry, we don't do God.

Alastair Campbell, when Tony Blair was asked about
his Christian faith by *Vanity Fair* magazine

But without God, the universe is meaningless. Life is meaningless. We're meaningless... I have a sudden and overpowering urge to get laid.

Doris Levine, *God*

It is stupid of modern civilisation to have given up believing in the devil, when he is the only explanation of it.   R.A. Knox

The devil is an optimist if he thinks he can make people meaner.

Karl Kraus

Maybe there isn't a devil; perhaps it's just God when he's drunk.

Tom Waits

RELIGION
– GENERAL

For them that don't have football, there's always religion.

Nick, *Night Moves*

Religion is the venereal disease of mankind.   Henri de Montherlant

It's hard to be religious when certain people are never incinerated by bolts of lightning.   Bill Watterson

Say what you like about the habit of unquestioning faith. I consider the capacity for it terrifying.   Kurt Vonnegut

I pray and do meditation. But not religion. That's close to organised
crime.   **Robin Williams**

Men never do evil so completely and cheerfully as when they do it from
religious conviction.   **Blaise Pascal**

Christian Science is notoriously a menopause religion ... that sounded better in German.

V.S. Pritchett

A Mormon told me that they didn't drink coffee. I said, 'My friend, a cup
of coffee every day gives you wonderful benefits.' He said, 'Like what?' I
said, 'Well, it keeps you from being a Mormon.'   **Emo Philips**

I have heard cynics who say the Dalai Lama is a very political old monk
shuffling around in Gucci shoes.   **Rupert Murdoch**

Many people think they have religion when they are merely troubled with
indigestion.   **Robert Ingersoll**

But, Marge, what if we chose the wrong religion? Each week we just
make God madder and madder.   **Homer Simpson**

All religions die of one disease; that of being found out.
                                                          John Morley, *attrib.*

The more I study religions the more I am convinced that man never
worshipped anything but himself.   **Sir Richard Burton**

No matter what our faith, we are all members of the human race. And
can one say worse?   **Henry David Thoreau**

What do atheists scream when they come?   **Bill Hicks**

CHRISTIANITY

Two guys knocked at my door and said, 'We'd like to talk to you about Jesus.' I said, 'Oh, no, what's he done now?'
Kevin McAleer

Jesus was a carpenter. You can tell he was a tradesman because he disappeared off the face of the earth for three days with no rational explanation. And he had his twelve mates hanging round expecting lunch.
Al Murray, the Pub Landlord

The good news is that Jesus is coming back. The bad news is that he's really pissed off.
Bob Hope

Christian: one who believes that the New Testament is a divinely inspired book admirably suited to the spiritual needs of his neighbour.
Ambrose Bierce

I'd like to point out that during the twentieth century, white, God-fearing, predominately Christian Europe produced Lenin, Stalin, Franco, Hitler and Mussolini.
George Carlin

On a visit to Paris, Evelyn Waugh made a beeline for the Musée Grévin, which in those days was like Madame Tussauds Chamber of Horrors, only much more horrible. There was a particularly dreadful tableau of Christians and lions, and although even then Evelyn was a keen Christian, he was obviously sympathetic to the lions.
Lady Mosley

The Archbishop of Canterbury, Rowan Williams, looks like one of those trick pictures you look at – an old man with a big beard then if you turn him upside down you'd see a picture of a woman with a bouffant hairdo.
Sandi Toksvig

I don't like those televangelists. I woke up yesterday morning, I turned on the TV, lying in bed, and this televangelist's screaming at me, 'You may not know this but today you have already sinned!' I've just fucking got up! What could I possibly have done? I turned to my sister – she didn't know...
Danny Bhoy

Don't Let Worry Kill You – Let the Church Help.
Notice on a church noticeboard

Swedes have more faith in their local IKEA store than in the Church.
According to a survey, 80 per cent of Swedes said they trusted the
furniture chain. Only 46 per cent said they trusted the Church.
Ananova news website

I have no objections to churches so long as they do not interfere with
God's work. **Brooks Atkinson**

Beverly Hills' churches are so posh that at communion they offer you a
wine list. **Bill Poston**

A Sunday school is a prison in which children do penance for the evil
conscience of their parents. **H.L. Mencken**

BIBLE

I've been away at Bible Camp learning to be more judgemental.
Maude Flanders, *The Simpsons*

The Bible – written over a period of a thousand years by men who
believed the earth was flat. **Clarence Darrow**

I always carry a bullet in my breast pocket. Someone threw a Bible at me. That bullet saved my life. Woody Allen

There's a Bible on the shelf there. But I keep it next to Voltaire – poison
and antidote. **Bertrand Russell**

CATHOLIC

I was raised Catholic and received the Body and Blood of Christ every Sunday at Communion until the age of thirty, when I became a vegetarian.
                                                                    Joe Queenan

We were sceptical Catholics. We believed Jesus walked on water. We just figured it was probably winter.
                                                                    John Wing

She had once been a Catholic, but discovering that priests were infinitely more attentive when she was in the process of losing or regaining faith in Mother Church, she maintained an enchantingly wavering attitude.
                                                                    F. Scott Fitzgerald

I'm giving up for Lent.
                                                                    Richard Pearson

What is Catholic Alzheimer's Disease? It's when you forget everything but the guilt.
                                                                    Anon

What you say: 'Forgive me, Father, for I have sinned.' *What you are thinking*: '…especially the lies I am about to tell you.'
                                                                    Chris Doyle

I stepped into the confessional today and said, 'You first.'   Dennis Miller

A Catholic priest, a Boy Scout leader and a lawyer take some boys out on an adventure trip. On the flight over, there is engine trouble and the plane is about to go down. 'We have a problem,' says the pilot. 'There are only three parachutes!' The Boy Scout leader suggests they give them to the boys. 'Screw the boys,' shouts the lawyer. 'Is there time?' asks the priest.
                                                                    Anon

The Catholic clergy: God's storm troopers.   Dave Allen

Father, your sermons are like water to a drowning man.
                                                                    James Montgomery

101 Ways to Survive a Dull Sermon No. 102: Slap your neighbour. See if he turns the other cheek. If not, raise your hand and tell the minister.

Ben Schwalb

I have had a good many more uplifting thoughts, creative and expansive visions, while soaking in comfortable baths or drying myself after bracing showers in well-equipped American bathrooms than I have ever had in any cathedral.

Edmund Wilson

JEW

Two Jewish guys are walking down the street when a very attractive girl passes by. Hymie turns to Ben and says, 'I'd lend her one!'

Anon

—Are you Jewish?
—You want to check my penis?

Man and Larry David, *Curb Your Enthusiasm*

[*On the phone*] No, I'm not Jewish. I'm not Jewish. I keep telling you, Ma, I'm *not* Jewish.

Joy Behar

I can tell if you're a Jew with one question: 'What is your cholesterol level?' Every Jew knows their cholesterol level.

Jackie Mason

I was born of the Hebrew persuasion, but I converted to Narcissism.

Woody Allen

I drive a Yom Kippur Clipper. That's a Jewish Cadillac. It stops on a dime and picks it up.

Kinky Friedman

—What do you do with a Jew with ADD?
—Put him in a concentration camp.

Anon

That's the trouble with being Jewish – you haven't got a foreskin so you need a lot of balls to make up for it.

Esther Rubins, *Sixty Six*

I think I said, 'All men are Jews except they don't know it.' I doubt I expected anyone to take the statement literally. But I think it's an understandable statement and a metaphoric way of indicating how history, sooner or later, treats all men.   Bernard Malamud

—I'm not Jewish.
—Well, nobody's perfect.
                          Albert Nimzicki and Julius Levinson, *Independence Day*

MUSLIM

Jews and Muslims have more in common than any other religions: we both don't eat pork, we both don't celebrate Christmas, we both use 'ucghhh' in our pronunciation, we both yell on the phone when there's no emergency. The only difference between Jews and Muslims is that Jews never like to spend money and Muslims never have any money to spend.
                                                           Ahmed Ahmed

A guy goes into a sex shop and asks for an inflatable doll. The assistant says, 'Would you like a Christian or a Muslim doll?' The customer says, 'What's the difference?' 'Well,' says the assistant, 'the Muslim one blows itself up.'   Anon

I'm astonished at the failure to identify Islamism as dangerous, to see it for what it is: a millennial death cult with us very much in its sights. There is a tendency in England to see anyone with darker skin as a victim of repression, or some past crime committed by our empire or government and not for who they are. We respect Muhammad, but not Mohammed Atta.   Martin Amis

Tricky, isn't it, if you're in a mosque and everyone's praying and you really enjoy leapfrog.   Milton Jones

IMMORTALITY

If man were immortal, do you realise what his meat bills would be?

Woody Allen

Friedrich Nietzsche said that the life we lived we will live over again the exact same way for eternity. Great. That means I'll have to sit through the Ice Capades again.

Woody Allen

The first ten million years are the worst. And the second ten million years, they were the worst too. The third ten million I didn't enjoy at all. After that I went into a bit of a decline.

Douglas Adams

—What do you think of the next life?
—I don't think much of this one.

James Joyce and Samuel Beckett

If I were reincarnated, I would wish to be returned to earth as a killer virus to lower human population levels.

Prince Philip

In my next life, I'm going to come back as a rather good-looking well, even quite fat and plain – 50-year-old man who's just been widowed or divorced. I would get a bonk every night of the week.

Jilly Cooper

I want to be reincarnated as a sofa – something warm and quiet, just sitting in the corner, covered in dog hair and unidentifiable bodily fluids.

Alex, *Waiting for God*

If there is such a thing as reincarnation, knowing my luck I'll come back as me.

Rodney Trotter, *Only Fools and Horses*

It may be that we have all lived before and died, and this is hell.

A.L. Prusick

HELL

Hell is other people.   Jean-Paul Sartre

Hell is other people's children.   Gail Collins

Hell is four men in a car talking about football. I hate manly men.
                                                            David Bailey

Hell is any Jack Nicklaus-designed golf course.
                                                            David Feherty

Hell is like a bad tooth that gets worse and worse through eternity.
                                                            William Rees-Mogg

Hell is in hello.   Ben Rumson, *Paint Your Wagon*

Hell is a place for the wicked. The wicked are quite comfortable in it; it
was made for them.   George Bernard Shaw

I do believe in hell – but I don't believe anyone is in it.
                                                            Abbé Arthur Mugnier

Hell is full of musical amateurs: brandy is the music of the damned.
                                                            George Bernard Shaw

—What? You have air-conditioning in hell?
—Sure! Fucks up the ozone layer!
                            Harry Block and the Devil, *Deconstructing Harry*

Oh no, we gave up stoking fires ages ago. You'll be working in the call
centre now.   Don Hatcher

HEAVEN

I'd like to believe in heaven, not least because I'd like to meet my mum and dad again. I'd like to know whether the Welsh dresser was meant to go to me or my brother, really.   John Peel

If there's a heaven for homosexuals it'll be very poorly lit and full of people they can be pretty confident they'll never meet again.
                                                            Quentin Crisp

Is this what I've been good for all my life? It's more like Liberace's bedroom.   Peter Cook

Please use the stairs. Pearly lift closed for repairs.   Victoria Wood

[*Saint Peter to a man at the Pearly Gates*] If you don't mind throwing tennis balls for eternity, I do have an opening in doggie heaven.
                                            Frank and Ernest, by Bob Thaves

TIME

Life to me is like boarding-house wallpaper. It takes a long time to get used to it, but when you finally do, you never notice that it's there. And then you hear the decorators are arriving...   Derek Marlowe

Life is short; Italian salamis are long.   Kinky Friedman

Nothing lasts, neither Mr Money nor Mrs Cunt.   Thomas Berger

I'm gonna live my life right now. I'm not gonna wait for it to come out in paperback.   Henry Willows, *Home to Roost*

There is never enough time – unless you're serving it.   Malcolm Forbes

A lifetime is more than sufficiently long for people to get what there is of it wrong.   Piet Hein

We moved back yesterday from glorious British Summer Time to equally glorious Greenwich Mean Time, which meant that I had to waste the extra hour I'd just saved adjusting all the clocks in the house. That's quintessentially British.   Victor Lewis-Smith

Are you aware that rushing towards a goal is a sublimated death wish? It's no coincidence we call them 'deadlines'.   Tom Robbins

A motto: do it tomorrow; you've made enough mistakes today.
                                                                                Dawn Powell

What do we want? PROCRASTINATION! When do we want it? NEXT WEEK!   Anon

I expect to pass through this world but once and therefore if there is anybody I want to kick in the crotch I had better kick them in the crotch now, for I do not expect to pass this way again.   Maurice Bowra

Time doth flit. Oh, shit!   Dorothy Parker

THE WORLD

I'm sitting on top of the world – and I've got haemorrhoids.
                                                                        Rodney Dangerfield

In the battle between you and the world, back the world.   Franz Kafka

The world needs an enema.   Mason Cooley

Believe everything you hear about the world; nothing is too impossibly bad.   Honoré de Balzac

—You're a bitter little lady.
—It's a bitter little world.

John Muller and Evelyn Hahn, *Hollow Triumph*

Have you ever tried to take the world in your arms? It resists being snuggled. **James Broughton**

I have one share in corporate Earth, and I am nervous about the management. **E.B. White**

The world would be a better place if it was half-dark, indoors, and air-conditioned. **Larry L. King**

I've just spoken to Mum. She said she's read somewhere the world's coming to an end Saturday morning and do we want to buy her electric kettle? **Margaret Meldrew,** *One Foot in the Grave*

It happened that a fire broke out backstage in a theatre. A clown came out to inform the public about it. They thought it was a joke and applauded. He repeated it; people laughed even more. This is the way I think the world will end – with general giggling by all the witty heads, who think it is a joke. **Søren Kierkegaard**

The world is ending and everyone is getting cosmetic surgery and watching debutantes getting fucked up the arse. **Claire Fisher,** *Six Feet Under*

The world is always ending; the exact date depends on when you came into it. **Arthur Miller**

Have a Nice End of the World. **Tagline,** *Evolution*

—It's the Seven Horsemen of the Apocalypse! Bart, are you wearing clean underwear?
—Not any more. **Marge and Bart Simpson,** *The Simpsons*

—Morticia, we may indeed have just saved the world.
—Oh, Gomez, do you think we did the right thing?

Gomez and Morticia Addams, *The Addams Family*

THE MEANING
OF LIFE

I'll tell you the meaning of life, but first you have to promise not to laugh.   **Frank and Ernest, by Bob Thaves**

Imagine the Creator as a low comedian, and at once the world becomes explicable.   **H.L. Mencken**

—I never thought of God as humorous.
—The creator of the platypus, the camel, the ostrich, and Man? Oh, come now!   **Ray Bradbury**

Suppose the world were only one of God's jokes, would you work any the less to make it a good joke instead of a bad one?   **George Bernard Shaw**

The world is indeed comic, but the joke is on mankind.   **H.P. Lovecraft**

INDEX